Improving Classroom Behaviour:
New Directions for Teachers and Pupils

Denis Mongon and Susan Hart
with Chris Ace and Anne Rawlings

TEACHERS COLLEGE PRESS

Teachers College, Columbia University
New York

© 1989 Cassell Educational Limited
Artillery House, Artillery Row
London SW1P 1RT

Published in the USA by
Teachers College Press
1234 Amsterdam Avenue
New York, NY 10027

Library of Congress Cataloging-in-Publication Data
Mongon, Denis
    Improving classroom behaviour.
    1. Problem children—Education. 2. Teacher–student relationships.
    3. Special Education. I. Hart, Susan II. Title
    LC4801.M59   1989
    371.93   89–4893
    ISBN 0–8077–2995–7

Typeset by Activity Ltd., Salisbury, Wilts.
Printed and bound in Great Britain by Biddles Ltd., Guildford and King's Lynn.

Contents

Acknowledgements   iv
Terminology relating to the British Educational System
(England and Wales)   v
Introduction   1

Part One   PROBLEM BEHAVIOUR: WHOSE PROBLEM?   7

1   A Multi-layered Epic   9

2   Towards a Preventive Approach   25
    Susan Hart and Denis Mongon

Part Two   STRUCTURE, STRATEGIES AND STEREOTYPES   43

3   Historical Developments   45
    Denis Mongon

4   Strategies and Explanations   61
    Denis Mongon

5   Environmental Factors and their Implications   72
    Susan Hart and Denis Mongon

Part Three   INITIATING CHANGE: CASE STUDIES   95

6   Everest in Plimsolls   97
    Susan Hart

7   Rejecting the Rational   116
    Chris Ace

8   The Cock-eyed Optimist   135
    Anne Rawlings

9   If we'd known then …   150
    Susan Hart

Part Four   TOWARDS A WHOLE-SCHOOL APPROACH   157

10   Questioning Classrooms, Questioning Schools   159
    Susan Hart

11   Psalm CXXI   182
      Denis Mongon

      Appendix 1   Questioning Classrooms   202
      Appendix 2   Questioning Schools   211
      Appendix 3   Galloway (1985)   215

      Bibliography   216

      Name Index   224

      Subject Index   227

Acknowledgements

The format, style and general content of this book were developed initially by Chris Ace, Susan Hart and Denis Mongon, joined subsequently by Ann Rawlings whose substantial experience of primary work helped to elaborate that dimension. The main task of writing, editing and co-ordinating the text was undertaken by Susan Hart and Denis Mongon.

We include a short quote in the book from Tim Joyce, a former colleague, and we are also grateful for the contribution his work with us made to our ideas. Thanks are also due to Brian Jones and Stuart Scott who were closely involved in the work described in Chapter 6. They have kindly confirmed that our assessment fairly reflects their own.

Last, but not least, we owe thanks to other colleagues and pupils in the schools where we worked. We hope they will not mind us drawing upon experience of which they were an essential part. Criticism, such as it is, is directed towards our limitations, not theirs.

> Teaching is … like all arts of high ambition, a strategy in the face of an impossible task.
> Lawrence Stenhouse, 'Research as a basis for teaching'. Inaugural lecture, University of East Anglia (February 1979)

Terminology relating to the British education system (England and Wales)

1. AGE RANGES AND THE ORGANISATION OF SCHOOLING

Age	Class title	School		Alternative forms of organisation
	Nursery	} Pre-school		
4–5	Reception			
5–6	Middle infants	} Infant*		
6–7	Top infants		} Primary	
7–8	1st year junior			
8–9	2nd year junior	} Junior*		
9–10	3rd year junior			
10–11	4th year junior			
Secondary transfer				} Middle schools (8–13)
11–12	1st year secondary			
12–13	2nd year secondary			
13–14	3rd year secondary			
14–15	4th year secondary			
15–16	5th year secondary	} Secondary		
Statutory school-leaving age				
16–17	1st year 6th			} 6th form colleges
17–18	2nd year 6th			Tertiary colleges (16–19)

*In some primary schools, these age ranges are 'vertically' grouped as a matter of policy, i.e. they contain a balance of children in each age group. In others, mixed ages are a necessity because of low numbers.

2. ADMINISTRATION OF EDUCATION

Comprehensive reorganisation: This term applies only to secondary schools, since primary schools have always been 'comprehensive', in the sense that they accept all pupils within a given geographic area, irrespective of 'ability'. Most state-maintained secondary schools now also accept a balance of pupils from across the whole 'ability' range. Only a few local education authorities retain (or have reinstated) a selective system based upon examination or assessment of pupils at 11+ to obtain entry to 'grammar schools' (academically oriented secondary schools).

DES: The Department of Education and Science is the government department which oversees the organisation and some parts of the funding of the education service.

HMI: Her Majesty's Inspectors of Schools are appointed to inspect the provision of education and report to the government on educational standards.

ILEA: The Inner London Education Authority is the local authority which administrates the education service of ten inner-London boroughs. In 1990 it will be dissolved, and the duties devolved to the local boroughs.

LEA: Local education authority. There are about 100 of these in England and Wales. Their role is to manage the education service for a particular geographical area. Many of the responsibilities currently fulfilled by local education authorities are shortly to be devolved to the schools themselves.

3.   ARRANGEMENTS FOR GROUPING PUPILS FOR
     TEACHING PURPOSES

Banding: A system of grouping pupils on the basis of two or three broad 'ability' bands (upper and lower ability or upper, middle and lower ability).

Mixed-ability: A system of grouping pupils on the basis of a balance between pupils of differing 'abilities' (e.g. 25 per cent top ability, 50 per cent middle, 25 per cent lower).

Setting: A system of grouping and re-grouping pupils on the basis of 'ability' or levels of attainment in each area of the curriculum. In theory, a pupil might be in Set 1 for Maths, but Set 4 for English.

Streaming: A system of closely grading pupils for all teaching purposes into classes based on their assessed 'ability' on entry. A large school might have ten or twelve streams from the top to bottom ability levels.

Unstreamed classes: Groupings in which no particular attempt has been made to identify or structure classes on the basis of 'ability' (this is the situation in many primary schools, but is unusual in secondary schools).

4. ARRANGEMENTS MADE FOR OVERSEEING PUPILS' GENERAL WELFARE AND EDUCATIONAL PROGRESS

Pastoral: This describes the aspect of teachers' work which is concerned with a broader view of pupils' welfare and development than their specific progress in academic subjects. All teachers are expected to fulfil a 'pastoral' as well as an 'academic' role within the school. In Britain, commitment to the 'pastoral' side of education has recently been extended to include specific teaching programmes relating to personal and social development. In its traditional mode, the work has tended in practice to concentrate on discipline and other 'problems' experienced or presented by pupils, in support of the academic curriculum. These have become the concern of groups of identified people with specific responsibilities (see more detailed history, structure and discussion in Chapter 3).

Tutor: The teacher who has specific responsibility for the general welfare of a group of about 30 pupils (usually of similar age, known as a **tutor group**). The basic idea is that in a large school there needs to be at least one teacher who knows each pupil really well, and to whom the child can turn for help with a problem. The tutor's responsibilities (at secondary level) include taking the daily register, following up absences, monitoring of homework, overseeing general academic progress, looking after personal, emotional or academic problems. The tutor is usually the first point of contact between school and parents. At primary level, all these responsibilities are fulfilled by the class teacher, who works with the same group of pupils all day, every day, throughout the year.

Unit teacher: Some schools have received additional resources or have used their own resources to set up 'units' to support pupils whose behaviour makes it difficult for teachers to pursue their work constructively with other pupils. Pupils whose behaviour causes concern, and who have not responded to various other systems and sanctions in operation, may be referred through the year head to spend time in the unit instead of attending those lessons in which particular difficulties are occurring. More details of the work of such units (and other kinds of provision for such pupils) are contained in Chapters 3, 4 and 7.

Year head: The teacher who has oversight of a team of tutors for a whole year group (sometimes more than one year group). Responsibilities include taking on problems that tutors have identified but do not feel able to deal with themselves, organising activities relating to personal and social development for the year group during tutorial periods (periods spent in home room), liaison with outside agencies concerned with truancy, liaison with social services, with hospitals, with special units, etc.

5.   ARRANGEMENTS FOR THE PROFESSIONAL DEVELOPMENT OF TEACHERS FOLLOWING INITIAL TRAINING

INSET: Stands for inservice education of teachers. In general, it refers to any arrangements and opportunities provided for teachers to reappraise current practice, develop new skills, pursue research interests, refresh their own particular area of curricular expertise, etc. The current trend is for more school-focused in-service work, with funding made available to allow teachers to be released from teaching commitments, during school time, to pursue aspects of professional development on a coherent and planned basis relating to the school's identification of its own needs.

GRIST: Stands for Grant Related Inservice Training. Known officially as Local Authority Training Grant Scheme, this is a grant from central government to the local authority. It is a new arrangement for funding inservice work introduced in April 1987. In place of central funding for inservice courses, local authorities are now required to identify their training requirements and submit these to the DES (see above) for funding. Schools are required to determine their needs and negotiate them with the local authority as part of a policy of staff development and appraisal. The government sets out a list of national priorities for funding to guide local authorities. Special needs is currently one of these.

6.   OTHER

GCSE: The examination at 16+ which has replaced the former two-tier system of GCE O (Ordinary) Level and CSE (Certificate of Secondary Education). Pupils take the examination in each subject they study, and receive a grade for each subject separately.

PACT: Stands for Parents and Children and Teachers. It is a 'scheme' for involving parents in reading with their children and encouraging their children to read at home. In an effort to do more than merely send books home with the children, the scheme provides some means of two-way communication between teachers and parents about how the children are progressing and specific guidance for parents in how to conduct read-together sessions.

ROSLA: Raising of the school leaving-age. In 1972, this was raised from 15 to 16 years.

ntroduction

1 the mid-1970s, one of us was employed as a teacher in a school vhich was then described as for 'maladjusted' children. One of the upils, a bright teenage girl approaching school leaving, asked vhether she would always be maladjusted. 'I mean,' she said, 'will eople always call me maladjusted?' It was a provocative question, lthough it was not asked with that intention. She was not the asiest of young people with whom to choose to spend one's time, ut her mistrust of adults and her scepticism of the human condition vere not inappropriate. Her attitudes had enabled her to survive, hysically and psychically, a childhood which would have des- :oyed a less resilient personality. With hindsight, it is possible to ay that her survival was then preparing the basis for a much more atisfactory young adulthood. However, at the particular moment ɔ which we refer, she was worried about the label with which she new she had been endowed by an education service unable to ɔlerate the very behaviour which enabled her to survive.

The label itself is only of interest in so far as it is one of the many vords we have available, ranging from the pseudo-scientific to the nsultingly vulgar, to describe – or more accurately to *label*, since the ɛrms have only marginal descriptive value – children whose ehaviour we see as troublesome. What is important is that the girl's ircumstances showed how difficult it is to be dogmatic about ehaviour. Behaviour which allowed her to survive in one area of er life was condemned in another; it was 'maladjusted' and nappropriate' at school, but well adapted outside.

This book is mainly, but not exclusively, about children like that oung girl, whose behaviour causes distress and difficulties for eachers in primary and secondary schools. However, that empha- is is, in a sense, an admission illustrating how, like most authors nd practitioners in this field, we allow ourselves to be dominated ɔy the problems which cry out loudest for solution. It does not ollow that those are the most urgent or the most desperate cases nd it should be recognised from the outset that there are other hildren whose behaviour does not apparently cause problems for eachers but does at the time, or eventually, cause distress or ifficulty for the children themselves. The terms 'disruptive' and ɪggressive' are commonly used to describe many of the children vho do cause difficulties. Many of those whose own distress is less

obvious are described as 'withdrawn' or 'neurotic'. We hope that
the needs of that latter group are represented in what we say and
that if we are not constantly explicit about this point, the reader
will be able to draw conclusions for both groups from our
suggestions. In fact, we hope the reader will be able to draw
conclusions for a much larger group of children than those usually
thought of as 'difficult'. The strategies and methods we advocate
are more likely to benefit the minority if they are at the same time
adopted for the benefit of the majority. They are not marginal
aspects of school life or philanthropic afterthoughts; we hope they
are recognisable as sound approaches to catering for all young
people in school.

That brings us to what is, in our view, an equally important
feature of the book. We cannot overemphasise that the book is
only in part about children, and that it is equally concerned with
teachers and with the organisation of schools. Although it would
be absurd to deny that some children do bring enormous difficulties to school with them, it is equally absurd to pretend that
schools and teachers do not play a part in creating the circumstances in which problems arise. If that is the case then it follows
that the difficulties which teachers and pupils have in working and
coping with one another cannot be resolved by examining only one
element, children, in an equation with two other components,
teachers and schools.

At the time of writing a fourth element is being added to that
equation as central Government proceeds with a Bill designed to
give the Secretary of State sweeping new powers. The Bill makes
passing reference to the exemption of children who are the subject
of a statement from aspects of the national curriculum including
testing arrangements. As we write, the Government is committed
to amending that reference but it is difficult to predict quite what
form that could take. There is very little belief in the education
world that the Bill will make it easier for schools to meet the special
educational needs of young people. We share that concern.
However, the approaches we outline in the book are not prescrip-
tive solutions to problems; they are ways of working on them.
Thus, they are not constrained by our preference to see them
implemented in a genuinely comprehensive education system or
by our belief that they operate best in such a system. The
approaches are those which, in our own experience, have been
effective, as well as others which are worth consideration on the
basis of reported research or experience. When the national
timetable, national syllabuses or national testing are in place, it will
still be the responsibility of teachers to work out the curriculum,
the day-to-day activities of a school. For that purpose, the

approaches in this book will continue to be of value to teachers in a variety of circumstances.

There are, and will continue to be, many paradoxes and contradictions surrounding the work which teachers and pupils do, or don't do, together in schools. The anecdote with which we began illustrates only one of them. We, like most teachers, can produce more anecdotes to illustrate some of the others, for example:

- children whose behaviour is seen as a problem only at school or only at home;
- teachers who unwittingly make behaviour worse by their attempts to make it better;
- quiet children whose desperate needs go unrecognised in the hurly burly of school life;
- teachers who feel desperately in need of help and are discouraged from seeking it.

We could go on, because these are not simply matters of discipline or misbehaviour. They are threads through the whole fabric of learning, teaching, care and welfare which our society expects of teachers who are given responsibility for nurturing the mental and physical health of young people. Given the present anomalies, it would be remarkable if we could not improve the ability of teachers and pupils to work constructively together so that the former can exercise their responsibilities successfully. This book aims to provide some ideas about how that might be done and to plot some of the pitfalls on the way.

THE MAIN ELEMENTS OF THE BOOK

It seemed to us that the majority of books which deal with the subject of behavioural difficulties in schools fall into one of two categories. The first of these is the general critique, usually providing an analysis of the definitions, statistical material and insight into the general issues. The second approach is the teacher handbook, a more or less tightly structured set of guidance notes for teachers. Both these approaches have their place in the wider scheme of things and many of these books have provided us with ideas and strategies. A number of them are referenced in the text and some are recommended for further reading.

We wanted to provide a different sort of book, which would combine the following three elements:

- firstly, a *framework from within which problems can be tackled*, rather than claiming to produce the answer;

- secondly, a *format that would encourage active reading* so that you consciously use your own experience and opinions to explore the issues and can act as a participant rather than as a recipient;
- thirdly, a *structure that would recreate a sense of journey*, with the emphasis upon a continuing process of exploration and discovery, rather than a particular set of solutions.

1. The framework

Any social arrangement which requires the co-operation of the whole cohort of the population of a given age, which is what, in effect, schooling does currently require, is going to run into some difficulties. *The* complete answer is not available, we believe, because some difficulties are the inevitable consequence of the kind of enterprise which is universal schooling.

That is not to suggest that nothing can be done about the problems faced by schools; far from it. More of the solution may lie in the hands of teachers than is suggested by either the common belief that the cause, and so the cure, is somewhere outside school, or the common expectation that these problems can, and should be, handed on to specialists who, after all, know how to deal with 'this kind of thing'. We have something to say about the ways in which teachers who are not 'specialists' in dealing with 'problem behaviour' can go about making the initial response to problems. We will claim that those initial responses need not be essentially special; they are inextricably tied to the ways in which all children learn successfully and teachers teach effectively.

This is still not recognisably *the* answer or even *an* answer to the problems. What we are suggesting is that there are better or worse ways of working at the tensions, paradoxes and downright contradictions which these problems create for us and we believe that the better ways are those to which the participants have some commitment and over which they have some sense of ownership. We will outline the areas of school and classroom activity in which we believe these better ways can more successfully operate and describe our own, not always entirely successful, efforts to introduce strategies for change in some of these areas.

2. Active reading

We wanted to produce a book, the content and style of which would reflect the general view of learning which is implicit throughout it, drawing the reader into an alliance with us, based on a sense of equivalent status and commitment, and presenting our ideas in a form that would encourage and expect critical reflection.

At some stages in the text the material is clearly and explicitly set out in the form of 'activities' which invite the reader to make a response other than just reading. Although it is possible for the reader to pass over the activities and still make sense of the following pages, it would be equally regrettable. The point of the activities is that they act like major points of punctuation in the text. They are a moment in which to draw breath and either to reflect on what has been presented up to that point or to anticipate what might come next.

A sense of journey

There is still much to learn about effective responses to behavioural problems in schools. We are not, therefore, offering a neatly rounded-off package which is the product of our experience. We are taking stock of the point to which our experience has brought us, which is, in turn, a new starting point for the next stage of the journey.

We begin, in Part One, with an acknowledgement of the sheer complexities of life in a large school; the frenetic pace and conflicting pressures which make it difficult for teachers to respond to 'problem behaviour' in any except the most immediate and direct way. We explore how things look from the pupils' point of view, and how accepting the legitimacy of different perceptions provided us with a starting point for seeking more effective long-term strategies for tackling 'problem behaviour'.

We examine, in Part Two, how the structure and history of special provision tends to maintain and reinforce teachers' sense that a substantial minority of pupils are beyond our help and 'need' specialist teaching which ordinary teachers cannot be expected to provide. We offer our own critique of these assumptions and present theoretical grounds to justify the alternatives which we began to explore in our own practice.

We describe, in Part Three, our attempts to initiate changes in our own work with children, and in the features of the organisation and curriculum of our schools that we thought might be effective in reducing or preventing 'problem behaviour' in the long term. We analyse the strengths and shortcomings of the strategies we adopted, and draw out the process lessons to guide future efforts.

In the final section, we consider what has been learned over all and what the implications are for our immediate responses to individual pupils' difficulties. We look at the question of what kinds of special provision will realistically still be required to supplement, rather than substitute for, schools' own efforts to meet all their pupils' needs.

OURSELVES

The co-authors of this book are teachers (or have been for most of our professional careers), so whenever teachers are referred to in the text, for better or worse, we include ourselves. Although we have read and have been influenced by research and literature in the field, we have not attempted a second-hand description of the work of others just to ensure a comprehensive overview of current developments. Instead, we have constructed a substantial part of this book around our collective experience of working in a variety of capacities in primary and secondary, mainstream and special provision, in the belief that this can be of value to others concerned with the same issues. It might be said that our personal experiences however valuable and interesting in their own right, are too context-specific to be of more than limited value to the general reader, that it is not possible to generalise from what worked or did not work with one child, one class, one teacher or one school to make general statements or prescriptions about approaches that might prove effective in any other situation. Our reply would be that there are many books which present theoretical arguments and draw conclusions from them about what should happen in practice but few go into any detail about the reality of using those ideas. To bring our ideas to life, we need to tell readers what it was like when we tried to develop them in our day-to-day teaching so that they can participate in assessing the successes and shortcomings and in judging what lessons or conclusions of general relevance might be learnt.

The fictionalised accounts of a day in the life of a comprehensive school, which constitute the first chapter of our book, are written directly from that experience, as well as from our knowledge of the issues which have been the subject of much research in the field. They will, we hope, set the scene for the discussion that follows and draw readers into a consideration of the question of 'problem behaviour' viewed from different, sometimes conflicting perspectives.

Part One
Problem behaviour: whose problem?

1

A multi-layered epic

> ... any incident is a climax or crisis in a number of 'stories'. Both pupils and teachers carry their stories with them into school, the clash of stories makes a multi-layered epic.
>
> (Shostak, 1983, p. 113)

From the start our discussions about this book were beset by problems of terminology and definition — how to signal clearly to readers what the book was about without prejudicing the case we wanted to put forward about the nature, causes and most constructive strategies for dealing with 'problem behaviour'. The series of fictionalised accounts with which this chapter begins emerged as an idea from our attempts to resolve this dilemma. They tell the story of a 'day in the life' of an imaginary, but familiar, large comprehensive school, in which a sequence of events combine to create a crisis and a boy is suspended. The events of the day are reconstructed through the accounts of a number of participants, teachers and pupils, who are either directly involved with the incident themselves, or come into contact with those directly involved at some point before or afterwards. As each person struggles to make sense of, and cope with, the complexity of demands made on them by the school day, their stories will, we hope, raise in readers' minds a range of issues which permeate the literature in the field and which help to explain the problems of presenting the subject matter of this book in a more orthodox form. An activity accompanies each person's account, to help to draw attention to specific issues which we intend to take up in the next chapter and in the book as a whole. However, we would encourage readers first and foremost to respond to the stories in their own way, to use them as an opportunity to relate and reflect upon their own experience in preparation for the more focused discussion which follows.

PILGRIM'S WAY SCHOOL: SETTING THE SCENE

The summer term is drawing to a close and the atmosphere at Pilgrim's Way is becoming increasingly festive and frenetic. The ritual end-of-year activities — sports days, concerts, day trips, parents' evenings, reports, prize days, fêtes, concerts and plays — are all taking their toll, while teachers struggle to find the extra energy to attend to the final details of next year's timetable, option lists, tutor groups, teaching rooms, planning of new courses, ordering and printing of materials and preparations for the new intake for the coming September. In the midst of it all, of course, teaching is expected to go on as usual.

The people

1. **Mary:**   second-in-charge of the school's on-site 'disruptive unit'
2. **Fred:**   suspended pupil
3. **Sheila:** history teacher involved in incident
4. **Carol:** the real culprit
5. **Bob:**   primary teacher visiting school
6. **Dan:**   adviser for special educational needs

1. Mary's story

Mary is a (formerly) Scale 2 teacher, second-in-charge of the school's disruptive unit. She has been working with Fred (the boy who is suspended) for some time and is feeling optimistic about the possibility of his successful reintegration into lessons. However, her day begins not with thoughts of Fred, but with another pupil who has been truanting and whom she has been asked to call for at home and bring into school.

Discussion points

What are the consequences of placing those with designated responsibility for pupils with 'behavioural difficulties' on the fringes of mainstream education:

(a) for the pupils?
(b) for the specialist teachers?
(c) for mainstream teachers?

8 a.m.
Today I have to leave early to collect a school refuser from his home. I hope that this will enable him to settle in to coming to school on a more regular basis. However, listening to the weather forecast, it looks like it will mean me getting and staying wet for half an hour longer than usual.

8.30 a.m.
The steady drizzle turns into steady rain, and as I arrive at the house I am met by a rather large dog wagging its tail and baring its teeth at the same time. Jack's brother opens the door and the dog goes in, but it is obvious that I'm not going to be let over the doorstep. All manner of strange noises come from within the house, including the sound of Jack trying to fight whoever is using forceful persuasion to get him to come and meet me. Eventually, amidst much cursing from the upstairs of the house, Jack appears and we start the journey to school. Little conversation happens on the way, partly because Jack refuses to talk to me. I can't say I blame him. I feel that I have intruded on his privacy.

9.00 a.m.
We arrive safely in the unit. I had taken Jack to see his year head before registration period had begun so that they could become reacquainted with one another. This was a partial success. It seemed fairly obvious to me that the year head was biting her tongue over something that had happened in the past but was desperately trying to appear as if she was pleased to see him. I didn't witness the whole of the interview because I had to go and remind the head of fourth year about another pupil from the unit who has been out of humanities for two months and is due back to lessons today. On the way back to the year head's office, I bumped into Fred himself and reminded him about going to humanities. He appeared to be quite relaxed and said that he was looking forward to going back to the lesson because they were going to watch a video. His manner confirmed my feeling that he would be all right in lessons from now on. He had made significant progress in managing his own behaviour, or perhaps he had just grown up. When I finally returned to collect Jack, he had a slight smile on his face. The year head looked decidedly grey.

9.15 a.m.
Teaching for the morning is under way. Two children are doing maths, one reading, one English, one humanities and two are setting up the computer instead of doing French. I am trying to fill in some admittance details with Jack. After doing this, which takes rather a long time because I keep having to answer questions about which lead goes where on the computer and what this particular maths problem really means, the first double period has nearly gone and it is time for break.

10.15 a.m.
Break time. Take Jack back into school explaining that he has now got to go back to his lessons for the morning because I am support teaching next lesson, and after that I am teaching my own English group. He gives me a slight smile, only the second time I've seen it today, and makes off towards some friends of his. I go in search of a cup of tea.

10.35 a.m.

Support teaching with a second year group, perhaps the most enjoyable session of the week. I'm supporting this group in lessons because it has three unit pupils in it, and potentially more on the way. It has always struck me that many of the pupils I see in the unit would be better dealt with in the context of their tutor group and the curriculum presented to them. It can be a very enjoyable experience producing new work for the group and seeing it going down well. And there are always lessons to be learned from seeing it fail miserably! The lesson today is a success. The children work well in their groups and appear engrossed in the work.

1.00 p.m.

A fairly normal morning. Not so the lunch hour! All interest in my salad roll evaporates when Fred's humanities teacher comes up and tells me she has had a bad time in the lesson with Fred. Apparently, she sent him to the year head for swearing at her. I just don't believe Fred could have reacted like this without provocation. It transpires that he was accused of stealing some money by one of the girls in the group and it grew from there. I set off in search of the year head, and after ten minutes spent scouring the building, discover him back in the staff room telling jokes. He tells me in an off-hand way that the head has decided to suspend Fred for leaving school premises without permission and for using threatening and abusive language to a member of staff. I feel extremely irritated that nobody has bothered to inform me, let alone ask me how the situation should be handled. It is two hours since the head made that decision, but no note or communication from anyone to me. The year head's reaction is that we are all better off without Fred; he's taken up more than his fair share of everyone's time and patience already, and deserves all he gets. He turns back to tell the next joke.

1.45 p.m.

I catch up with the head, who confirms to me that Fred has been suspended because she has had enough of him. I try to point out that several good things have been happening with him as well, but the matter is already closed. The head is more interested in telling me about a meeting next week which appears to mean that there are going to be larger first year groups next year because of falling rolls, and that we can have no INSET time for special needs next year because the fourth and fifth year curricula have priority. I try to argue that working with an advisory teacher on classroom management will eventually be of benefit to the fourth and fifth years. In return, I receive a speech about who has to carry the can.

1.55 p.m.

I go back to the staff room feeling very disillusioned with life and find a note in my pigeon hole telling me that Jack did not turn up for his lesson after break. There is no time to do anything about that now. I suppose I will be back on his doorstep tomorrow morning. I leave the staff room thinking that I have one of two choices, getting muddy going back to the unit in the rain or following my pupils' example and going home quietly without telling anybody. I choose the mud only because I'm not as brave.

2. Fred's story

Fred is fourteen years old. He is a fourth year pupil, and has a long history of difficult, disruptive behaviour stretching back to his primary school days. His teachers have 'tried everything' with him, but apparently to no avail. He seems to have difficulty in grasping what it is about his behaviour that the school finds so objectionable, and feels that he is victimised by teachers because they regard him as a troublemaker. He looks back on the incident that got him suspended and expresses, with some bitterness, his feelings about it.

Discussion points

   (a) How do certain pupils acquire identities as 'troublemakers' or as being 'maladjusted'?
   (b) How do these 'identities' affect the way they behave and the way their teachers treat them?

My name's Fred and this is my story, although you probably won't believe me. Nobody ever does. I've been at this school for nearly four years now and I quite like it really. No, not the lessons (I think they're boring), but I like coming to see my mates.

When I was in the first year, they sent me to see this Ed. Psych. bloke. I don't think they wanted me to stay at this school, but I said I wanted to and he said that I could. Since then things have been all right really. Mind you, I've been kicked out a few times – you know – excluded, but they were for things that weren't really my fault. Once you've drawn their attention to you and you've got a face, you get picked on. Like there was this time when I was fooling around with me mates in the gym. We'd asked to go to the toilet during the maths lesson and the teacher let us. Anyway, we found this tennis ball in the gym which was on the way to the toilet, and we were kicking it around like, when it hit the fire alarm and the alarm went off. I got three days out for that. Nobody else did. Something about it being their first offence, or some excuse like that. Anyway, it just goes to show that once you've got a face, they'll do you.

I'm supposed to be telling you what happened yesterday. The school that I go to has got this unit, and I've been in and out of there for the last few years. It's where they send you when your subject teacher has got fed up with you. I've been in there for science because they said I was dangerous. I ask you! And just recently I've been in there for humanities. I don't know why that was, but it gave me a chance to catch up on me homework and the work in class. Last week, the teacher says to me 'Do you think you are ready to go back to the lesson?' I says 'Yes', because I've caught up with all me work and that. Anyway, they were going to have this video next lesson, and I'm not one to miss a good show, so I agree to go back. Just before registration, the teacher from the unit saw me and told me to be a good boy and all that stuff. I said I would, 'cause it was the video, see. I went off to register, but I didn't stay in the room because I've got mates all over the school, and it is one of the times of the day that you can see them.

I got to the lesson and everything seemed to be OK. The teacher was in a bit of a huff, but that was because she was a bit late setting up, and there was this girl surrounded by other girls. There was a lot of chattering and the girl in the middle was crying. The teacher went over to them. I suppose she had no choice really, but I bet she thought it was a pain in the neck, first lesson and all that. Then suddenly out of the blue she comes over to me and asks if I was out of my tutor room this morning. I said 'Yes', because I'd been out seeing my mates. Then she tells me in this really snooty voice that some money has gone missing from one of the lockers, £10 to be precise. She asks me again what I was doing out of my tutor room. I've already answered that question, so I guessed she was accusing me of taking it. Well, I'm not having that. I might be a face, but I'm no thief, so I told her where to get off. We had this slanging match, and she told me to get out and go to Mr Hardaway. Fat chance of me going anywhere near him. He'd spit at me as soon as look at me. I decided to go home and let them all cool off.

Anyway, this morning my mum got this letter telling her I'd been suspended until further notice, not because I'd stolen the money – I hadn't, so they can't do me for that – but because I'd used bad language to a teacher. Honestly, who's ever heard of anybody being suspended for swearing when they've been wrongly accused of theft? You ought to hear some of the teachers' language! It goes to show that if you've got a face, they'll do you in the end.

3. Sheila's story

Sheila is an experienced main scale history teacher. She is also a tutor of a third year class and tries to take her pastoral responsibilities seriously, although there is never enough time to fulfil them properly. Today turns out to be one of those days when the pressure just gets too much and she loses her temper with a pupil, a confrontation occurs and the pupil is subsequently suspended.

Discussion points

(a) What conflicting expectations imposed upon teachers by

themselves and by others add to the pressures and stresses of the job?

(b) To what extent is it legitimate to hold either the teacher or the pupil solely responsible when an incident of 'problem behaviour' occurs?

8.30 a.m.

There's a cover slip with my name on it lurking by the head's daily notices, and I discover that I have won the dubious privilege of an hour's drama with 3Lr last thing this afternoon in the year base immediately facing the head's office. I'm just getting accustomed to that thrill in prospect, when Lyn, my class's geography teacher, comes beaming into my field of vision. I feel my defences rising. I know when she looks like that it means my class has been playing up again (and somehow there's always a sense that it's a reflection on the tutor when a class is badly behaved). It turns out that she's given the whole class a detention, which she knows is officially against school policy, but she couldn't sort out who the ring leaders were and they drove her to the point where she couldn't think what else to do. She wants to come into my registration period this morning and warn them in front of me to be sure to turn up. (Her confidence in the deterrent effects of my influence is gratifying but, I fear, ill-founded.)

The first pips go as she speaks, and everyone starts pushing past us towards the door. I should be going too, of course, but I can't exactly abandon Lyn in mid-sentence, so I avoid noticing the deputy head in charge of registers who is trying to attract my attention by waving my register in the air. I feel a bit awkward because I want to help but I know that if she comes straight in with me now it will look to my class like I'm taking her side without listening to their point of view. I stall for time to think by asking her to tell me exactly what they were getting up to in her lesson. At the same time, I'm uncomfortably aware of the deputy head's increasingly frenzied gesticulations in my direction.

The scene Lyn describes is all too painfully familiar, but if it was me I couldn't be quite so sure that it was only the kids who were at fault. Still, it's not my place to say so, and anyway if I try to hold out a moment longer I think the unfortunate deputy head might become locked into permanent spasm. Moving backwards towards the door, I suggest we leave it until tomorrow. She agrees, somewhat reluctantly, and I escape down the corridor. It's a nuisance because I've already got more than enough things to get through in my tutor period today. There's Sukhjit and Helen for one thing. I've been trying to find time to talk to them about homework for days. I've got a suspicion that the problem is that they've got nowhere quiet to work at home, and I might be able to get some arrangement made for them at school. I also intended to get the journals signed up to date this morning. The familiar sense of too much to do and too little time to do it is beginning to build up again. It takes another surge forward as, half-way to my tutor room, I remember I haven't got the video I need for my first lesson. Oh well, I'll have to collect it from the faculty room after registration.

8.50 a.m.

'Late detention for you, Miss!' my kids heckle self-righteously as I scurry towards the tutor room. They pile through the door and I'm grateful that for once they seem prepared to settle down quite calmly. I decide to ignore surreptitious chewing and non-regulation attire for once – much to the annoyance, no doubt, of those who were angling to get sent home to change. There's a limit to what you can tackle constructively at any one time, and I need to keep the atmosphere positive for the discussion to follow.

After the register, I tell them all to bring their chairs into a circle round my desk, and in my best pastoral manner try to open up a responsible discussion about the problem in geography. The response is predictable, if disappointing. Their faces assume that familiar expression of wide-eyed innocence which they've perfected over years of experience of dealing with such situations. Then they launch into a tirade about how boring the lesson is and how moany the teacher is, etc., which is highly embarrassing and exactly what I don't want to happen. I try to steer them off that and get them to consider what they could do themselves to improve the situation, but they just look blank as if they don't see that it's up to them. I find myself saying things like: 'Just because you don't like a lesson, it doesn't give you the right to be rude or to stop other people from learning', but they don't look any more convinced than I feel. I try not to show it, of course, but underneath I wonder if it isn't more worrying if children *don't* act up when they're bored, but just sit there compliantly and take whatever is meted out to them. I am at a loss to know how to bring the 'discussion' to a constructive conclusion, but the pips solve that for me. I wonder if anything has been achieved by this small foray into pupil participation and democracy. I have my doubts.

Just as they're all bundling off towards the door, glad to escape, no doubt, I remember the notice about lining up for dinners that I'm supposed to have read out to them. I can imagine the chaos (and complaints from colleagues on dinner duty) if my class don't know what the new arrangements are, so I frantically call them all back and make them write the information down in their journals, fending off the groans and complaints as good humouredly as I can manage as the minutes tick relentlessly on. By the time they've finished, the second years due to come into the room have already started arriving outside and are falling over each other trying to press their noses against the glass panel of the door. They think it's a huge joke to hold on to the door handle so that my class can't get out. I issue a few threats and manage to wrench the door open, and then, of course, both lots of children push forward simultaneously so that the sea of bodies presses itself to a standstill. I yell at them to use their common sense, and expend more energy restoring them to some semblance of order before I can make my getaway. I finally head off down the corridor already more than five minutes late for my lesson.

9.12 a.m.
Today being one of those days, my lateness does not, of course, go unobserved. Rounding the final bend, I spy, with sinking spirits, yet another of the ubiquitous senior staff in the process of subduing my fourth year history group outside my teaching room. She looks pointedly at her watch as I scramble up the corridor, still clutching the register which both she and I know should by now have been sent to the general office. I mutter my apologies to her supercilious departing back, remembering I still haven't collected the video that I need to start the lesson.

I'm beginning to feel like I've done a day's work already. The fourth years seem to be pretty 'high', too. Maybe it's only because I'm late. I decide to give us all a chance to calm down, and just mark the names quietly in the register instead of calling them out as I usually do. Fred's back, I see. I wonder if he's the reason for the mood they're in. He always used to have a bad effect on them when he was there before, but he hasn't been in my lessons for a while because he's been going to the unit. I wonder if I should choose him to go down to the faculty room for the video. The others might settle down better without him there, and it might give him a chance to start again on a positive note. I decide not to risk it. He might not feel like doing me any favours yet.

There's a commotion going on in one corner. Sacha appears to be in tears and all her friends are fussing round her trying to comfort her. I don't exactly relish the thought of sorting out another problem, but it doesn't look like any work is going to get done unless I do. I take a deep breath and go over to the group.

Apparently someone has taken her school-journey money from her locker during registration. They say they think it was Fred because he was wandering about the school during that time. I turn to Fred, and before I know what's happening, he starts shouting and swearing at me. The shock of his reaction makes me flip my lid too and before I can stop myself I've told him to get out and report to the year head. As soon as I've said it, I wish I hadn't, because, of course, he just sits there refusing to budge and I've got another problem on my hands about how to make him go short of using physical force (and he's bigger than me, anyway). He stares at me threateningly for what seems like hours, and I'm panicking inside wondering if there's any way I can give in gracefully without losing face with the other children. Just as I'm thinking I'll have to do something, he gets up and slams out of the room with a gesture of defiance in my direction which leaves no one in any doubt as to what he thinks of me.

The relief I feel at his departure is more than compensation, but I'm shaking inside too. It really upsets me to have a confrontation with a kid. Deep down, I'm on their side, but that's not the way they see you. It's so hard to strike the right balance with some of them. If you're nice, they think you're soft. If you're not, they treat you like the enemy. I wish I'd been more careful with Fred, but he just caught me off my guard. I really wasn't accusing him of stealing the money; he just chose to take it that way. And I had to react to him swearing at me. School policy is if they swear at staff, they're out – all the kids know it. I'll go and see the year head at break and explain what happened. Except I'm on duty, so I'll have to settle for a note instead.

The rest of the class are a bit shocked and hushed after Fred's departure. Should I talk to them about the incident or not? I really can't face it, or the video for that matter. I feel completely drained. Better for all of us to escape behind an anonymous worksheet until the pips go to release us.

1 p.m.

I've been so busy for the rest of the morning that I haven't had time to think about Fred again until now. I wonder if the year head got my note. The unit teacher is in the staff room eating her sandwiches, but she doesn't seem to have heard anything about it at all. In fact, she's very upset and I can quite see why. She's spent a lot of time working with Fred, and now she feels it's all been wasted. She rushes straight off to find the year head, and I feel even worse.

4 p.m.

I've just heard that Fred was suspended because of the incident with me. It turns out that he never reported to the year head (surprise, surprise), but just ran out of school. The head said it was the last straw, that he'd had all the chances it was reasonable to give, not to mention costly one-to-one individual support in the unit. She said you had to draw the line somewhere. I tried to explain that the incident had been partly my fault, but she didn't want to know, nor did the year head. I've got a feeling they're both quite glad to see the back of him really. But I'm left with a terrible sense of guilt and responsibility.

4. Carol's story

Carol is fifteen years old and a pupil in Sheila's fourth year history group. She rarely gets into trouble because she is always one step ahead of everyone else. She appears to have no scruples whatsoever about the money she has stolen, and takes great delight in watching the incident with Fred, enjoying the sense of power she gets from being the one in the know.

Discussion points

(a) How do we know if problems such as theft, vandalism, bullying, etc., are:
  • signs of individual disorders;
  • manifestations of pupils' alienation from schooling; or
  • a reflection of wider social problems?

(b) In what ways does gender affect schools' responses to 'problem behaviour'?

It's been a right laugh in history today. Quite a little *drama*, if you get my drift. I could tell Miss was over the top the minute she appeared. Must have got out the bed the wrong side or something. You'd think that would be a warning to the rest of them to keep their heads down, but not the boys, oh no! They go headlong for a confrontation every time.

If you ask me, Fred had it coming to him. Boys are so thick. They act all flash to the teachers as if to say 'You can't do nothing to me', but they're about as useless as a hippopotamus in a strawberry field when it comes to picking their way out of a tight spot. You'd have thought Fred would have learnt by now that the best thing to do when anyone tries to pin anything on you is to stay cool, look them straight in the eye and deny it. After a bit, they start to wonder themselves, and then you're home and dry. Anyway, you can be sure I had my excuses ready if anyone happened to inquire how come I'd got ten quid on me when a ten pound note had just done a disappearing trick. But I don't think I'll be needing them now somehow, after the way Fred carried on.

The point is you've got to beat teachers at their own game. It's no good looking for trouble, because they'll always get you in the end. What you have to do is pretend to do all the things they want you to do, like behaving all deferential. They love that. Some kids just can't help smirking and shrugging their shoulders when they get told off, to show they don't care. That really gets teachers going. You should watch me and my mate Alison operate. We can stop just about any teacher in their tracks, no matter what we've done. What you do is: you *smile*, you *apologise*, and you *look as if you mean it*. Magic. Like snuffing out a candle.

Getting done for swearing is too stupid for words. Still, it's even more stupid the way these teachers act so touchy when anyone swears, as though it offends their sensitive ears. They must hear people saying the same words every day outside of school and they can't send *them* to the year head. I sometimes wonder how these high-and-mighty teachers manage outside of school, when they can't order people around and give them detentions to make them do what they want.

Anyway, the excitement's over. Fred's gone and Miss looks like she's about to burst into tears. She's handed us this mind-blowingly boring worksheet and told us to get on with it, and now she's sat at her desk with her head in her hands like a relic from a silent movie. Well, I'm not about to waste my time doing some stupid questions when she's being paid to teach us. They go on and on about how important our 'education' is, and this is what we get! Out of the window, I can see the second years clodhopping it round the netball pitch, but it's more than my delicate eyes can stand. I nudge my mate to pass me the magazine she's reading under the desk. She doesn't want to, but she's hoping to get a share in the takings so she can't ignore me. I flip through the pages until the pips go. Some education!

5. Bob's story

Bob is a teacher from one of the feeder primary schools. He is visiting the school today to pass on information about some of the pupils who may have difficulty in settling when they arrive in September. Unfortunately, the head of first year will be a new appointment, and so is not yet at the school to receive the information personally.

Discussion points

(a) What information about pupils, whose behaviour has caused concern at primary school, should be passed on to secondary school?
(b) How can that transfer of information be most effectively achieved?
(c) Under what circumstances is it appropriate to give the pupils a chance of a completely 'fresh start'?

8.00 a.m.
Today is the day for my yearly visit to the local secondary school about the pupils transferring in September. One and a half hours is all I'm allowed to pass on the information on 50 or so kids! The records we send on are worse than useless really, despite all the time it takes to fill them in. I mean, where is there space to put down the individual things that really make a difference, like 'gets irritable when hungry – needs to be first in to lunch' – and would secondary schools take any notice? What could they do, anyway, about a child who 'can't cope with large numbers of children', or 'can't cope with lots of changes in activities' – that's what secondary schools are all about. So, if you don't fit in, tough!

They're a good lot going up this year, really. My main worry is that I've found out they're going to get a head of first year who's a new appointment from outside. Quite apart from the fact that she won't be there today to hear about all the treats in store, how on earth is she going to be able to appear reassuring and welcoming to a new lot of kids when she's feeling all tense and strange herself and hardly knows her way around? It's bound to take her time to settle in, and that's just when they need her most. Especially kids like Andy. I just can't imagine him coping at secondary school. He's such a baby still, needs looking after, making special. Who will there be to give him that sort of attention at Pilgrim's Way? Secondary teachers don't expect to have to cosset kids like we do at primary school (not all of them, of course, but some of them do still need it even in the fourth year, and why not?).

8.30 a.m.

I bet secondary teachers don't have to do early morning playground duty either! The playground is already quite busy, and the caretaker informs me that the Robson girls have been there since before eight o'clock. I must tell the head that this is happening more and more often. Andy is standing watching some boys kicking a ball around. He looks miserable, as if he'd love to join in, but doesn't know how to suggest it. He sees me and comes straight over. A ghost of a smile as I greet him. He looks pale and undernourished. He tells me a story about his dog (the same one as yesterday), and then asks to blow the whistle. Who will he talk to when he gets to Pilgrim's Way in the morning? Will he ever get there, after the first few days?

9.00 a.m.

As the kids line up, I notice Vincent towering above them all and remind myself to make a point of mentioning him, too, when I get to Pilgrim's Way. Just his size alone always gets him noticed, and since he's usually around where there's any trouble brewing, he tends to be the first to get blamed for it. He gets resentful because he feels everyone is picking on him, and then he behaves so objectionably that you really do have to pick on him! It could get out of hand at secondary school, where nobody knows him really well. He might feel picked on all the time. Come to think of it, though, just by making a point of picking him out on my visit today, I'm starting the whole process rolling again. You can't win, can you?

9.05 a.m.

Find the head's room to remind him I'm out this morning. He's talking to the school nurse, but beckons me to join them. It's Andy they're discussing. He's lost weight, and they're deciding how to make sure he gets extra helpings at dinner time if he wants them. I ask the head for the list of notes on kids we've compiled together for me to take along today. Some bits and pieces of information are still missing from the record cards, but I am to promise that these will be sent on to them within a week. While I'm there, he asks me if I'd like to go on a course on behaviour problems. I wonder if I should read anything into that?

9.45 a.m.

Managed to get a cup of coffee and the Fun Day Banda sheets run off before I left school. Remembered about Himansu's case conference, but there's not a lot I can do about that because the outcome won't be available until next week, and by then Pilgrim's Way will be completely tied up with their end-of-term activities and certainly won't want any more visits from me. He's another one who will need watching out for, but I can't see him surviving the rough and tumble somehow, no matter how much extra help he gets. But what can you do?

I'm feeling a bit depressed about the whole thing as I pull into Pilgrim's Way car park. The only space is one which says No Parking, so I drive back out and park in the street. I'm just walking back in at the gate, when this large character comes storming past me, virtually knocking me off my feet, makes no attempt to stop and apologise, just goes storming off up the street issuing a torrent of expletives. Am I supposed to do anything? The rate he's going, I'd never catch him anyway. I've got to go to the office to let them know I'm here, so I'll report it to them.

9.50 a.m.

That kid running out made me think of Vincent a few years on, and started me off worrying about him again. The pastoral deputy is not in her office and no one can find her. I'm sitting here waiting, and wondering if it's all just a waste of time.

6. Dan's story

Dan works for the local education authority as its senior adviser for special educational needs. A large part of his work is with special schools, but for the past ten years he has continually spent more time in primary and secondary schools. They have been admitting a small number of children with physical impairments or learning difficulties, who might previously have gone to special schools. However, Dan thinks their main concerns are with general staffing levels and worries about behavioural problems. He starts this day with an advisers' meeting to discuss the new LEA plan for reorganising special schools. In the afternoon he is due at Pilgrim's Way School with the secondary adviser, Jean, to talk to the head about 'disruption'.

Discussion points

> We need not deny that some children are emotionally disturbed and need help … [but] … *many features of maladjustment can be interpreted as an artifact of the procedures and practices of local authority administrators.*
> (our emphasis; Woolfe, 1981)

In the following anecdote, what decisions are made – or not made – by local authority advisers or officers which might affect:

1. the way in which the teachers at Pilgrim's Way respond to behavioural difficulties in school;
2. the number of children they expect to be dealt with outside their usual classrooms;
3. the number of children who might be transferred outside the school?

8.35 a.m.

The Assistant Education Officer for Special Education (AEO/SE) thanked us for making a prompt start and summarised the briefing papers which were our one item for discussion. The rolls of many of our special schools have fallen rapidly to the point where it is arguable whether they can provide a reasonable curriculum; the number of pupils outside special schools for whom we are holding a statement and making some provision is increasing; and some features of the new assessment procedures are still not understood by the schools. There has been no fall in the roll of the special schools for children with emotional and behavioural difficulties (EBD), even though the total number of children in the LEA has fallen by a quarter.

I was ready for a discussion about the number of schools for children with moderate learning difficulties (MLD), because there are just not enough children who now need to go to them, but the AEO/SE moved us straight into behavioural problems.

'I want', he said, 'the discussion to encompass an additional but, I think, related issue. There is some concern amongst the elected members about the current rate of suspension in secondary schools and also about the value in educational and fiscal terms of our off-site units programme.' These pupils always soak up more time than you expect; it is so difficult to know what to do about them. The rest of the business was pushed to one side and did not do justice to the MLD reorganisation issue. We will have to meet again soon on that one.

I am worried as well about the rate of suspensions. They are not really justifiable, but their present level might look small beer after the Education Reform Act. Schools just will not want anyone around who might pull down their published test-attainment scores. As for the units, well it true that they are a mixed bunch, and although the DES circular said that statutory assessment is not necessary when a child attends a unit for disruptive pupils, I'm not sure that that is a distinction we can maintain forever. And if we have to concede the point, the resource implications are horrendous.

11.13 a.m.
Not only did we fudge the MLD issue, I was late for my next meeting with the area psychologist, Rob. Advisers and educational psychologists are always late, so I know he will not have been waiting. My breathless apologies were only half-sincere. We meet once each month for a working lunch to go through the recommendations for extra teaching or welfare help. The annual budget for our area is heading for overspend and we have no really rational way of deciding which cases are 'worth' five hours and which are worth ten.

One of the points I noticed this morning was that Pilgrim's Way had requested ten teaching hours for a pupil causing them some difficulty. I told Rob I would be there this afternoon and take it up with the head. Bit of a cheek really, since we are helping from central budget to fund their unit.

1.30 p.m.
No sooner was Rob out of the room when my secretary was in. 'I

thought I should warn you before you go. Divisional office have been on the 'phone. Pilgrim's Way suspended a pupil this morning. The DO knew you were going there to talk about problems and thought you should know.'

Well, that was going to make the afternoon sticky. This would be pushed down my throat as 'proof' when I asked them why it was that one of the most favourably staffed schools, with a unit to boot, was after extra teaching hours. It was hard to see how we would find the common ground to talk about INSET and staff development.

2.45 p.m.

Which is exactly how the meeting was going. I was fairly livid about this Fred story. He is suspended from a school which has a unit (why hasn't that worked?) for a pretty petty-sounding reason; his behaviour will make it difficult to place him in an MLD school and his age would put off the schools for emotional disturbance – if they had places, which they don't. Anyway we cannot pull statements and special schooling out of the hat as a form of crisis management. In the longer run it would be educationally stupid, in the medium term it is managerially inept and in the foreseeable future we cannot get away with it. On the other hand, we have to provide education for Fred – the elected members expect that we should provide; his mum and dad will want to know why we're not providing, and no doubt the teachers will tell me that they cannot provide.

Jean saved the bacon. She had said that she wanted to mention the DES funding for the classroom management course before we left, but she slotted it in nicely. She might have had another idea for it but, again, time, energy, emotion or money – difficult pupils soak it up. Still, suggesting that the school could use the money to send someone on the course to look at classroom management of problems was an inspiration. We had something to offer the head, the head had something to offer the staff, and we could all think again about what to offer Fred.

2

Towards a preventive approach

Our use of 'stories' in the opening chapter borrows from current developments in 'action research' (Winter, 1986). Fictional writing is increasingly being used as a strategy for seeing familiar, everyday experiences in a new light and, through critical analysis of the material, finding a focus for professional development. In a similar vein, our 'stories' offer us the opportunity to step outside our immediate professional role and consider the *whole context of schooling* in which 'problem behaviour' occurs. They are an attempt to acknowledge the existence of difficult situations in schools without focusing exclusively or predominantly upon the pupils, and without adopting a label or euphemism which concentrates attention on the pupils as 'the problem' to the neglect of other contributory factors. In the first part of this chapter, we consider in more detail the problems of definition which led us to present our subject matter in this form. In the second part, we analyse the central incident of our 'stories' as a basis for introducing the main themes of the 'preventive' approach developed in this book.

1: WHAT IS PROBLEM BEHAVIOUR?

ACTIVITY

Write down a short definition of each of the following terms in a way which distinguishes their individual meanings:

- conduct disordered
- difficult
- disruptive
- emotionally disturbed
- maladjusted
- neurotic
- troubled
- troublesome

Although words like those in the exercise are common currency, they are rarely used with any precision and it is arguable whether they can be. Precise causes and responses cannot be attributed to these terms as they are used in describing children. On the other hand, they are often used as if they were categorical and ever self-explanatory.

Like all labels, these help us to understand a diverse and complex world. By grouping together sets of phenomena, we can save ourselves from the overwhelming task of trying to identify, interpret and understand every available stimulus as if it were something completely new. We group things so that by recognising a few salient characteristics, we can allocate a stimulus to a category and understand it implicitly as a member of that category. This is not only true of the categories of children who might be described with the labels above. It is generally true of our attempts to make sense of the human condition.

This can work well so long as there is substantial agreement about the nature of the category being used. We could, for example, probably gain some kind of general agreement amongst ourselves about the category 'blond', including a rough description of the main characteristics required for a man or woman to be included in the category. Given colour photographs of a selection of men and women, we could probably reach some agreement on which should reasonably be called 'blond' and which should not. Agreement would probably not be universal unless the criteria used became highly technical in terms of light and colour, thus illustrating the important point that the more precise and unambiguous the criteria, then the easier and more accurate it is to allocate members of the category.

All that is simple enough but the labels which we presented in the activity above constitute a quite different kind of category, most obviously because of the absence of clear criteria. Although they are often used in apparently similar ways, these labels and categories are not analogous to medical diagnoses based on measurable, observable characteristics about which there is at least a broadly agreed interpretation. In the field of behaviour, things are not as easy as that.

- Behaviour is more than just an observable phenomenon which can be simply reported; (for example, *the emperor has no clothes on*).
- The appropriateness of a particular piece of behaviour can only be considered if its context is known; (*the emperor with no clothes on is not in his bathroom but on the street*).
- Even then the behaviour will have different meanings and therefore elicit different responses from different people; (*who dare tell the naked emperor in the street that he is a fool?*).

This really means that when judgements are made about pupils whose behaviour is causing concern, they are not made on the basis of 'hard' or 'objective' technological data, but instead on the more or less well-informed opinions and interpretations of teachers who themselves have an interest in both the cause and the outcome.

That said, we would not want to give the impression that problems in schools would simply evaporate if teachers were somehow better at their work or did it differently. Although we believe that the use of labels like those in the activity is generally inappropriate and unhelpful, we do not deny the existence of difficulties in schools or claim that those difficulties are never caused by particular children. The labels are unhelpful, despite their common usage and far-reaching effects on pupils' careers, because they individually lack a substantive basis and collectively have no clear points of differentiation.

When a teacher uses 'disruptive', 'maladjusted', 'delinquent' or some similar adjective to describe a young person, then we have to accept implicitly that there is some difficulty in that teacher's relationship with the child. The description itself does not allow us to conclude that there are more widespread difficulties and offers nothing in terms of knowing the cause of the difficulties, or their present state, or what might be done about them.

Technical or common-sense approaches?

Many teachers assume, with some justification, that there is either a technical or at least a common-sense authority for these categories. They expect technical authority because these are terms used by 'experts' and are part of the discourse of their teacher training. Therefore, it seems, there must be some degree of accuracy with which they can be applied so that pupils can be allocated to the appropriate kinds of provision which are, after all, called schools or units for the maladjusted, emotionally disturbed, disruptive or whatever. The idea of common-sense authority derives from the belief that since we 'know' that some children are 'irremediable rogues', what we call them is largely irrelevant, provided that something is done about them, for preference their removal to somewhere different and, if possible, special.

The simple fact of the matter is that there has never been a clear-cut, agreed definition for particular kinds of behaviour in school. There are, of course, check lists of behaviour which enable teachers to give pupils a 'score' and allocate them to a particular category defined by the score. The Bristol Social Adjustment Guide (Scott, 1978) and the Rutter Behavioural Scale (Rutter, 1967) use phrases like over-reacting and under-reacting (BSAG) or neurotic and anti-social (RBS) to describe children with particular scores. However, these techniques are limited in their application and are not commonly used by schools. It is more common for teachers to be exposed to generic words like 'maladjustment' and 'disruption' in descriptions of pupils' behaviour. These are usually translated into an adjective describing the pupil rather than the behaviour – 'maladjusted' or 'disruptive'. It follows that we should ask what technical validity or common-sense value these words possess?

One of the commonest terms, 'maladjustment', is largely a legal artefact given statutory backing in the Regulations which followed the 1944 Education Act. Its earlier origins will be referred to in Chapter 3, but Bridgeland (1971) provides a fuller review of the definitions used by pioneers in this field. These reflect how diverse their interpretations were and show a notable degree of indecision, if not disagreement, about the boundaries between maladjustment and delinquency – if, as some argued, there were any boundaries. In the 1945 Regulations, however, maladjusted pupils were defined as those who

> ... show evidence of emotional instability or psychological disturbance and require special educational treatment in order to effect their personal, social or educational re-adjustment.

This description lasted for only ten years before it was rejected as inadequate by a Ministry of Education Committee of Enquiry whose predominantly medical members offered these generalisations:

> Maladjustment is not a medical term diagnosing a medical condition. It is not ... to be equated with bad behaviour, delinquency, oddness or educational subnormality. Nor is it the same as a deviation from the normal; while it is true that many deviations are signs of maladjustment, some may involve only one side of a child's development and may not affect his mental health.
> ... [maladjustment] is a term describing an individual's relation at a particular time to the people and circumstances which make up his environment. In our view, a child may be regarded as maladjusted who is developing in ways that have a bad effect on himself or his fellows and cannot without help be remedied by his parents, teachers and other adults in ordinary contact with him.
>
> (Underwood, 1955)

Over twenty years later the term came under close scrutiny again when the Warnock Committee (DES 1978a) suggested the removal of the statutory categories of handicap of which maladjustment was one, but recognised that '...for the sake of convenience descriptive terms will be needed for particular groups of children...'. As a result the Committee decided that 'maladjusted' was a serviceable form of description. However, the phrase 'emotional or behavioural disorders', which the Committee did not endorse, now seems to be the favoured terminology in the field.

It is evident that there is a recurring difficulty of relativity. Since behaviour only acquires a meaning in context, maladjusted behaviour cannot be easily circumscribed by a list of behavioural attributes. This is particularly true in relation to young people whose behaviour carries a strong element of age appropriateness. So, for example, the acceptable sexual interests of an adolescent would cause concern if displayed by a six year old, while the six year old's attachment to a comforting blanket could seem inappropriate in the sixteen year old. As a result, the available definitions of maladjustment have been confined to generalisations which, in practice, rely upon locally idiosyncratic interpretations by adults.

Because 'maladjusted' was a description with some implicit and some explicit administrative and procedural consequences, it was unsuitable for use when there was the rapid increase of provision in and around schools to respond to behavioural problems (described in greater detail in Chapter 4). Suggesting that a pupil was 'maladjusted' drew the child and teachers into a set of procedural requirements which decelerated the rate at which the case could be dealt with and the pupil transferred into the special provision. It was at this point, in the mid-1970s, that the term 'disruptive' entered popular usage. *The British Education Index*, an index of articles on education or related topics, and therefore a guide to educational fashions, first adopted 'disruptive' as a separate index entry in 1977. Prior to that it had subsumed a very tiny number of references to 'disruptive' under the headings of 'discipline' or 'maladjustment'.

Over a decade later, it remains the case that 'disruptive' does not even possess the kind of quasi-authoritative definition provided for 'maladjustment' and that it remains very much in the eye of the beholder. Although some examples of behaviour would be considered disruptive in the vast majority of classrooms, there is an enormous grey area in which behaviour which is treated as disruptive in one school or even in one department within a school, will not be treated as such in another. One of us is reminded of a time spent working with the on-site provision established by a secondary school. Teachers could send pupils to this provision, a designated room within the school, if they 'disrupted' the lessons and a pupil sent there three times would be sent home for a short period. This system produced many anomalies, not least the different interpretations by departments of what constituted 'disruption'. Closer examination of the varying rates of referral from departments to this room showed that pupils would be sent there by one PE teacher if they did not have full kit, but that teachers in another department were always reluctant to send children to the room in case it was their third time and the consequence then exceeded the importance of the particular incident.

For reasons associated with either research programmes or administrative organisation, there have been attempts to create a definition for 'disruptive' behaviour. For example, Young (1980) reports an LEA definition of the pupils for whom a unit was being established as:

> ...[those showing] a gradient of level of disturbance from occasional episodes of truancy or outbursts in the classroom, to totally disruptive behaviour in any group situation.

In that instance, a disruptive pupil would be one showing disruptive behaviour, a tautology which, of course, begs the formidable and initial question, 'What is disruptive?'.

An attempt to answer at least part of the question (reported in Tattum, 1982) was made by the 1977 DES York Conference which produced the following list:

1. aggression to other pupils and staff;
2. rudeness and insolence;
3. horseplay in the classroom and behaviour designed to disrupt the work of others;
4. refusal to obey school rules, written and unwritten;
5. general hostility to authority.

As Tattum points out, these categories do not get away from the essentially descriptive element and maintain the situation in which the definition is made by a figure of power and authority who is 'an integral participant in the interaction'. However, researching the referral of pupils to a 'disruptive unit', McDermott (in Lloyd-Smith, 1984) reported that the definitions used by Tattum's 'integral participants' are equally imprecise about the acts committed by the pupils. A disruptive pupil was:

- Anyone who prevents a normal [sic] class operating.
- Someone who will not allow a lesson to continue properly.
- Someone who is not psychologically disturbed but just badly behaved.
- Abnormal behaviour of any kind.

Pressed to describe particular pupils being referred to the unit the teachers made similarly generalised statements:

- Basically non-cooperative.
- A constant disrupter.

- He was quietly self-willed.
- He was a thorough-going nuisance.
- She just enjoyed disrupting the school.

If there is in all of this a common-sense definition or, more accurately, explanation of what teachers define as disruptive behaviour, it can be found in Lawrence's survey, which asked the staff of two secondary schools to report on all the disruptive incidents they encountered. Lawrence concluded that:

> ... disruption amounted to anything which prevented the teacher from achieving worthwhile results with the pupils. Teachers therefore stress disruptive behaviour as a 'general refusal to be taught', 'general disruption', 'doing no work', 'tardiness in settling', 'refusal to obey' and 'insolence'.
>
> (1984)

What emerges from all this is that whatever it feels like to individual teachers in the middle of trying to make sense of a day at school, there is no technical or even common-sense definition of general application or value for the kind of problem with which we are concerned in this book. Indeed, even if there were general agreement among teachers about the nature of the 'problem' and the behavioural characteristics associated with it, the definition inevitably remains a *partial* one as long as the pupils' own perspectives on schooling and the quite different meanings which they may give to the same set of events remains unacknowledged. There are now many illustrations – for example, in the literature on absenteeism and disruption – that one person's *problem* may be another person's *solution*. From Holt (1965) to Hargreaves (1982) we find evidence to suggest that what we as teachers perceive as worrying or troublesome behaviour in pupils might, from another point of view, be interpreted as legitimate protest or, at least, their response to, or strategy for coping with, those aspects of the experience of schooling which create problems for them. This is nowhere better illustrated than in Paul Willis's claim that the behaviour of the 'lads' which caused so many difficulties for their teachers was not only a means of weaving 'a tapestry of interest and diversion through the dry institutional text' (p. 62), but was also a form of preparation for life after school (Willis, 1977).

Our fictionalised accounts of a 'day in the life' of a comprehensive school set out to create a context in which pupils' perspectives on 'problem behaviour' can be included and legitimated without discounting those of their teachers, and without shifting 'blame' for the existence of problems from pupils onto teachers. They represent an acknowledgement that *both points of view* need to be taken into account if we are to plan strategies for responding effectively to 'problem behaviour'. Problems need to be understood in terms of the complex relationships which make up the 'social world' of the school (Pollard, 1985), and the structure of these relationships themselves understood in terms of the expectations and constraints imposed on teachers and pupils both from within school and from outside. Through our 'stories', we hoped to illustrate why problems cannot be regarded as something which individuals carry or bring or own by themselves; to show that they are the product of the social activity that people are engaged in together. In the incident between Fred and Sheila, neither person's actions can be understood in isolation, but only as they relate to one another and to the network of events unfolding in the classroom. At the same time, they have a history and a meaning which extend way beyond the boundaries of the immediate situation.

To relate 'problem behaviour' to the *whole context of schooling* is an essential starting point for the approach we shall be developing throughout this book. It enables us to raise questions about the efficacy of methods of *treatment* which focus all effort and activity upon the child, often in isolation from the context in which the behaviour occurs. It also opens up the possibility of *prevention*, since it may be possible to influence or change features of the context of schooling once their link with 'problem behaviour' is recognised.

2: FROM TREATMENT TO PREVENTION

'Problem behaviour' creates such stress for teachers that it obviously makes sense to look for approaches which resolve problems and prevent them from recurring, rather than simply struggling on from day to day trying to keep them in check. In the remainder of this chapter, we take up the question of prevention – its possibilities and limitations – in relation to the confrontation between Fred and Sheila described in our first chapter. We look at how Fred's perceptions of the incident help to highlight features of the situation of which the teacher is unaware. More generally, we consider how looking at schooling through the pupils' eyes helps us to recognise potential for preventing 'problem behaviour' through improvements to aspects of the organisation and curricula of our schools.

If prevention is to be a realistic possibility, we must have reason to believe that at least some of the significant factors contributing to the problem we hope to resolve or prevent lie within our control.

ACTIVITY

Look back at Fred and Sheila's accounts of the events leading up to Fred's suspension:

1. Make a list of the factors which appear to have contributed to it.
2. Which of these do you consider to have been within the teacher's control?
3. How inevitable do you consider Fred's eventual suspension to have been, even if the teacher had managed successfully to avoid confrontation on this particular occasion?

(a) The immediate incident

The confrontation between Fred and Sheila represents a crisis in two quite different stories. For Sheila, it is about professional commitment and the frustrations of not being able to achieve her ideals and aspirations. For Fred, it is a crisis of acceptance and rejection; of himself by the school and vice versa. Thus the immediate classroom events are simply providing a scenario for a clash whose real significance lies elsewhere. None the less, confrontation was by no means inevitable. Despite the stresses of their respective situations, both Fred and Sheila were in control at the start of the lesson. In their initial comments, both show signs of sympathetic awareness of how the other might be feeling. It was the immediate classroom events which precipitated the incident, and these events were, at least to some extent, within the teacher's control.

Sheila

Sheila readily admits that she mishandled the situation. She is prepared to acknowledge the fact publicly and intervene on Fred's behalf later on, because she knows he caught the brunt of her particularly stressful start to the day. Since first thing that morning, she had been buffeted to and fro between a series of seemingly irreconcilable professional dilemmas:

- loyalty to 'her' pupils *v.* loyalty to colleagues;
- her disciplinary role *v.* her supportive pastoral role;
- responsibility for education *v.* necessity for control;
- attention to administrative procedures *v.* attention to pupils' needs.

Not only had she, inevitably, been unable to resolve them to her own satisfaction, but her efforts to do her best by all of them had brought home to her yet again the painful irony that, given the circumstances in which teachers have to work, the more conscientious you try to be, the less you succeed in doing anything well. A sense of despair is evident in her comments about having to deal with the theft of the money on top of everything else, and this no doubt clouded her judgement when she made the move to tackle Fred directly. Under less fraught circumstances, Sheila would have been able to acknowledge her mistake and take steps to sort it out without loss of face on either side. In her present frame of mind, the unexpected violence of Fred's reaction provokes a defensive response. Disregarding the extenuating circumstances, she focuses her feelings of anger and disappointment onto the 'disrespect' which his language displays towards her as a teacher. Although she instantly regrets ordering him to report to the year head, she finds it difficult at this stage to back down since by now the situation has hardened into a public confrontation in which both her personal dignity and professional authority are on the line.

Sheila knows that she had a number of opportunities to rescue the situation after her initial false move, but in the heat of the moment she was unable to take advantage of them. However, her admission of responsibility for her own part in the confrontation misses a significant feature of the situation which we only discover when we look at the same set of events from Fred's point of view.

Fred

From Fred's account, we realise that what he is reacting to so violently is not the injustice *per se* of the teacher's implied accusation (as she assumes), but rather the injustice of the *assumptions which enabled it to be made*. In other words, Fred realises that the teacher would never have made the veiled accusation on such slender evidence if he had not been a 'face', and, therefore, in her view consciously or unconsciously, a possible culprit. He sees that if the girls' suspicions had fallen on someone whom Sheila regarded as basically 'honest' and 'reliable', she would automatically have dismissed them as speculation and referred the matter to the appropriate senior member of staff. Her action confirms his suspicion that 'once a villain, always a villain' as far as the school is concerned. It destroys in an instant any fragile optimism he might secretly have been harbouring about trying to reform ('be a good boy and all that stuff') following his time in the unit. Not for a second does he consider the possibility of reporting to his year head. To do so would be to rob himself of the initiative so vital for the preservation of his own dignity, in that it was he, not the school, who made the final choice.

(b) Long-term prevention?

As far as Fred's own 'story' is concerned, Sheila is merely acting out a symbolic role which could potentially have been filled by any representative of the school's authority. Had she acted differently, the incident might have been prevented on this occasion. But it has to be recognised that the likelihood of a confrontation that would provoke Fred's suspension occurring on another occasion would be an ever-present possibility as long as the vicious circle continued to operate, through which Fred, in turn, rejected and was rejected by his school. Our experience suggests that the crisis which occurred on Fred's return to class after a 'successful' period in the unit is typical of what so often happens. A colleague formerly working in an on-site unit for 'disruptive' pupils describes the problem as follows:

> It was as though the pupil would come to us for a boost of confidence. We would spend six weeks or so healing the wounds of shattered confidence only to return the pupil to circumstances in which we could predict the scab would be picked and festered in very little time.
>
> Why would pupils who could work hard, behave sensitively and appear to enjoy coming to school when in the unit, behave so differently in the atmosphere of the main school? At least one pupil a year would end up expelled for their behaviour on the main site, despite the work they had put in with the unit. We were failing to prepare them for the 'real world' of school and, in retrospect, too much of our time was spent trying to teach the students strategies which might enable them to foresee or circumvent potentially difficult situations without bringing teaching staff or the pupils' peers into the process. Consequently, the emphasis for blame and remediation lay squarely on the shoulders of the referred pupil who ended up doing an awful lot of the work in isolation and out of the context of where the problems appeared to manifest themselves.
>
> (Tim Joyce)

Our experience of working with the many 'Freds' with whom we have come into contact over the years, suggests that as long as so much of the onus is on a pupil to adjust his or her behaviour to fit in with the school's scheme of things, the chances of successful long-term assimilation are small. If there is to be any hope of interrupting the self-reproducing process of rejection and response, or preventing it from getting underway in the first place, then schools, as well as pupils, must be prepared to adapt and change. Schools must accept their own responsibility for examining *how* the dynamics of schooling may be contributing to 'problem behaviour', and *what* might be done both to ease the problems pupils are currently experiencing and, where possible, to prevent the same problems arising with the next generation of pupils.

Identifying features of schools' organisation and curricula, which might be adapted or improved to promote more constructive patterns of behaviour, is undoubtedly that much easier at one or more removes from the sometimes threatening immediacy of the classroom. Teachers like ourselves, who have chosen to work with 'problem' pupils, find that we are uniquely placed to look back in at the curriculum *from their point of view*. Release from the relentless pressures of whole-class teaching, coupled with the opportunity to direct our thoughts and energies single-mindedly to the needs of this group of pupils predisposes us towards adopting the *critical stance* which we shall argue is essential to a 'preventive' approach.

However, this 'critical stance' and the kinds of insights which it promotes are not, of course, the sole prerogative of teachers working with 'problem' pupils. For many mainstream teachers, a consciously reflective and critical stance is already an essential feature of the way they see their professional role (Stenhouse, 1975). Researching into one's own practice is a means of 'emancipation':

> ... the teacher is engaging in classroom research for the express purpose of improving the quality of educational life in that classroom. The motivation for doing so may be varied ... but the process and implications are essentially the same. The major consequence being that teachers take more control of their professional lives.
>
> (Hopkins, 1985)

Our aim is to harness and develop this approach to professional work in the cause of tackling 'problem behaviour', thereby discovering:

- the *scope* that exists within mainstream education for teachers individually and collectively to take action to bring about improvements in provision and practice which, in turn, will bring about significant improvements in pupils' behaviour;
- the *opportunities* that would otherwise be missed if schools follow the traditional practice of isolating and removing 'problem pupils' from mainstream classes.

This is the essence of what we mean in this book by a *'preventive'* approach. In applying a 'teacher-as-researcher' model to 'problem behaviour', the motivation is both to *reduce stress* on ourselves by reducing the time spent unproductively in policing and controlling pupil behaviour, and to *increase our sense of professional satisfaction* by discovering ways that we can resolve or alleviate seemingly intractable classroom problems through our own endeavours.

THE MISSING LINK

Few teachers would be likely to disagree with our first point; that there is scope for improvement in education provided in our schools, and that teachers can be, and are, instrumental in bringing those improvements about. What is less self-evident is that there is a causal relationship between the quality of education on the one hand and individual pupils' behaviour on the other, and thus that improvements in educational provision will necessarily lead to improvements in pupils' behaviour. Intransigent behavioural 'problems' are taken to be signs of individual 'disturbance' or a reflection of wider social problems which are outside the control of individual teachers and schools. Their potential as *warning signs*, drawing attention to where teachers might turn their efforts next to improve educational opportunities, is thus lost. The process of understanding and tackling 'problem behaviour' becomes dislocated from the overall process of developing and improving comprehensive education, a separation which is legitimated in theory by the ideology of 'different' 'special' needs, and reinforced in practice by the existence of separate units and schools to which such pupils can be referred.

The consequence of this split between the ideology of 'good practice' and professional development and the ideology of 'special educational needs' is that a whole host of opportunities are lost for creative interplay between the two; interplay which could provide special impetus for development and change which might not come from any other source. We shall provide grounds to re-establish the link in theory and illustrate the opportunities which applying it in practice can provide for improving the experience of schooling for both pupils and their teachers.

TWO DIMENSIONS OF PREVENTION

The two basic themes which constitute a 'preventive' approach are as follows:

1. Prevention

Not all problems are of a kind that could be anticipated and resolved through preventive measures. Nevertheless, to the extent that we do have control over features of schooling which affect pupils' behaviour, we have a responsibility, as individual teachers, as members of a school and of a community, to take action:

- to try to adjust what we teach and how we teach to better cater for the diversity of backgrounds and interests represented among the pupils we teach;
- to provide each with opportunities to contribute and to gain satisfaction in learning;
- thus to prevent as far as possible the alienation and disaffection

which research suggests, and our experience substantiates, are so often at the root of disruptive behaviour.

2. Response

A commitment to prevention in no sense implies a lessening of commitment to dealing with the individual cases of 'problem behaviour' that demand our immediate attention. Trying to resolve individual problems in our day-to-day teaching will provide one of our principal sources of insight into preventive measures. Even for those whose behaviour reflects difficult or stressful circumstances that lie outside our sphere of influence, a sensitive 'curricular' response can, as Hanko (1985) has so effectively illustrated, not only have a beneficial effect upon the particular child for whom it was intended, but have the spin-off effect of enhancing the curriculum for the whole class. Instead of being a debilitating drain on our resources, the challenge of 'problem behaviour' can thus become an *opportunity* for us as teachers to use our skills and professional judgement creatively, and find 'solutions' which may potentially improve learning opportunities for all.

SOME LIKELY OBJECTIONS

A 'preventive' approach to tackling 'problem behaviour' ought to be in the interests of both pupils and teachers. However, we can quite see that to many teachers it will probably sound like exactly the *reverse* of what they see as their own interests and those of the majority of pupils who have to suffer daily the constant disturbance and disruption created by certain individuals. Reactions may well mirror the disbelief of the reviewer of a book on disruptive behaviour in a recent issue of the *Times Educational Supplement* who complained that no account seemed to be taken of ' ... those hulking fifth formers who use the classroom to limber up for Saturday afternoon's rumble on the terraces' (Alster, *TES* 15.1.88). The many objections and reservations likely to be in readers' minds need to be acknowledged and briefly responded to at this point.

ACTIVITY

What kinds of reservations do you have about the value and/or feasibility of a 'preventive' approach, on the basis of what you have read so far?

We have briefly summarised below our responses to some of the objections and reservations we have anticipated. In later sections of the book, we deal with these in more detail.

- *'Don't you think those with anti-school attitudes will reject anything we try on principle?'*
  Most of the young people concerned have an ambivalent, rather than an unequivocally hostile, attitude towards school and within this some common ground can usually be found or negotiated.

- *'Aren't the problems more to do with the home background or with lack of job prospects, which the school has no control over?'*
  A 'preventive' approach is not incompatible with a recognition of the wider social constraints within which schools operate. Even accepting those constraints, there is a growing body of research into school effectiveness which indicates that significant room for manoeuvre exists within schools to promote more constructive patterns of behaviour.

- *'Wouldn't you agree that there are some children who are genuinely disturbed and need individual help?'*
  A school where a 'preventive' approach is widely operated is more likely to be sensitive to, and able to distinguish, those cases of 'problem behaviour' which require specialist, individual provision, and make the appropriate support structures available.

- *'How can teachers give these "difficult" pupils the attention they need in a class with 29 others?'*
  How teachers use and create time for working with individual pupils is variable, and attention to group processes can free the teacher from time spent on pure 'disciplinary' matters.

- *'Wouldn't it be more effective to get rid of the minority who wreck lessons for the rest?'*
  As well as the difficulty of accurately identifying the main instigators of disruption, there is no evidence that levels of disruption in schools have been reduced by the huge increase in on-site and off-site provision for disruptive pupils in recent years.

- *'Isn't it just another form of social control?'*
  A 'preventive' approach is not concerned simply with suppressing 'problem behaviour', but in addressing, within limits, its underlying causes. It is, therefore, qualitatively different from approaches which aim, by whatever means, simply to 'sugar the pill'.

- *'Won't it mean more work for teachers?'*
  Our belief is that a 'preventive' approach should alleviate, not increase, the burden on teachers, by reducing the amount of class time spent in disciplinary matters.

- *'Isn't it just another justification for saving money on special provision?'*
  A 'preventive' approach should imply not a reduction in support, but a difference in the way support is offered, i.e., so that teachers can directly benefit from it.

UNDERSTANDING THE PROCESS

Rational arguments can, of course, prove to be a double-edged weapon as far as the process of innovation is concerned. They may do little in themselves to bring about changes in practice, and may produce the opposite effect of that desired if there is insufficient understanding of the processes needed to support proposed developments in practice. Resistance to ideas can be reinforced, leading to the rejection of new approaches before their potential benefits are demonstrated. We have considered it important, therefore, to give emphasis in this book to the *nature of the processes* involved in introducing or initiating a 'preventive' approach, as well as to the actual content of, and justification for, the procedures themselves.

However, the first step must be to present, in the next section, the theoretical grounds which justify our critique of traditional approaches to dealing with problem behaviour, set against some background information about the historical evolution of current provision. We shall, then, analyse more directly the *scope* that exists within schools for teachers to take action to improve pupils' behaviour. As we identify those aspects of the schooling process known to have a significant impact on pupils' behaviour and which do potentially lie within our control, it should equally become clear that we disassociate ourselves entirely from those who would blame 'problem behaviour' upon the 'failure' of comprehensive schools. Any process of selection within education (including *within* former grammar schools [Lacey, 1970]) implicitly devalues a section of the school population, increasing the risk of alienation and disaffection and hence the potential for 'problem behaviour'. Through comprehensive reorganisation, the necessary framework has been laid within which a more equitable and effective education for all can be developed. Our concern is to explore, within the limits of autonomy available to us, ways to further that development.

We would also wish to disassociate ourselves from those who would 'explain' problems in schools in terms of the lack of commitment, expertise or inspiration of their teachers. We are all too aware of the range of skills teachers need to be able to call on to do an even half-way respectable job, and of the drain on teachers' emotional and physical resources which the process imposes. When we appear to be critical of features of schooling, it is not the efforts of any individual or group of individuals that is in question. It is the inheritance of past practice in terms of teaching content, approaches and ways of organising schools that we want to bring under critical scrutiny, to decide what should be preserved and what transformed as our legacy for the future.

Of course, there are many constraints both from within school and from outside which limit the possibilities for change. We do not claim that the approach we propose can solve all problems, or that there will never be occasions or circumstances or particular pupils requiring separate or special treatment. What we are suggesting is simply that in trying to tackle the problem constructively, it makes sense to direct our initial and principal response towards those features of the situation which we are able to influence most directly. It is there that our efforts can and will *make a difference*.

Part Two
Structure, Strategies and Stereotypes

3

Historical developments

In this chapter we describe the development of provision and strategies for dealing with behavioural problems in schools, and in the following chapter we will describe the legacy of provision and strategy which this has produced for the education service. Our aim is to demonstrate that the outcome is a system which, because it is predicated on the ideas of individual pathology to be remediated in special provision, cannot provide effective help for primary and secondary schools with the wider range of difficulties which they currently experience.

It is common for the overall approach to behavioural difficulties in schools to be described as a 'medical model', initially a literal description in so far as the more difficult cases became the province of doctors, ranging from general practitioners to psychiatrists. As the direct impact of doctors has waned, their approaches and vocabulary have persisted, particularly through the work of educational psychologists. The 'medical model' has become a way of looking at problems of social/behavioural deviance/abnormality as a kind of illness of which an individual is the sufferer. It invokes '... the whole conceptual apparatus of symptom, syndrome, diagnosis, aetiology, pathology, therapy and cure' (Hargreaves, 1978). However, since the particular term 'medical model' has strong associations with 'medical techniques' (i.e., drugs, chemotherapy, psychiatry and surgery) with which we have only passing concern, and since notions of individual blame and deficit historically precede the emergence of modern medicine, we have favoured the term 'defect model'.

PAST DEVELOPMENTS

The development of the education service's response to behavioural difficulties is largely a history of separate, special services with a commitment to what Bowman (1981) calls *benign patriarchal change* and *moral training*. There are different ways of writing such a history; Bowman's (*ibid.*) broad sociological analysis, for example, is quite different to either the brief account within the Underwood

Report (Ministry of Education, 1955) or Bridgeland's (1971) mor
elegiac, biographical approach. Our approach is to show that th
history of specialist provision in this field is also the history o
intellectual and structural constraints which have made it increas
ingly difficult for teachers to respond effectively when faced witl
difficulties in schools.

The earliest days

Two features of current provision which can be traced back into th
nineteenth century are the roles of doctors and psychologists. Ir
that century these two groups established a pre-eminence whicl
enabled their professional ideas and, still to some extent, thei
activities to make a marked impression on the education services'
analysis and response to difficulties.

The nineteenth-century European development of what Foucaul
called, '... the myth of a nationalised medical profession, organisec
like the clergy and invested, at the level of man's bodily health witl
powers similar to those exercised by the clergy over man's souls ...
(1973) embraced a growing interest in mental health. In Britain
while Pasteur, Koch, Lister and Morton pursued the understanding
of physical organs and organisms through successive frontiers
there was a parallel search for physiological explanations of mental
moral and educational defects. Francis Warner (1896), a professor o
anatomy and physiology, used head measuring and the 'stigmata o
defect' to conclude that 15 per cent of children were 'defective'
while Maudsley (1879) propounded a physical explanation fo1
'moral defect'. Those biophysical approaches were then sup
plemented by studies of the unconscious mind and the develop
ment of psychoanalytical techniques, pioneered and controlled by
doctors. (Freud, a graduate of medicine in Vienna, was a specialis
in neurophysiology, Jung studied medicine in Basel and Adler hac
been an ophthalmologist.)

The foundation of what we now call educational psychology
owed a great deal to two nineteenth-century pioneers, Galton and
Sully. In 1884, Galton, firmly in the scientific medical tradition
opened an 'anthropometric laboratory' at University College
London. He devised a case history sheet which schoolmasters could
use for systematically investigating and reporting on children.
Sully, Professor of Philosophy at London University, argued (1896)
that although the pioneers had been medical men a new qualifica
tion was necessary for anyone concerned with the 'finer and fruitful
observation' of a child's mental life. Methodical, exact observation
required psychological training:

In very much the same way as physiology renders our everyday knowledge of muscular movement more precise by bringing light to finer processes in muscular and nervous tissues, psychology seeks to probe our mental processes ... so as to get at the more elementary constituent parts.

(Sully, 1913)

Thus the two disciplines of medicine and psychology were equipping themselves with the insights and techniques to which the Board of Education would eventually turn for dealing with problems in schools. The stage was set for some competition between the two groups even though their approaches had one outstanding common characteristic: they were, to a considerable extent, predicated on individual pathology and a 'defect model'.

1870–1920 – 50 years of state provision

1. General developments

In the early years of universal education, teachers receiving payment by results, and school boards incurring the comparatively considerable cost of £10 or £12 per year for each special school placement, represented a conflict of interests which is recalled by critics of the 1988 Education Reform Act. At that time, in the absence of the category 'maladjustment', a term which did not surface until early in the twentieth century (Sully, 1913), one pragmatic solution was to conclude that any children who did not, or could not, avail themselves of the new education system must be suffering from some kind of mental defect; and for that there was a category.

In 1899 the description of children as 'educable imbeciles' or 'feeble minded' was replaced by the Elementary Education (Defective and Epileptic Children) Act's broad definition of defective pupils who,

> ... not being imbecile and not being merely dull or backward are ... by reason of mental defect incapable of receiving proper benefit from the instruction in ordinary Public Elementary Schools but are not incapable by reason of that defect of receiving benefit from instruction in ... Special Schools or Classes.

The persistence of that definition, even when, in the 1920s, opportunities arose for its amendment, suggests that it provided sufficient criteria for school boards to use it as a response to most problems in schools. The evidence of teachers and other professionals' attitudes, outlined below, indicates that they, too, were able to employ the definition and its criteria to the same end.

2. *Professional attitudes*

During this period psychologists made small, but eventually significant, inroads into the education service. Binet and Simon provided the foundations of the eventually ubiquitous IQ test and London County Council became the first education authority to appoint a psychologist, Cyril Burt. On the other hand, the medical profession, despite criticisms of expense and faulty diagnosis (Burt 1964) and the persistent use of physical traits such as head shape for diagnosis (Dessent, 1978), was firmly established within the Board of Education's apparatus.

Following a number of critical reports on ill health, malnutrition and disability among school children, a Medical Branch was formed in the Board of Education and in 1907 local authorities were given the duty to provide for the medical inspection of pupils, and the power to make arrangements for attending to their health and physical condition. The Chief Medical Officer (CMO) began a series of annual reports which show the role of doctors, their interest in problems of behaviour and the use of 'mental defect' to cover a variety of problems. By 1910 the CMO was writing that:

> Disturbances of Emotional balance are frequently associated with mental defect and may assume positive or negative phases in respect of depression and excitement, apathy or interest, submission or aggressiveness, isolation or cooperation, cruelty or affection, spite or pity. To these may be added manifestations of sexual disturbance.
>
> (Board of Education, 1910)

Teachers adopted a similar vocabulary and approach, represented in the following description by a teacher of a 'moral defective'.

> ... crime is out of all proportion to the temptation, the moral shortcomings are not influenced by ordinary discipline and punishment. There is usually some sign of defect but this is not necessarily of an intellectual nature. Often there is a certain eccentricity of character and a dislike of family habits; there is frequently a tendency to lying, together with bad sexual habits and cruelty towards companions and animals ... These cases may be difficult to deal with though something may be accomplished by prolonged training in favourable surroundings.
>
> (Shuttleworth, 1916)

A. C. Cameron (1931) refers more directly to the use of the deficiency clauses in the relevant Acts to remove difficult pupils from schools:

> The tendency in many areas therefore has been that *harmless defectives have stayed in their schools and only those who are anti-social or a nuisance*

have been certified and then either B or C (Educable or Ineducable) according to whether a place has seemed more probable in a Special school or in a Mental Deficiency Act Institution ... there has been a general though not a universal tendency to admit first of all to the day special school children whose presence in the ordinary school was detrimental to other children.

(our emphasis)

The strategies and structures introduced in the early years of the state education service, as a response to only a tiny number of cases, were establishing a paradigm which would persist and expand to become the model on which the majority of responses to problems in schools would be based through to the present day. As a result, although the terminology would have changed, the basis of Cameron's allegation would have been familiar to teachers 50 years after he first made it.

State provision 1920–44

During the 1920s and 1930s there were significant developments in the education service's response to difficulties in schools.

- the development of the term 'maladjusted' in the Chief Medical Officer's reports;
- the creation of Child Guidance Clinics;
- the work of educational pioneers in the small but growing number of special schools for 'disturbed' children.

These developments have to be set against a growing conviction that children in general could be categorised and allocated to predictable and predicting groups. Thus the Spens Report on Secondary Education (Spens, 1938) concluded with reassuring certainty that ' ... it is possible at a very early age to predict with some degree of accuracy the ultimate level of a child's intellectual powers'.

The Norwood Committee (Norwood, 1943) recorded its belief that 'the evolution of education has in fact thrown up certain groups each of which can and must be treated in a way appropriate to itself'.

This belief in a measurable determinism, which led Spens to reject 'multilateral' (i.e., comprehensive) schools, is a persistent theme moving in and out of fashion and renovated by the 1987 Education Act.

Reports from the Chief Medical Officer

By 1927 the CMO's concerns had moved on from the 'spurious' or 'nervous' defect (1908) past the 'neuropathic child' (1921) to a report on 'nervous, unstable and "difficult" children'. In that last report, the CMO noted (Board of Education, 1928) that allied to the problem of the mentally retarded, '... is that of the nervous unstable, *maladjusted* and difficult child'. Thus maladjustment, the term which would provide a generic classification and a staff-room catchphrase in this field, crept into official language. However, throughout the first twenty years of their reports, CMOs had taken the status quo for granted; children, not schools, had difficulties and should change. The proper duty of the CMOs had been to discover what the children's problems were and they had finally arrived at the diagnosis of maladjustment.

2. *The Child Guidance Clinic movement*

During the 1920s, the Child Guidance Council and the Jewish Health Organisation each founded a child guidance clinic in London (Sampson, 1980). The model spread, typically staffed with a psychiatrist in charge, a psychologist and a psychiatric (or mental welfare) social worker. The medical director took the predominant diagnostic and treatment role, while the psychologist would assist by administering tests and working with schools. Expenditure was justified by using the 'Medical Inspection and Treatment Sections' of the 1921 Act and children could only attend the clinic in school time if the head of the clinic was medically qualified. These arrangements tended to enhance the medical or clinical aspects of the clinics' work and to diminish the educational and social.

> Clinics *treated*. As child psychotherapy developed, children whose problems were thought to be internally caused became the preferred clients, the rest, including most delinquents, created problems.
> (Bowman's [1986] own emphasis)

In the absence of a satisfactory administrative or legal structure the main impetus for provision in this field came from philanthropic individuals or institutions. Nevertheless, by the end of the 1930s enough local authorities had exploited the rules to create 22 child guidance clinics provided wholly or partly from public funds and 4 schools for 'nervous, difficult and retarded children' (Min. of Ed. 1955).

3. *Educational pioneers*

While the state system struggled with the difficulties uncovered by universal, compulsory provision, some educationalists, mainly in the private sector, struck out on their own to live and work with disruptive or delinquent young people. The wealth of provision they created, celebrated in Bridgeland's account (1971), was as varied as their philosophies and ideals. Generally they had a psychoanalytical orientation, often committed to the creation of communities – frequently residential – in which children's needs could be recognised and resolved. These later provided the most common models for provision within the state sector. However, like the CMOs' reports and the Child Guidance Movement, their recurring theme was that difficulties should be solved outside the mainstream and by therapies directed at individual pupils.

Already, the creation of segregated provision, and the parallel segregation of professional skills competence was creating an atmosphere of 'bitterness' between psychiatric and psychological perspectives (Moody, 1952), of conflict between psychologists and physicians (Burt, 1942) and of indecision or doubt among teachers (Barons, 1938) which has persisted, to some degree, into the lives of primary and secondary schools at the present time.

The 1944 Education Act to the present day

The 1944 Education Act supplemented moral or educational commitments to children's welfare with a statutory framework. It provides an overall context by placing upon local authorities the duty to '... contribute towards the spiritual, moral, mental and physical development of the community ...'. There is also a reference to LEAs' responsibilities for pupils' well being in terms of cleanliness, health, transport, nutrition, clothing, main-tenance allowances and provision for recreation and social and physical training.

More explicitly, the Act allowed the creation (through Regula-tions introduced in 1945) of the category of 'maladjustment' and, in 1950, the Ministry of Education established the Underwood Committee (chaired by the Chief Medical Officer and dominated by physicians) to report on the treatment of maladjusted pupils; in effect, to define the group and appropriate treatment. It reported in 1955, acknowledging that the definition in the Regulations had the sole purpose of legalising the provision of special education treatment to a particular, but until then ill-defined, group of children. Although the committee's own definition (see page 28) did not move beyond the realms of subjective, context-bound assess-ment, the word became a common, acceptable description of pupils, *She/he is maladjusted*', as if it encompassed a clear and clinical analysis.

The committee's major preoccupation (37 of its 97 recommenda-tions) was with the child guidance clinics and their personnel. It recommended, unsuccessfully, that the clinics control entry into, and 'discharge' from, special classes as well as the day and boarding special schools in which the education authorities would be expected to provide additional places. There were no recommendations for any developments within a mainstream context.

Even during austere periods since the 1950s, provision for children in difficulty has been a constantly expanding part of the education service. The more notable features of that expansion, in an order which approximates to the crude notion of 'closeness' to schools and classrooms, includes:

- the rise and subsequent development of 'remedial' or 'support' departments in secondary schools;
- the introduction of the 'pastoral system' into secondary schools;
- the growth of Education Welfare Services;
- the increasing employment of educational psychologists;
- a massive expansion in the numbers of special schools and units in this field;
- further increases in the provision of Child Guidance Units.

1. Remedial education

It is a 'spurious distinction' and 'psychologically and educationally false assumption' (Galloway, 1985) which divides children into 'disruptives' or 'remedials'. Croll and Moses, for example (1985) found that two-thirds of the children described by teachers as having behavioural difficulties were also said to have learning difficulties and Lawrence et al. (1984) claim that,

> If the school helps the child to learn successfully and to progress, improved self-esteem and security in the learning situation may lead to improved conduct. It is in this context that cut-backs in staffing which lead to cut-backs in remedial teaching ... need to be seen.

It is also apparent that the predominantly individualistic defect model which formed the basis for much 'remedial' teaching is being reconsidered and restructured (Hinson, 1985), much as responses to behavioural problems are. Perhaps the common element in both situations, the existence of *teaching difficulties*, requires a common strategy.

Nevertheless, quite recent surveys (DES, 1978b; Clunies-Ross, 1983) continued to report the widespread use of the withdrawal of individuals or small groups as the most common approach to 'remedial' work. Particularly in primary, but also in many secondary schools, this was achieved by the deployment of female, often part-time, teachers with no directly relevant specialist qualifications.

In 1971 a third of secondary schools visited by HMI had a special department (DES, 1971), but by 1979 Clunies-Ross (op. cit.) found that over three-quarters of the secondary schools in a sample of 600 had such a department. A more recent survey (DES, 1984) found the individualised withdrawal approach still dominant and described work in the special provision as too often narrow and uninteresting. HMI described one pupil obliged to sit through an enjoyable, exciting English lesson, completing a tedious exercise set by the remedial teacher.

2. Pastoral systems

'Pastoral structures' allow secondary schools to perform a 'pastoral role' which might be described loosely as the expression of a broader concern beyond the teaching of 'subjects', or as 'looking after the total welfare of the pupil' (Marland, 1974). The HMI survey of secondary schooling (1979) reported that pastoral systems were created to:

- attempt to co-ordinate consideration of the pupils' personal, social and academic development;
- facilitate the development of good relationships between pupils and teachers;
- try to ensure that each pupil knows and is known by a particular adult;
- make available relevant information through the development of effective communication and record systems;
- involve parents and outside agencies in the work of the school where appropriate;
- enable someone to respond quickly and appropriately to pupils' problems or, indeed, to anticipate problems which may arise;
- improve, by these means, the learning of pupils.

It is a notable difference between this form of provision and others to which we have referred that the emphasis here, at least in theory, is on the well being of all pupils rather than of a particular group. However, in reality, '... the disciplinary and administrative aspects ... are more apparent than their counselling and guidance functions' (Johnson, 1980).

Theoretically, pastoral care teams provide a coherent framework within schools to support all pupils. Inevitably, the nature of their work brings certain pupils to their attention more than others. These include pupils with major behavioural problems, learning difficulties and those who manifest disaffected tendencies through their

non-attendance, lack of effort in class and poor peer group relationships.

(Reid, 1986)

Although considerable resources, in terms of time, energy and
promoted posts, sustain pastoral systems alongside academic
systems in secondary schools, many developments in this field have
been more opportune than planned.

> ... by 1974 the majority of large secondary schools had adopted
> pastoral structures of varying levels of complexity.
>   What is perhaps most interesting and alarming is that this
> revolution in secondary school organisation appears to have occurred
> without any theoretical underpinning or national debate. To find any
> mention of pastoral care in the literature prior to 1970 is virtually
> impossible.
>
> (Clemett and Pearce, 1986)

Yet these structures now perform such a central role in secondary
schools that HMI have reported that heads of house and heads of
year '... could exert a great deal of authority, acting almost
as Headmaster within the group' (DES, 1979).

The expansion and increasing 'professionalisation' of pastoral
systems demonstrate the enduring problems associated with
personal relationships in secondary schools. In large institutions
populated in the main by adolescents, difficulties might be
expected, but it is remarkable that they persist to the extent they do
despite the continued extension of a variety of special services to
help those institutions. Ken Reid sums up the conclusions of many
observers:

> The separation of pastoral and curriculum work in the 1960s and
> 1970s was arguably one of the greatest disasters for schooling. There
> is very little evidence to show that the employment of vast numbers of
> pastoral workers in schools has reduced alienation, underachieve-
> ment, disruptive conduct or absenteeism. ... Arguably the move has
> been divisive, creating academic and pastoral empires, reducing the
> effectiveness of form tutors and resulting in more and more
> bureaucracy and administration.
>
> (1986)

3. Education welfare services

The Education Welfare Service (EWS) has been involved with pupils
whose behaviour causes difficulty ever since Section 28 of the 1870
Education Act gave school boards the power to employ visitors to
enforce attendance. Although school attendance has never been

strictly speaking, compulsory, the titles 'school board man' and 'attendance officer' persisted among parents and children long after the changing work of Education Welfare Officers (EWOs) had been reflected in the changing title of their professional association. The pre-1939 title, 'School Attendance and Investigation Officers' National Association', gave way in 1977 to 'National Association of Social Workers in Education', showing a more generic concern for children's welfare.

Describing the work of EWOs, Macmillan (1977) draws a useful distinction between their *duties* and their *role*. Duties he categorises as:

(a) *allocation and support duties* in the fields of nursery education, handicapped children and school placement;
(b) *provision duties* in respect of clothing and school meals;
(c) *regulation duties* in relation to school attendance, court procedures, child employment and neglect.

The role, he writes,

> ... provides for frequent contact between EWOs, parents, children and schools, based on a diverse range of issues. ... Analysis of the work of EWOs in relation to these issues reveals a role of *discovery*, *first aid*, *counselling* and *progress-chasing*, rather than lengthy social case work. It is a liaison, support and preventative role rather than specifically remedial.

4. *Educational psychologists*

Since 1944 there has been a marked growth in the work done by psychologists in schools, and a shift from doctors towards educational psychologists in their relative influence over the identification and assessment of children with difficulties. It appears that during the 1950s a sense of dissatisfaction with their Child Guidance Clinic role drew psychologists into closer working contact with schools. In turn, schools began to see psychologists as a useful resource and to increase the demand for their services.

The Summerfield Report (DES, 1968) described the work of LEA psychologists and made recommendations about training, qualifications, numbers required and service organisation. It did not satisfactorily resolve questions which are still being asked about the underlying philosophies and purposes of the services. Nevertheless, there are now over 1,300 full-time equivalent educational psychologists employed by LEAs in England and Wales and a statutory requirement to obtain advice from an 'educational psychologist employed ... or engaged by the LEA' when a child's special educational needs are being assessed under the provisions of the 1981 Act.

In some areas educational psychologists are responsible for the administration and inspection of teaching services. This growing involvement is illustrated by *The British Journal of Educational Psychology* which indexes 'teachers' only six times between 1930 and 1954, but 27 times in the next quarter-century. Gillham (1978) claims that there is no more simple index of the drift of change than that of demarcation disputes between educational psychologists and advisers, replacing those between educational psychologists and medical officers or child psychiatrists.

5. *Expansions in special provision*

(i) *Units*   The HMI Report on 'Behavioural Units' (DES, 1978b) recorded 239 known units offering 3,962 places, 85 per cent of which were opened between 1973 and 1977. A later survey by the Advisory Centre for Education (Where? 1980) received replies from 63 LEAs, 44 of whom operated a total of 386 behavioural units providing 5,857 places. The Social Education Research Project at City of Birmingham Polytechnic, in a study confined to *off-site units only*, located 400 units which provided around 7,000 places (Ling, 1984).

The distinctions between units 'specifically for the accommodation within school hours of truants and/or disruptive pupils' (DES, 1978b), and other classes in or out of school, are not clarified by the many titles – more or less descriptive or euphemistic – under which units operate. We are concerned with the full range of units and classes which aim to reduce stresses between pupils and teachers and have been established, initially at least, to achieve that by removing children from classrooms or schools.

Units are usually characterised as either 'on-site' or 'off-site' as if their geographical relationship to schools is their outstanding characteristic. In which case, terminology may reflect an underlying truth, that the most important thing to know about any unit is how far it will remove pupils from the regular classroom. More specifically, 'off-site' is not simply a physical description of the base from which a unit operates, but also an expectation of the work its staff will do. They will work off-site, usually removing pupils from the school(s) to a separate place for teaching or treatment. The staff of some off-site units have recognised inconsistencies in this model and are attempting to reorientate their work towards a preventive or recuperative role within schools. This is one source from which peripatetic services supporting schools are beginning to develop.

Units can also be characterised by their location within the administrative structure of the education system, a different, but equally significant, measure of their distance from primary and secondary schools. In this context, units are either 'attached' or 'unattached', depending on whether they operate within the administrative structure of a school (attached) or whether they operate outside such a structure and are established under Section 56 of the 1944 Education Act (unattached). An *attached* unit can also be *off-site* if it is located away from the main campus. Although the physical separation of school and unit will have some implications, the administrative connections can reduce some undesirable consequences of isolation. On the other hand, an *unattached* unit which is *on-site*, i.e., within the physical boundaries of a school, may have neither line management to that headteacher nor a catchment area confined to that one school. In this case, the physical proximity can be exploited to advantage, although the administrative boundaries can cause problems. In reality, various degrees and combinations of these arrangements operate.

An *unattached* unit does not operate within the administrative structure of the education service if it is a social service or a voluntary services provision. A national survey of 380 off-site units (Ling, 1984) showed that almost one-quarter were not administered by education departments. Nearly one-fifth were administered by social service departments and more than one in 25 were administered by voluntary or independent agencies.

Mel Lloyd-Smith (1984) has suggested three typologies by which units could be grouped – therapy, radical social work and education – but units are rarely characterised either individually or collectively (for example, in research material) by their ideologies or methods. Though difficult, this kind of grouping and analysis of units' work would be especially useful in considering whether any features of the work of units could be beneficially employed within schools in a preventive way. The rarity of this approach to characterisation may well reflect a disinterest in whether the methods used in units are transferable. We return to this point in the next chapter.

(ii) *Special schools* The number of pupils whose main category of handicap was 'maladjustment' and who attended special schools, rose from a few hundred in 1950 to over 13,000 by 1980, doubling and doubling again between 1966 and 1976 (DES, 1977). Around 25 per cent of these pupils attended schools for the 'educationally subnormal' (DES, 1980). On the other hand, in 1980 only two-thirds of the 21,000 children ascertained as maladjusted were attending a special school of any kind. In the main, those who were attending special schools for the 'maladjusted', now usually called for the 'emotionally and behaviourally disturbed', would be attending a small school with between 40 and 60 pupils and a pupil–teacher ratio of around six or seven to one.

In some areas schools for the 'delicate' have also been used to provide for children said to have emotional and behavioural difficulties. Three-quarters of the children attending schools for the delicate in Inner London were reported to be in this category (ILEA, 1985, para. 2.9.46). That in 1980 there was not a single category of special school which did not have at least one pupil who was primarily categorised as 'maladjusted', shows the extent to which special schools of different kinds are used to accommodate pupils whose behaviour causes concern.

Although an increasing number of special schools can point to more or less extensive or effective contact with primary or secondary schools, their essential characteristic is that they are a separate institution.

(iii) *Home tuition*   Primarily to provide teaching at home or in hospital for children who were too ill to come to school, Section 56 of the 1944 Education Act empowers local authorities, when a pupil is unable to attend a suitable school for the purposes of receiving primary or secondary education, to make special arrangements for such education otherwise than at school. In reality, 'home tuition' has become a euphemism for a variety of circumstances in which education is provided outside school. Both DES figures (see Ford et al., 1982) and local authority records (e.g., ILEA, 1985) confirm that the majority of children receiving 'home tuition' are those whose behaviour has been unacceptable at school.

> The increasing use of centres (for home tuition) is resulting in their taking on the characteristics of part-time, off-site centres, particularly as the behaviour of the majority of the children receiving home tuition has resulted in their being unacceptable at school.
>
> (ILEA, 1985, 11.50)

It is apparent that this service has been increasingly diverted into providing education away from schools for pupils whose behaviour has troubled their schools, but for whom other placements have not been found.

6. Child Guidance Service

The service had continued to operate typically through a clinic-based, multi-disciplinary team, including a child psychiatrist, social workers, child psychotherapists, educational psychologists and a teacher, offering therapy sessions to 'disturbed' children and their families, who had either self-referred or agreed to referral. The 400 Child Guidance Clinics operating in 1970 were more than double the number in 1950.

During the early and mid-1970s the clinics suffered from confusion over their administrative position as the Departments of Education and Health and Social Security tried to accommodate their multi-disciplinary character within an overall reorganisation which intended to demarcate school health services as clearly under the control of area health authorities, and not as education services controlled by education authorities (DES Circular, 3/74).

More importantly, against a background of research which questioned the effectiveness of many of their approaches (e.g., Shepherd, 1971; Glavin, 1972) clinics were criticised as ineffective and inadequate. Their highly selective intake, irrational referrals, and contact with such a small proportion of the child population were, it was argued, indefensible (Rehin, 1972). Jack Tizard, an eminent figure in child psychology, concluded that,

> ... the individual treatment of maladjusted children is a pessimistic one. Psychotherapy, play therapy and other forms of individual therapy based on dynamic beliefs have not proved successful in practice.

Tizard believed that the whole enterprise of child guidance in its historical form was 'expensive, ineffective and wrongly conceived' (1973).

Consequently, there has been a trend within the child guidance services to develop consultancy and systems analysis models (ILEA, 1985), one of which is summarised as follows by Denise Taylor (Dowling et al., 1985).

1. The focus of attention was no longer on the individual client ... but was enlarged to include the *setting* in which the difficulty occurred, i.e., the pupil–teacher relationship, the relationships in the class group and the organisational context of the school.
2. The consultant worked with the consultee, i.e., the teacher, not the child ...
3. The aim of the consultation was limited to enable the consultee to contain and resolve the difficulties encountered with the client, not to reform, cure or treat the child, nor for that matter the consultee.

Summary

The historical description given above has been largely an account of the development of services outside primary and secondary schools. Services and responses have been developed on the basis that the greater difficulties are attributable to an individual pathology, and a defect model has been applied to the pupils concerned. The assumption has been that if the correct *individual* pupils can be identified and assessed, then individual programmes for remediation are the best, if not the only appropriate, response. It is expected that this 'treatment' or intervention can only be performed with specialist support from within a continuum encompassing at one end the special school and, at somewhere near the other end, teachers with special responsibility for pastoral care or special educational needs in primary or secondary schools.

Towards the end of the nineteenth century, teachers in the elementary schools, faced for the first time with the responsibility of schooling an entire generation of children, began to look outwards towards psychology and psychiatry for assistance. Keen to show their paces, the new disciplines took on a wide range of problems and established a particular perspective on intervention. Despite its continuous expansion, that perspective has never satisfactorily resolved the problems within schools. The focus, and in various ways the pressure, are again on schools, classrooms and teachers. The question we can reasonably ask is, what legacy has this history provided for teachers facing up to the kind of problems with which we are concerned?

—4—
Strategies and explanations

In Chapter 3 we described the development of units, schools and other services which together form a structure responding to children's difficulties in school. In this chapter we look more closely at the work within that structure and at the legacy of ideas and strategies which that historical development has passed on to schools today. We hope to establish the extent to which the more common approaches adopted by the specialist educational establishments have been generally successful and the extent to which they can be usefully transferred into the work of primary and secondary schools.

INTRODUCTION

It is difficult to know where to set the limit as to who should be included in, or excluded from, a list of the services which help and support schools with problem behaviour. However much we emphasise the specialist elements of various services, solutions, in most cases, will not be provided by specialists. Instead, they will be worked out by teachers within the structure and activity of daily school life emphasised in this book. Arguably, therefore, anything which enhances the quality of a school's work could be included.

The difficulty faced by teachers, responding in the first instance to problem behaviour in school, is that it can have a variety of meanings and consequences, both immediately and in the longer term. When Lewis Carroll wrote:

> Speak roughly to your little boy,
> And beat him when he sneezes;
> He only does it to annoy,
> Because he knows it teases.
>
> (*Alice in Wonderland*)

he demonstrated that it is the meaning we attach to behaviour and its immediate consequences which most influences our responses to it. In the following section we illustrate how that maxim applies to teachers in primary and secondary schools as well as to those who work in specialist services.

PERSPECTIVES AND OUTCOMES IN SCHOOL

ACTIVITY

At the end of the school day you dismiss the third year class but ask one pupil, who has been causing some difficulty in the lesson, to stay behind. The pupil, who is of the same sex as yourself, refuses and heads for the door.

Consider your own most probable response if you were the teacher in the above incident. Make a list of the possible responses which come to mind and try to identify the most desirable and least desirable outcome of each.

There are no simple or necessarily correct answers to this activity, given, as it is, without any of the contextual clues of, for example, whether this was a third year junior or third year secondary class, which influence teachers' judgements. However, some teachers would prevent the pupil leaving the room, using physical restraint if necessary. This has the advantage of responding to the challenge immediately, but runs the risk of escalating it dangerously. Other teachers might let the pupil go, but take the matter up the following day. They risk delay and an apparent loss of face, but may gain by allowing the incident to be dealt with at a less public and pressing time.

It is not possible to say which of the variety of possible responses is best or even, perhaps more important, whether such confrontations are absolutely avoidable. What we need to consider is that a single action – *the pupil heads for the door* – can have quite different consequences depending upon the meaning which the teacher attributes to it. Not all of the different consequences are predictable and we cannot be sure that any of them will be sufficient to settle a particular problem. However, since there is an element of choice for teachers in these circumstances, it is reasonable to ask how it can be exercised with as much insight and purpose as possible. Above all, insightful and purposeful choice requires a prior awareness that choice exists at all. Yet, perhaps because their views of their proper role or the proper ethos of their school are so strongly held, some teachers would argue that, in certain circumstances, there is no choice.

C. Wright Mills wrote that:

The differing reasons men give for their actions are not themselves without reason ... When an agent vocalises or imputes motives he is not trying to describe his experienced social action. He is not merely stating 'reasons'. He is influencing others – and himself.

(1971)

It is in the context of influencing and being influenced by their colleagues, particularly those with authority and senior status, that teachers make and explain decisions about discipline and control. As a result some will have learnt that it is necessary to stop the pupil who is heading for the door; it would be absurd to let the pupil leave the room. Others will have learnt that it is absurd to risk a physical confrontation with any pupil and that some other approach is necessary. These different positions reflect, at least in part, different ideas about the responsibilities of the teacher which are, in turn, reflections of ideas about the nature and purpose of schooling.

Just as the outcome of a particular incident will be affected by the meaning attached to it, so the existence and character of specialist services are moulded by the ideologies and methods which the education service uses to explain and to respond to behavioural difficulties. Current thinking determines the development of institutional arrangements but, in turn, institutional arrangements constrain and contribute to the development of thinking. This is illustrated in Lloyd-Smith's discussion of units, referred to in the previous chapter, in which he suggests that three orientations, *therapy, radical social work* and *education*, could provide the basis for grouping units according to methods used. However, because most school staff and local authority officers may be more concerned about the units' real and metaphorical distance from schools, what happens within them is of less consequence. The result, a system with considerable diversity, left very much to its own devices, is confirmed in HMI's comments that formal local authority documents 'gave little guidance' on the programmes to be pursued and that the day-to-day approach 'depended on the qualifications, previous experience and interests of the staff' (DES, 1978b).

THEORIES ABOUT CAUSES OF BEHAVIOURAL DIFFICULTIES

Methods for solving problems are inextricably linked to views about their causes. Reinert (1976) groups the latter into four categories;

- *biophysical*, in which the pathology is believed to be part of the child's physical constitution;

- *psychodynamic*, in which it is claimed that the child has not successfully negotiated the various intra-psychic and external conflicts associated with the processes of maturity;
- *behavioural*, which argues that unacceptable behaviour is essentially maladaptive behaviour learnt through inappropriate feedback;
- *socio-ecological*, concentrating on the social dynamics of the interaction between the child and its environment.

ACTIVITY

Make a list of familiar words used to describe pupils whose behaviour causes concern (you may wish to refer back to the activity on page 25).

Now allocate each of your terms to one or other of Reinert's four categories. Which categories attract the highest number of terms? (You may compare your list with Reinert's, reproduced as Appendix A to this chapter. There is, of course, no right or wrong answer to this exercise, you may have produced labels which Reinert omits and vice versa.)

The lists you produced for the activity above may reflect how uncommon biophysical explanations of children's behaviour are in educational circles. One example, hyperactivity, is sometimes used as an explanation for difficult behaviour, although, as a diagnosis, it has been severely criticised for cultivating what Schrag and Divoky (1975) call 'the myth of the hyperactive child'. There has also been a growing interest in the behavioural consequences of lead and food additives. *Socio-ecological* explanations have a more recent history to which we will return in the next chapter. This has left the *psychodynamic* and *behaviourist* as the dominant responses in specialist education provision. Although the majority of readers will have some idea about the general orientation of these two approaches, a brief comment on each is necessary.

The *psychodynamic* approach has its educational roots in the pioneer work done in the first schools for 'maladjusted' children and in the Child Guidance Movement. The approach accords a primary significance to what is often referred to as the child's *internal* experience.

Not that psychodynamic theorists ignore, or are indifferent to the outer circumstances of a child's life, such as the presence or absence of parents, family, home. It is rather that they recognise that any external provision is likely to be ineffectual without an accompanying effort to engage in the task of helping the child to utilise the changes in external circumstances through addressing those feelings and reactions of the child which have been caused by earlier privation, and which, unacknowledged, will militate against all efforts at purely external remedying.

(Reeves, 1983)

The approach draws, to varying degrees and with varying local interpretations, on the work of Barbara Docker-Drysdale, Anna Freud, Melanie Klein, Rudolph Steiner and D. W. Winnicot, among others. The therapeutic intervention can take place in a variety of establishments, ranging from residential communities through to classes or units in which pupils spend only a part of their school week. The particular form of intervention inevitably reflects, to some extent, the particular features of the immediate environment and the particular interests of the workers there. The common elements of the approach include the provision of opportunities for a child to establish a close relationship with one or more adults, who become the focal point for unresolved emotions of love or hate which are preventing the child from finding its own enabling sense of security and self-respect. The adults must perform the difficult balancing acts of accepting the child without reserve but also without collusion, of providing structure but also avoiding punishment in its common forms. It is not easy to employ this approach within anything like a traditional form of schooling. The balance – more recently the interweave – between *education* and *therapy* has been a longstanding debate between practitioners of this method. Nonetheless, such was the original strength of the psychodynamic orientation in schools for the maladjusted that it arguably led to 'a neglect of alternative methods of approach' (Bridgeland, 1971).

The Schools' Council project on the education of disturbed children confirmed the continuing use in special schools of 'treatments' based on psychodynamics, but also found a growing use of approaches derived from *behaviourist* theory (Wilson, 1980). In a review of these findings, Dawson (1981) points out that of the four areas of 'common ground' in the pioneer work – unconditional affection, freedom of expression, self-discipline through self-government and a psychoanalytical orientation – only 'freedom of expression' had not experienced a decline in usage. On the other hand, Dawson writes,

> Specific behaviour therapy with individual pupils ... is reported as being used in 14% of the schools, techniques of classroom management derived from learning theory as being used in 22% of schools and the systematic use of incentives and deterrents as being used in no less than 42% ...

The growing popularity of the behavioural approach based on the learning theories of, among others, J. B. Watson, E. L. Thorndike and B. F. Skinner, has been attributed to its comparative parsimony, both as an explanatory device and as a source of working techniques (Brown, 1979).

> The behavioural model suggests that what can most constructively be done for the troubled or troublesome child, is not to care, treat, punish or to give insight, but to teach the child a more adaptive and extensive repertoire of skills ... [behavioural treatment] ... is not based on an historical analysis of the problem, particularly not on speculative statements about the link between earlier experiences and current problems, but at the same time it is not a formulation which is out of any context. [It] consists of identifying relevant features of the social environment, carefully manipulating those features and evaluating the effects ...
>
> *(ibid.)*

The approach presumes that, for better or worse, all behaviour is learnt and can therefore be retaught.

> A person behaves in a certain way because he has been taught to behave in that way or because he has not been taught to behave differently.
>
> (Westmacott, 1981)

Current behaviour can be extinguished by removal of the reinforcement which sustains it or replaced by alternative behaviours which are equally well, or better, reinforced.

Central to the behavioural approach is the establishment, in any intervention, of clear objectives which will be examples of desired behaviour from the pupils. Ainscow and Tweddle (1979) write that the two important qualities of a behavioural objective are that it is an *action* which is *observable*; it would otherwise be impossible to know when or if the objective is attained. Once the objectives are settled the programme of intervention will attempt to alter the *antecedents*, *background* and *consequences* of the pupil's behaviour so that the desired behaviour, or other behaviour leading to it, are encouraged, while undesired behaviour is discouraged. It may well be that most of us would claim to be doing just that for most of the time. A central tenet of the behavioural approach is that we should methodically and purposefully check, and if necessary amend, our practice to ensure that we are actually doing what we think we are doing. The application and outcome of some of the common techniques in this field with which teachers may be familiar, including, for example, social reinforcement, token reinforcement and modelling, are neatly but succintly reviewed by Kolvin et al. in the report of a research programme to which we will make further reference later in this chapter (Kolvin, 1981).

THE LIMITATIONS OF SEPARATE, SPECIALIST PROVISION

Teachers seem receptive, at least at a generalised level, to psychodynamic and behavioural approaches and there is reference to them in much of the learning and education theory to which all teachers are exposed. However, the approaches are not usually identifiable as distinct, operational ideologies in schools, except when they are used by special schools, units or peripatetic services. In this context, specialisms have acquired their own status, although little priority has been given to evaluating their effectiveness in terms of either remediating or alleviating the individual or systemic difficulties in schools. There have been only limited attempts, to which we refer later, to compare the outcome of intervention with non-intervention or the outcome of one intervention with another. The absence of momentum and funding to acquire this data implies that the outcome of the work of special provision is less important than its actual existence; i.e., its main purpose is achieved by its existence, relieving immediate pressure on schools by removing pupils. We are not unsympathetic to the circumstances which create this position, but would argue that this should be a more public element in a wider debate about the actual purposes of this kind of provision.

In his comprehensive review of data concerning the effectiveness of special provision, Topping (1983) begins with a review of the considerable research showing high levels of 'spontaneous remission' among young people when there is no formal intervention to change their behaviour. He concludes that,

> A 'persistence rate' of around one-third, and a 'spontaneous remission rate' of about two-thirds, appear with stunning regularity in the research literature.

One implication of this might be that, as a general rule, any form of intervention designed to be a therapy for individual cases should demonstrate a success rate of around 66 per cent before it can claim to fulfil that particular intention.

Topping then goes on to review the available material on provision outside primary and secondary schools and draws the following conclusions:

- Residential special schools show average learning gains and poor behavioural gains within the school, and have poor reintegration rates ...
- Day special schools show worse learning gains and worse behaviour gains within school, and have similarly poor integration rates ...

- Separate units show varied learning gains, but curricula are restricted and overall results poor. Reintegration rates are very poor on the whole and subsequent adjustment is well below spontaneous remission rates ...
- Separate units with transition facilities and part-time attendance have shown equivalent academic gains and better reintegration rates and subsequent adjustment, but only in the USA ...

Overall, it appears that specialist provision has not been as successful in alleviating individual difficulties as the commitment of resources to it would lead us to hope. Whether it successfully relieves pressure on schools is, as Topping also acknowledges, another matter. Two indicators might show the extent to which it successfully does so:

1. evidence of a decline in the demand for specialist services in this field;
2. some recognition from within schools that problems have reduced.

Neither is available.

We have already noted, in the previous chapter, the increases in special school and unit provision which occurred through the late 1960s and early 1970s. Despite the rhetoric of 'integration', the momentum to separate provision in this field has persisted and DES figures show that the population of schools for the 'maladjusted', which was 13,334 in 1978, had increased very slightly by 1983 to 13,395. At the same time the population of the other two categories of special school said to accommodate children with behavioural problems, delicate and moderate educational subnormality, declined slightly in total but became an increasing proportion of a more rapidly declining overall school population (DES, 1985). There is no evidence in the data for schools, or in those available for units (Ling and Davies, 1984; ACE, 1980) that there has been anything other than a proportionate increase in the demand for the use of separate provision as the general school population has declined.

It is more difficult to know whether the actual or perceived levels of problems in schools have reduced in the recent past, simply because of the lack of comparable data. It is certainly our impression that teachers believe that there has been a steady increase in the problems they face as a result of children's behaviour, and at the time of writing the Secretary of State for Education has convened a committee of enquiry into discipline in schools. The equivocal nature of the data and the role of the media in promoting 'moral panics' have both been reviewed by Laslett who concludes:

Certainly, evidence collected carefully and thoroughly points to problems in schools which are more frequent than they were some years ago … [but] … does not suggest that schools are about to be overwhelmed by violence and disruptive behaviour.

(1977)

Overall, we conclude that the available evidence shows disappointing outcomes for identified pupils and for the education service generally from the commitment made to specialist services operating specialist or pseudo-specialist approaches.

THE TRANSFER OF METHODS

As it has become clear that the specialist structure is not providing anything like a satisfactory solution to the difficulties experienced by schools, it has been suggested that more might be achieved if the teachers in primary and secondary schools could acquire as many of the specialist skills as could be usefully transferred into the regular classroom. As well as having an immediate pragmatic appeal, since this proposal would facilitate early intervention and make skilful help available to a wider range of pupils, it also has a firm basis in the specialist theories which suggest that intervention is more likely to be effective in the classroom than away from it. In both behavioural and psychodynamic models, specialist – and particularly separate – provision takes pupils away from the reality with which they eventually have to cope. To reintegrate the pupil's psyche into that reality or to teach the pupil skills for coping with it is more difficult in comparatively unreal circumstances. Our own experience and that of many of our colleagues has been of a notable number of referred pupils who, once they are placed in special provision, show little if any of the behaviour which led to their referral, although that behaviour recurs if the pupil is 'reintegrated'.

IS TRANSFER POSSIBLE?

Although there is evidence that specialist approaches can be applied to pupils in primary and secondary schools with some resultant improvement in their behaviour (Kolvin, 1986), we are not satisfied that this amounts to a case for using the methods as the major, or primary, response to problems in schools. Kolvin and his colleagues studied the effects of several kinds of treatment on a minority of pupils identified as 'maladjusted', after screening all the pupils in about a dozen primary and secondary schools in the north east of England. Outcomes for groups, then treated by different methods, were compared with one another and with the outcomes for control groups who received no treatment. A central hypothesis of the research was that one or more of the treatment regimes would prove more effective in reducing 'maladjustment' than the no-treatment regime (the controls). In a set of what Kolvin calls 'complex and interesting results', every one of the treatment regimes relative to the controls did show '*some* improvement on *some* measures' (Kolvin's emphasis). On many scales the 'untreated' control groups also showed improved behaviour over the period of Kolvin's study, although, it must be said, the treated groups often showed improvements which were greater by a statistically significant amount. However, it remains arguable whether the treatments as treatments were the only effective element or whether the additional interest and activity of a research project were themselves also a catalyst.

Be that as it may, there are other important difficulties with the transfer of specialist methods into primary and secondary schools, which are not confined to the approaches explored by Kolvin and will arise whenever methods remain special and therefore limited in application. Kolvin's work and conclusions, while illustrating the possibilities, also illustrate the persistent limitations. The pupils in the project were identified by a thorough screening procedure which would be beyond the resources of most schools and local authorities. Unless that could be generally replicated, any exercise based on the findings could still only be a marginal event directed at pupils whose identification would continue to be haphazard. In addition, the strategies themselves remain focused to a great extent on individualistic reactive, rather than preventive, measures. There is no suggestion that they deal with the causes of the problems and so could prevent the emergence of the next layer or generation of difficulty. The treatments were introduced or supported or even carried out by additional non-teaching personnel, teachers' aides, social workers or psychologists. Notwithstanding the resource implications of this additional assistance, as Kolvin notes, it does require commitment or effort from schools, which might not be universally forthcoming. Even where that goodwill is available, it may lead to the teachers 'not owning' (which is not the same as disowning) the approaches. The consequence, in our experience, is that it is difficult to ensure that the changes in the teachers' behaviour are maintained. Unless they are maintained, of course, the incremental benefits in pupils' behaviour may also be lost.

Conclusion

Over all, we conclude that the possibility of transferring specialist techniques, in anything approaching a specialist form, into primary and secondary schools is severely limited and that there is no reason to believe such a transfer could provide the basis for a satisfactory response to the generality of problems which teachers and pupils face. This does not mean we believe that there is nothing to be learned from the experience of staff and pupils in special schools and units. Kolvin's research demonstrates that if we improve our knowledge of how and when the specialist approaches can be effective, then they may be of value in a small number of identified cases. We will return to that point in our concluding chapter.

More important, both the psychodynamic and behavioural approaches offer insights or techniques which can be of value to teachers in the construction of their general approach to pupils. The former provides a perspective which illustrates the importance of a sympathetic response to the individuality and diversity of the pupil population. The role of the teacher *in loco parentis* need not be simply a legal artefact but could be such that the relationship of teacher to pupil cannot be extricated from the simultaneous relationship of adult to child. The behavioural approach provides techniques which can place both curriculum planning and classroom management within the context of learning theory. It provides the wherewithal for teachers to identify their curricular goals and objectives and then to implement purposeful classroom strategies for their achievement. At this level we do not believe that the two approaches are necessarily exclusive or contradictory, nor is either of them an approach which should be employed only when there is some kind of 'problem'. On the contrary, they both contain potential means for making the whole business of teaching and learning more enjoyable and effective for all concerned. However, we maintain our view that they are at best only a partial response to the difficulties which occur in schools because they address only a part of the causes.

In the following chapter, we go on to consider the last of Reinert's four categories – *socio-ecological* – and explain why we think that category of analysis offers teachers their best opportunity for identifying and responding to difficulties in schools.

APPENDIX A

Terms labelling deviance from a variety of viewpoints.

asocial	autistic	behavioural problem
character disorder	delinquent	disruptive
emotionally disturbed	learning problem	nervous
neurotic	personality disorder	psychopathic
psychotic	schizophrenic	sick
socially maladjusted	sociopathic	spoiled
uninhibited	unsocialised	withdrawn

Source: Reinert (1976)

Environmental factors and their implications

The consistency with which behaviour at school has been found to be relatively independent of the pupils' families and social backgrounds could be seen as extraordinarily encouraging for teachers.

(Galloway and Goodwin, 1987, p. 135)

Socio-ecological perspectives set 'problem behaviour' in the context of all the different 'environments' (home, school, peer group, etc.) with which children come into contact and which exert an influence upon them. The complex processes which constitute these 'environmental' influences have been the subject of much research and analysis by sociologists and educational theorists whose work over the past 25 years has far-reaching implications for schools' responses to 'problem behaviour'. Not only have they provided new sources of insight into the aetiology of 'problem behaviour' in individual cases, but because they have treated the issues as social rather than as individual phenomena, they have been able to identify relationships between individual cases, which give us cause to question some of our existing assumptions and practices and consider different kinds of 'solutions'.

One important relationship which has received much attention is that between socio-economic background and educational achievement/successful adjustment to school. It has consistently been shown that, as a group, children from semi-skilled, unskilled or unemployed families tend to do less well and are considered by their teachers to be less well adjusted to school than children whose parents are in skilled manual or non-manual occupations (see, for example, Table 5.1).

It has also been shown that the former group of children are more likely to be referred to special units for disruptive behaviour or to special schools for learning or behavioural difficulties (Table 5.2).

A similar pattern has been identified for pupils of an Afro-Caribbean background, whose over-representation in certain special schools has been a source of much concern (e.g., Tomlinson, 1982; Francis, 1979; Coard, 1971; ILEA, 1986). Our understanding of, and response to, 'problem behaviour' must thus be adjusted to

Table 5.1 *Comparison of pupils selected (as having disturbed behaviour) in parental and teachers' questionnaires*

Family characteristics		Selection source	
		Parents	Teachers
Social class I and II		16.5%	14.5%
	III	15.0%	9.2%
	IV and V	21.2%	32.3%

Source: Rutter et al. (1970) Table 10.7.

Table 5.2 *Parental occupation of pupils in different types of educational provision*

	Non manual	Skilled manual	Semi/ unskilled manual	Unemployed	Not known absent	N (100%)
ESBD schools	8.9	13.8	28.7	44.1	4.5	1,265
Tutorial classes	13.5	18.5	23.0	37.2	7.8	769
EGC	16.1	18.8	26.8	37.5	0.9	112
Primary schools	22.1	21.0	25.4	25.3	6.1	131,415
Secondary schools	21.3	24.7	24.8	18.3	10.8	133,450

Source: Jay and Kysel (1986) p. 48.

encompass the idea that children whose behaviour causes concern are apparently not randomly distributed among the school population as a whole, but concentrated among particular low-status socio-economic or ethnic 'minority' groups.

Explanations of this relationship have generally drawn attention to particular features of the children's 'home background', which make them less able to take advantage of what school has to offer. Increasingly, however, factors within the process of schooling itself have been brought into the reckoning. It would certainly be true to say that the circumstances which give rise to this relationship are so woven into the whole social fabric, including the process of schooling, that it would be impossible to try to isolate any one factor as 'the cause'. Our purpose, in this chapter, in reviewing those factors now known to be significant in the genesis of 'problem behaviour', is to identify among them those which may be susceptible to change by teachers, and which could thus provide a starting point for developing more effective strategies for prevention and response. The chapter is divided into three sections, looking at:

1. 'home background' factors and the relationship between social deprivation and problems at school;

2. 'school' factors and the contribution to 'problem behaviour' made by pupils' negative experiences of schooling;
3. the practical implications to be drawn from both earlier sections, to guide our professional activities.

1. THE HOME BACKGROUND

A recent survey reports that the majority of teachers consider 'home background' to be the most significant factor in 'problem behaviour' (Croll and Moses, 1985). However, this apparent consensus may conceal differing interpretations of the specific 'home circumstances' thought to be contributing to the problem.

ACTIVITY

In what ways might these features of the 'home background' create problems for a child, which might lead to 'problem behaviour' at school

- family finances
- living conditions
- size of family
- parents' attitudes to school
- cultural/linguistic resources of home
- family health
- family circumstances
- parent–child relationships
- sibling relationships

Choose one or more of the above which you regard as particularly significant and describe how it may give rise to problems at school.

Laslett (1982) interprets 'problem behaviour' at school as a reflection of tensions in relationships between parents and children, or between the parents themselves.

> We know that disruption in the home, unpredictable discipline, or no consistent discipline, marital tensions, parental rejection and indifference are prime causes of conduct disorder in children. In such circumstances, children are more likely to be worrying about what is going on at home than thinking about their lessons. Furthermore, conduct-disordered children will act out the anxieties associated with unsettling events.

(p. 10)

However, this account is unable to explain why 'problem behaviour' should apparently be concentrated among certain sections of the population, unless we are prepared to make a urther, highly questionable inference that problems of this kind are predominantly to be found among particular socio-economic and ethnic minority groups.

A second interpretation, which focuses more directly on factors common to the groups concerned, is one which relates 'problem behaviour' to *social disadvantage*. This link has been extensively researched and documented by the National Children's Bureau (Wedge and Prosser, 1973; Wedge and Essen, 1982), drawing on information provided by the National Child Development Study. Social disadvantage was defined in terms of a combination of three 'social factors': 'a-typical' families, low income and poor housing. These were used to identify the most disadvantaged section of the school population at the ages of seven, eleven and sixteen, and to study their progress and behaviour in relation to the achievements of their peers. The reports confirm that the most socially disadvantaged children do less well and their behaviour is regarded as less acceptable than non-disadvantaged children at every stage, and that these differences increase during the secondary period. They show that social disadvantage has enduring effects, so that a child who has been disadvantaged at any point in his or her childhood, will continue to be disadvantaged educationally even if social circumstances improve. They conclude,

> ... the combination of poor housing, low income, uncertain health, insecure employment, coupled often, no doubt, with limited knowledge of parenting skills, offers a prescription for low achieving, poorly behaved, disenchanted and alienated young people.
> (Wedge and Essen, 1982, p. 93)

The effect of combinations of 'disadvantage' factors on educational outcome has been further investigated in an ILEA study of secondary pupils (Sammons et al., 1982; see Table 5.3). It was found that the more 'disadvantage' factors experienced by a child, the greater the risk of that child falling into the lowest achievement band and/or being rated as having some kind of disturbed behaviour at school. Because it is children whose parents are semi-skilled, unskilled or unemployed who are those most likely to be affected by these various 'disadvantage' factors, low socio-economic status of parents is useful as an indicator of children most 'at risk' educationally (Mortimore and Mortimore, 1985). The Swann Report reminds us that, in addition to the deprivation and disadvantage suffered by their white counterparts, children of low-income ethnic minority groups have to suffer 'racial prejudice and discrimination on the part of society at large' (DES, 1985).

Table 5.3 *Percentages of pupils affected by different numbers of factors*

Number factors	% pupils in VR band 3	% pupils with disturbed behaviour
0	10.8	5.6
1	16.7	9.4
2	25.5	14.7
3	32.2	20.4
4	38.6	25.1
5	49.1	28.6
6	61.5	32.7
7	91.7(N = 12)	42.3(N = 2)
	(N = 22, 241)	

Source: Sammons et al. (1982).

However, researching in more detail the association betwee particular 'home background' factors and 'problem behaviour' not the same as providing an explanation. As the reports of th National Children's Bureau are themselves at pains to point out, n direct causal link can be inferred from their findings. We still need ask *how* this association comes about and *why* some children ar affected but not others. After all, read another way, the figure show that the majority of children who come from poorer families who belong to ethnic minority groups do 'adjust successfully' school. While it may be important, therefore, to be aware of th difficulties which some children have to contend with at home, it equally important not to assume any simple determinism.

> ... socio-cultural factors soon become *explanations* of educational failure. Poor performance is accounted for by factors external to the schooling system ... Instead of considering possible malfunctions in the education system, teachers and administrators look for explanations in terms of cultural deprivation or deficits.
>
> (Widlake, 1986, p. 15)

Such 'explanations' led, for instance, to the 1960s' 'solution' 'compensatory education' for assumed cultural and linguisti 'inadequacies' of the working class home background, in preferenc to a consideration of how the language and culture of the schoo might be adjusted to respond more adequately to the cultura and linguistic diversity of its pupils. Certainly, the recent suc cessful involvement of parents in traditional 'deprived' inner-cit areas in reading with their children at home suggests that, contrar to what is often supposed, 'working class' parents are interestec

1 their children's education and that their reticence to become involved may be due more to a sense that they lack appropriate knowledge rather than lack of basic concern (Tizard et al., 1981). Similarly, the commitment of Afro-Caribbean parents to education is amply demonstrated by the growth of Saturday schools to supplement what are seen as inadequate educational opportunities made available for their children within the state system, about which that community is increasingly prepared to voice its criticisms.

The point is that we can acknowledge the significance of socio-economic factors without transforming them into 'explanations'. They contribute to our understanding of 'problem behaviour', but the crucial question is *how do they interact* with features of the process of schooling? The picture necessarily remains incomplete until we have explored the part played by pupils' experience of schooling in the genesis of 'problem behaviour'.

THE PROCESS OF SCHOOLING

A number of empirical research studies, carried out since the mid 1960s, attest to the powerful influence which schools exert upon their pupils' achievements and behaviour. Comparative studies of rates of exclusion, suspension and disruptive behaviour in schools with pupils of similar background have consistently shown marked differences between schools in terms of behaviour outcomes. In a thorough review of the evidence, Galloway and Goodwin (1987) summarise the findings as follows:

1. Whether a pupil is considered disruptive or maladjusted depends at least as much on factors within the school as on factors within the pupil or the family.
2. In general, schools which cater successfully for their most disturbing pupils also cater successfully for the rest of their pupils.

(p. 132)

ACTIVITY

In your experience, which factors of schooling have had the most notable effect on children's behaviour:

(a) at the level of organisation, management, structure and curriculum; and
(b) at the level of teacher–pupil interaction in the classroom?

In a school of your acquaintance, think of three factors which have had positive effect and three with a negative effect on pupils' behaviour.

(i) School ethos and teacher–pupil relationships

The general climate of a school, created by the methods adopted f
maintaining control, has been shown to have a major impact upo
pupil behaviour (Rutter, 1979; Reynolds, 1976; Galloway, 198:
Reynolds' study of eight secondary modern schools in Wales four
that schools using 'incorporative' rather than 'coercive' methods
enlist the co-operation of pupils and their parents had 'higher rat
of academic success, rates of delinquency roughly half of tho
shown by the coercive schools and rates of attendance about 6%
7% higher' (p. 52).

The 'incorporative' schools (five out of the eight) adopted
variety of strategies to encourage the positive involvement of pup:
in the life of the school:

(a) encouragement to take an active and participative role
    lessons;
(b) opportunities (such as prefect and monitor systems) f
    pupils to take responsibility and exercise some control ov
    their within-school lives;
(c) good interpersonal relationships between teachers ar
    pupils; avoidance of conflict/rule enforcement likely
    provoke rebellion;
(d) therapeutic, rather than coercive, responses from the schoo
    to individual instances of problem behaviour.

The support of parents was enlisted through encouragement
informal or semi-formal relations with teachers, informal visits
the school and frequent communications about pupil progress ar
school affairs.

In 'coercive' schools, on the other hand, relationships betwee
teachers and pupils were characterised by hostility and an ethos wa
created in which pupils expected repression by the teachers and th
teachers expected rebellion from their pupils. Teachers in the:
schools were found to overestimate the 'social deprivation' of the
pupils' background, to underestimate their abilities, and to regar
them as needing strong discipline and 'character building' to mak
up for the deficiencies of their upbringing.

Analysis of styles of interaction between individual teachers an
their pupils have produced similar findings. Aspy and Roebuc
(1977) found that:

> ... teachers who were highest in their ability to empathise with their
> students, who demonstrated respect (positive regard) in and out of
> classrooms and whose behaviour and intentions were congruent
> (genuine) were the teachers whose students showed most cognitive
> growth, most IQ gains, best attendance and fewest examples of

disruptive behaviour in the classroom.

Finlayson and Loughran (1978) identified the relationship between the teacher and the class as a whole, rather than individual pupil–teacher relationships, as the significant factor. The incidence of behavioural problems was shown to be greater when the teacher adopted rigid authoritarian methods of establishing discipline, rather than negotiation. Hargreaves et al. (1975) report a study by Jordan (1974) which distinguishes two types of teacher: the 'deviance-provocative' teacher whose handling of deviant pupils serves to exacerbate the problem, and the 'deviance-insulative' teacher whose handling of problem behaviour serves to inhibit it. The former type of teacher 'blames the pupils for their misconduct … believes that they are hostile, resistant and committed to their deviance … and refuses to believe that any signs of improvement are authentic'. The 'deviance-insulative' teacher assumes that if the pupils do not work, the conditions are at fault. 'He believes that these conditions can be changed and that it is his responsibility to initiate that change' (p. 261).

Thus, the studies reviewed suggest that the way pupils behave in school is importantly affected both by the general ethos of the school and the approach to classroom relationships characteristic of individual teachers. Are we therefore to infer that if all teachers were to become 'deviance-insulative' in their attitudes, or schools were to adopt 'incorporative' methods, a dramatic reduction in the incidence of problem behaviour, not to mention teacher stress levels, might then be achieved? It is not, of course, as easy as that. In the first place, beliefs, attitudes and institutional practices are deep rooted and not easily amenable to change. It is also an oversimplification to present individual teachers' behaviour towards pupils as uniform, aware as we now are of the myriad subtle ways in which our behaviour towards pupils can vary according to our different perceptions of them.

Nash (1973), for example, studied the effects of teachers' favourable and unfavourable perceptions of pupils upon the pupils' behaviour. He shows how children modify their behaviour for better or worse in response to the way they feel themselves to be perceived by their teachers. What causes us to perceive some pupils favourably and others unfavourably is a sensitive issue. Leach (1977) describes teachers' 'ideal' pupils as those who are:

> … enjoyable to teach and personally rewarding to their teachers. They are those pupils who try with some success to produce the quality and kind of work which they perceive to be required, who appear to be

involved in what their teachers think is important and who, in public at least, try to appear to be abiding by those rules in play ... They are likely to exhibit general social behaviour, appearances and personalities which closely match their teachers' own preferences for what constitutes an acceptable and likeable person.

In our experience, many teachers would disagree with this view, saying they prefer the more 'difficult', non-conformist pupils who present greater interest and challenge. However, the central point is that if pupils' behaviour is related to our favourable/unfavourable categorisations of them, then we need to look critically at the criteria influencing us in arriving at these judgements. There is a growing awareness of the extent to which judgements and categorisations of pupils may not be solely or objectively related to their behaviour but may also encompass other characteristics including gender, general 'ability', race and social class.

Gender provides a telling illustration. There is evidence that boys and girls are expected to behave according to sex stereotypes (Clarricoates, 1980; Clift, 1979; Frazier, 1973) in which: 'Any girl who is "aggressive" or "independent" and any boy who is "effeminate" or "sensitive" are the exceptions, the so-called deviants' (Clarricoates, 1980).

These expectations may be to some degree self-fulfilling. The 'same' behaviour may receive a different response on the part of the teacher according to the sex of the actor. Certainly there is overwhelming evidence that boys tend to be more aggressive and demanding in classrooms than the generally more diffident and compliant girls (Spender, 1982; Deem, 1978). Expectations of pupil behaviour may also condition our sense of being able to deal with it effectively. Anecdotally, teachers report that they find boys' overtly aggressive behaviour easier to deal with than the behaviour of 'difficult' girls, who are perceived to present a more complex problem.

It is fair to suggest that similar phenomena of patterned expectation and reaction also operate against other social, economic and educational criteria. The disproportionate referral of 'Afro-Caribbean' pupils to special provision for learning and behavioural difficulties (Tomlinson, 1978; ILEA, 1986) has to be set against the absence of evidence that the behaviour of 'Afro-Caribbean' pupils is generally of a worse standard and the presence of evidence that many teachers hold negative stereotypes of these pupils (Milner, 1975; Brittan, 1976; Driver, 1979; DES, 1985b).

Even if we are aware of the dangers of 'labelling' and believe strongly in the principle of equality of value of all our pupils, it is not necessarily easy to translate those good intentions into practice. Sharp and Green (1975), for example, report on the differences between the educational ideologies and 'substantive practice' of three primary teachers committed to child-centred approaches and egalitarian principles:

> ... those pupils whom their teachers regarded as more successful tended to be given far greater attention than the others. The teachers interacted with them more frequently, paid closer attention to their activities, subtly structuring and directing their efforts in ways which were noticeably different from the relationship with other pupils less favourably categorized.
>
> (p. 115)

Although these findings have not been substantiated by other observational studies in primary schools (e.g., ORACLE: Galton, Simon and Croll, 1980), the authors' point was not to suggest that teachers were at fault for treating pupils differentially (indeed, they saw some kind of differentiation as necessary and inevitable). Their main concern was to attempt to explain the gap identified between principle and practice. They argue that classroom practice has to be understood in the context of all the conflicting expectations and constraints upon teachers, from within school and from outside. Our espoused ideals have to be reconciled with these and with the demands of coping with large numbers of children, whose individual needs exert pressures of their own.

Thus, while the attitudes and behaviour of teachers undoubtedly have a significant effect upon pupils' responses to schooling, teacher–pupil relationships are a complex affair, which cannot easily be 'improved' by decree or conscious decision on the part of the teachers themselves or others. These relationships are, in any case, only one dimension of the experience of schooling which may affect pupils' behaviour. Holt (1965), for example, describes how, despite the kindliest intentions on the part of teachers, fear is the central debilitating characteristic of many pupils' experience of school. This problem could not be resolved by 'improved' teacher–pupil relationships, because it occurs even where the teacher sets out to be warmly supportive.

> They ... all said the same thing, that when the teacher, asked them a question and they didn't know the answer they were scared half to death. I was flabbergasted – to find this in a school which people think of as progressive ...Even in the kindest and gentlest of schools children are afraid, many of them a great deal of the time, some of them almost all the time.
>
> (p. 50)

Hargreaves (1982) argues a similar case for the effects of the 'hidden curriculum' of secondary schools. He suggests that what we as teachers interpret as 'problem behaviour' may, in fact, be a legitimate criticism of the schooling process which:

> ... exerts on many pupils, particularly but by no means exclusively from the working class, a destruction of their dignity which is so massive and pervasive that few subsequently recover from it ... It is not intended by the teachers, the vast majority of whom seek and strive hard to give their pupils dignity as I have defined it.
>
> (p. 17)

The implication is that the form, content and methods of presentation of the curriculum exert a powerful influence upon pupils irrespective of individual teachers' intentions or differences in their disciplinary styles.

(ii) The curriculum

To separate issues of discipline, control and teacher–pupil relationships from those of curriculum structure, content and pedagogy is, of course, to create a false dichotomy. At the level of classroom interaction, the teacher's management of classroom discourse fulfils both functions; simultaneously controlling the content, direction and nature of pupils' participation in learning what counts as valid knowledge and as appropriate behaviour (Barnes, 1976). Nevertheless, it is important to distinguish them theoretically at this point in order to bring into focus aspects of the schooling process which, while they are undoubtedly reflected in teacher–pupil interactions in the classroom, have their origins in features of the overall organisation and curriculum which are outside the control of any individual teacher. Some, indeed, like the examination system with its far-reaching effects, are beyond the control of any individual school.

The 'hidden curriculum' thesis referred to above suggests that the ways in which we select, organise and evaluate the official curriculum convey to the pupils a set of messages which combine to create a sense of their own differential worth as participants in the school community. For a substantial proportion of pupils, this means a sense that they are neither achieving nor contributing anything of value. Features of schooling through which such messages may be conveyed are, for example:

(a) **Ranking, sorting or grouping pupils by 'ability'** which assigns an inevitably inferior status to all but those at the very top, indicating to pupils that they are lacking to a greater or lesser degree in the very qualities most prized by the school.

(b) **The 'stratification' of knowledge** which accords superior status to knowledge which is abstract, remote from everyday experience, written and individualised (Young, 1971), denying the relevance of learners' existing knowledge and experience, and underplaying the importance of group, oral, practical and creative work.

(c) **The content of the curriculum** which presents a normative view of knowledge which implicitly devalues those who deviate by sex, race or culture from the 'norm'.

(d) **The language of the school** which insists that only knowledge and understandings which are embedded in abstract, impersonal, specialist language or expressed in Standard English are to be legitimate modes of communication for conducting school learning and assessing achievement.

According to this thesis, 'success' and 'failure' are not the natural products of differences in individual capacities and motivation, but are constructed through the processes of schooling which serve best those pupils whose interests, abilities, background and language are continuous with the values, language and culture of the school, and further disadvantage those for whom there is no such continuity. The effect is to create a 'pool of potential disaffection' (Booth, 1987) – a group of pupils who are alienated by their experiences at school and who objectively have little stake in conforming because their prospects of reaping any significant rewards are minimal. Not all of these, of course, become disruptive. Some accept their lot with resignation, some withdraw their interest and offer silent opposition, some vote with their feet and simply stay away, but the underlying problem is common to all. 'Problem behaviour' is thus interpreted as a *response to* the process of schooling, rather than a *reflection of* problems emanating from outside (although, of course, 'background' factors predetermine which children are likely to be excluded from the central purposes of the curriculum). From the pupils' point of view, rejection can be thought of as a *rational* decision (Ball, 1981), arrived at through weighing up the value of schooling in terms of their immediate life-goals and plans, set against the alternative opportunities now available to them for achieving dignity and status outside school.

If the school population is divided between 'advantaged' and 'disadvantaged' groups, any attempt to redress the balance in favour of the latter would seem likely to pose a threat to the achievements of the former group. This is the familiar dilemma facing teachers who wish to improve the opportunities for success of the one group, while avoiding charges of 'watering down' the curriculum and reducing academic standards for the high-achieving group. One way out is to devise more 'relevant' and 'appropriate' courses for the 'less academically oriented' pupils and, since ROSLA, considerable creative energies have been invested in producing imaginative curriculum packages for this purpose. However, these have, in many cases, had disappointing results because pupils are quick to spot that what they are being offered has only second-rate status compared to the education being offered to their peers. While it is important, therefore, to be aware that too much emphasis on 'book knowledge' (ILEA, 1984, p. 67) has alienating effects, and that failure to match tasks set to pupils' capabilities may be a key factor in problem behaviour (DES, 1978b), attempts to provide more 'appropriate' curricula suggest that these are likely to receive short shrift from the consumers if they continue to convey messages of inferior status.

The fate of one such innovation in the mathematics curriculum for fourth year 'low ability' pupils is described by Spradbery (1976):

> The pack was welcomed with enthusiasm and excitement. After a few weeks of using the materials, however, the pupils rejected them and demanded to return to 'proper Maths'. They refused to continue with the assignments on the grounds that they were 'childish' and 'slowing' them down. Their reaction contradicted both the intentions of the producers of the pack and the suggestion that pupils will welcome less alienating activities.
>
> (p. 238)

However, a more optimistic case is increasingly advanced that changes in the organisation of teaching and learning, required to provide opportunities for success for the 'disadvantaged' group, could result in a improvement in the quality of education for all children. The traditional grammar-school style curriculum has been severely criticised, not just for its failure to provide for the less 'academic' pupils, but for its limitations in terms of the learning opportunities which it provides for every pupil. It has been taken to task, for example, for the excessively passive role which it assigns to the learner, and for the lack of scope offered by formal teaching methods for learners to convert 'school knowledge' into 'action knowledge', i.e., knowledge which they use for their own purposes.

> Much teaching, especially in secondary schools, depends upon generating an artificial dependency in the learners, so that they can gain knowledge only by submitting to the teacher's view and not by thinking for themselves ... School knowledge is the knowledge which someone else presents to us. We partly grasp it, enough to answer the teacher's questions, to do exercises, or to answer examination

questions, but it remains someone else's knowledge, not ours. If we never use this knowledge, we probably forget it.

(Barnes, op cit., pp. 81/118)

The HMI Secondary Survey (1979) concurs with this view and its relevance to all pupils, questioning whether:

... the styles of teaching and learning which are widely employed are necessarily conducive to the best examination results or to the best education. Such styles typically include heavily directed teaching, a preponderance of dictated or copied notes, an emphasis on the giving and recall of information with little room for enquiry or exploration of applications.

(262.10)

A similar position is adopted in the ILEA report *Improving Secondary Schools* (1984), which identifies the following features of schooling as contributing to underachievement, dissatisfaction with school and uncooperative behaviour:

(a) fragmentation of the curriculum, leading to lack of coherence for the learner;
(b) overemphasis on theoretical knowledge and skills at the expense of practical applications in the curriculum areas;
(c) a too narrow definition of achievement, which excludes recognition of oral, practical and investigational skills, social and personal skills, and the capacity to persevere in learning;
(d) lack of choice for pupils in content and process of learning;
(e) teaching methods which do not engage pupils actively and collaboratively in learning.

'Problem behaviour' can thus be treated as the visible tip of a problem of disaffection which is widespread among the pupil population. Shostak's research (1982), for instance, reports that as many as '95% of 5th Year pupils voiced criticisms which called into question their school experience'. The implication is that 'problem behaviour' should not, and cannot effectively, be tackled *in isolation from a systematic programme of school improvement*.

This 'reactive' interpretation of 'problem behaviour' is convincingly borne out by our own experience of working with alienated young people approaching school-leaving age. However, accepting its relevance to our understanding of the issues does not in any sense rule out the possibility that some of the behaviour which gives cause for concern may be associated with traumatic or difficult circumstances which are unconnected with those children's experiences of schooling. We note that the ILEA Report specifically excludes 'maladjusted' pupils from its terms of reference, while admitting that no sharp boundary can be drawn between 'pupils who are "dissatisfied" or who become "uncooperative", and those deemed "maladjusted" and therefore in need of special educational provision' (1.2, p. 1). The reason for this is, presumably, that the problems of the latter group are not considered to be primarily attributable to features of the schooling process, and therefore are not so amenable to prevention through the kind of measures for curriculum improvement proposed in the document.

Yet even when pupils' problems do stem from circumstances unrelated to schooling, we still have a responsibility to consider whether their experiences at school are helping to alleviate those problems or whether they may, unfortunately, be adding to them. This means, in effect, attending closely to *exactly the same set of characteristics* within the process of schooling already identified as contributory factors in 'problem behaviour':

> ... a school by its conventions, discipline and curriculum can continue and confirm children's alienating experiences. On the other hand, a school can support, stimulate and demonstrate care for those children already in difficulties, thus preventing or arresting their maladjustment.
>
> (Laslett, op. cit.)

A study by Kounin et al. (1966) investigating the effect of teaching styles on the progress and behaviour of 'maladjusted' children in American primary schools, confirms that the approaches which are most effective in responding to 'disturbed' behaviour are not special or different, but are those which are most effective with all pupils. The teachers who were most successful in managing both ordinary and 'emotionally disturbed' children, were the 'with-it' teachers, those who provided variety in learning activities, who knew what was going on minute by minute in their classrooms and could intervene appropriately, who had effective techniques for handling group movement around the classroom, etc.

It makes no difference in the end, therefore, *as far as the implications for our professional practice are concerned*, what we believe the 'root causes' of 'problem behaviour' to be. If we acknowledge that children's experiences at school significantly increase or decrease the severity of any problem, however caused, a necessary condition for effective response in all cases must be to bring about improvements in those features of schooling known to have negative effects on behaviour. Recent work points optimistically to the possibility that such improvements need not be wrought at the expense of 'standards' or of the excellence of the few, but can be introduced for the educational benefit of all. The Swann Report (op.

cit.), investigating the underachievement of ethnic minority pupils, agrees with this conclusion:

> The fundamental change that is necessary is the recognition that the problem facing the education system is not how to educate children of ethnic minorities but how to educate all children.
>
> (p. 363)

3. MAKING A DIFFERENCE

From this survey of some of the research and analysis of the past twenty years, there are two crucial implications to be drawn:

Firstly, if we accept that children's behaviour is affected by environmental influences, then it cannot be regarded as justifiable to continue to direct our response to 'problem behaviour' uniquely towards children, leaving the environment itself unchanged. Unless we take the determinist view that in our capacity as teachers we have no power to alter the circumstances in which problems arise, our attention should be at least equally devoted to tackling aspects of the environment helping to sustain the behaviour and which are thought to be susceptible to change.

Secondly, since we are now able to identify in advance those groups of children who are most at risk and those features of schooling associated with underachievement and 'problem behaviour', we no longer have to wait until problems have arisen and then respond to each of them individually. We can set about introducing *preventive* measures which, within limits, will prevent those problems from arising in the future.

ACTIVITY

Which factors associated with 'problem behaviour', either in the home background or the school, do you consider to be open to change by:

    (a) an individual teacher working on his/her own initiative?
    (b) whole-school policy initiatives?

(i) The home background

Clearly, in our capacity as teachers we have no power to change the social conditions which give rise to deprivation and social disadvantage. Nevertheless, we can attempt to amend the organisation and curricula of our schools to prevent those social inequalities from being reproduced or exacerbated at school. This is the spirit of the equal opportunities' initiatives launched by some local educational authorities. While we would readily acknowledge the limitations of the concept of 'equal opportunities' (Daunt, 1975), these initiative have made an important contribution in recognising officially tha institutional practices can reinforce class, race and gender divis ions. In some cases, they have provided a framework of support encouraging teachers to develop anti-racist and anti-sexist teaching strategies in their own classrooms, and to engage in a thorough going critique of curriculum content, materials and taken-for-gran ted routine practices in their schools. They have required eacl school to formulate strategies which will help to prevent th devaluation, underachievement and potential disaffection o groups of pupils known to be at risk.

Another way in which schools may offer positive support fo such pupils is to provide after-school clubs, extended-day activi ties, extra classes, etc., or quiet areas for study for those witl nowhere private to work at home. As well as promoting ar increased sense of involvement in the school, such facilities help t convey to pupils a sympathetic awareness of the difficulties the may face in getting homework completed satisfactorily on time Such compensatory measures should, of course, be seen a: complementary, not alternative, to the curricular strategies men tioned above.

A third area of potential influence is the extent of parents involvement in their children's education. The success of th PACT reading projects has shown that it is possible to achieve th continued support and involvement of the majority of parents o any social or ethnic background. If we adopt a participatory, rathe than a compensatory, model of parental involvement (Widlake 1986), founded upon the assumption that most parents will war to help their children, given the right opportunities, informatior and encouragement, then our responsibility is to create th conditions which will foster maximum involvement. Encouraging the full participation of parents is not, of course, without it: problems, since parents' and teachers' views and expectations o education will not necessarily coincide. Nevertheless, awarenes: of the positive effects of parental support upon children's achieve ments and attitudes to school may help to convince us, despite these risks, of the potential value of such an undertaking.

(ii) The process of schooling

It is, of course, in this area that our greatest scope for interventior and prevention lies. If we accept that the environment of th school has an important influence, for better or worse, on pupils behaviour, then we must also accept our responsibility as indivi dual teachers and as members of a whole-school staff, to be ontinually questioning our own practice, so that whatever can be one is done to improve the experience of schooling for all children.

From the research and analysis of the past 25 years, which we ave only been able to touch on in this chapter, we have constructed wo 'frameworks' to support this process of *'critical self-questioning'*, vhich we believe must be at the heart of any programme of school nprovement and of any effective response to 'problem behaviour'. .ach 'framework' is supported by an appendix of further reading naterial, developing the issues referred to through each question in nore depth.

ı) At classroom level

igure 5.1 presents the range of questions we need to be considering t classroom level if we are to identify opportunities that exist to nprove the learning environment. Intervention may involve:

- either *remedying* features of current practice identified as contributing to problem behaviour (e.g., revising an activity to make the demands more accessible to the children's capabilities),
- or *extending and enriching* existing provision in a way which enhances the quality of learning for all children (e.g., creating more opportunities for children to engage imaginatively with curricular content).

The idea behind this 'framework' is hardly new. Every time we ılan a lesson, we take decisions which are, in effect, preventive neasures, selecting from a range of possibilities the combination vhich we think will stimulate and interest our pupils, promote ffective learning and, through appropriate design of tasks and lassroom organisation, prevent behavioural problems from arising. Yet, however experienced and skilful we may be, we know that he outcome is highly unpredictable. However well we have planned' a lesson, the children's responses will require moment-ry-moment intuitive responses from us, and the flexibility to adapt ur plan to take those responses into account. This framework is lesigned to help evaluate what happens, to explore the factors vhich may contribute to the success or otherwise of a lesson, or to he behaviour of a particular child who concerns us, and to plan uture lessons bearing those insights in mind. The interrelationship ıf factors reminds us that intervention in one particular area (say, mproving the readability of worksheets), although beneficial in its ıwn right, may have little impact on behaviour in the classroom if ther factors sustaining negative responses remain unchanged. It is ı process best carried out with the support and collaboration of

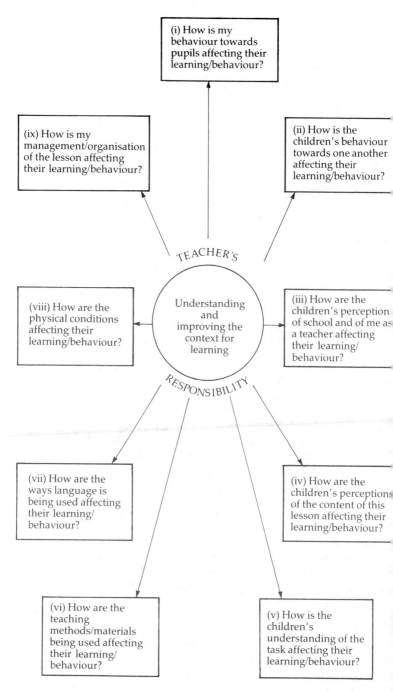

Figure 5.1 *Questioning classrooms*

olleagues who are evaluating their own practice in the same way, o that we can help one another to develop critical insights into eatures of our work which otherwise we might take for granted as nevitable or unchangeable. Professionalism demands not perfecion, but the willingness to accept that as teachers we are also earners, and that the response of our pupils – negative or positive – s one of the principal resources we have for our own learning and levelopment.

There are, of course, limits to teachers' autonomy (as well as to ur time and energy), and thus to the changes that an individual eacher can bring about on his or her own initiative. Decisions such is whether to abandon a reading scheme or a history syllabus are oolicy issues which cannot be taken unilaterally. It is also important o remember that some of the features of schooling, whose effects ipon pupil behaviour make themselves strongly felt at classroom evel, have their origins outside the classroom. The 'problem oehaviour' of a 'sink' group of fourth years timetabled for 'extra Inglish' in the dinner hall is unlikely to be resolved in the :lassroom, since the 'hidden curriculum' messages to which it is .urely a response are not amenable to change through an individual eacher's efforts, however well intentioned. This is one example of he kind of issues which need to be taken up at whole-school policy evel.

b) Whole-school policy level

Figure 5.2 presents the range of questions we need to be examining ointly as a staff if we are to identify those features of the context of ichooling which may be contributing to 'problem behaviour', and ntroduce changes which will increase the educational opportuni- ies available for all pupils.

In the majority of schools, the structures for carrying out the orocess of 'critical self-questioning' already exist and, indeed, are ilready in motion through the work, for example, of curriculum :ommittees, working parties and INSET programmes. In some .EAs, an official process of school review and self-evaluation has oeen instituted to take place every five years. The direct link is not ilways made, however, between the process of school improve- nent and the school's response to 'problem behaviour':

> … the most effective procedures for preventing, rather than treating, disturbing or maladjusted behaviour are a by-product of processes which aim to raise the overall quality of education for *all* pupils in the school.
>
> (Galloway and Goodwin, 1987)

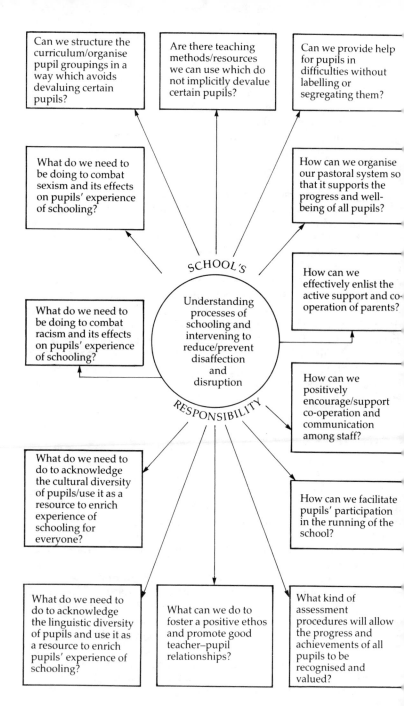

Figure 5.2 *Questioning schools*

It is this link which needs to be more clearly established, and the rationale of any additional provision, such as a special unit for 'problem behaviour', clearly explained in relation to it.

The scope for development within a school is, of course, limited by external influences which exert pressures on teachers and schools to function in particular ways. An example is the examination system which, even in its new form, presents a major limitation to the possibilities for change. 'For the school to succeed, it ironically can *not* educate all pupils, but rather must fail some' (West, 1979).

Recent developments in profiling, records of achievement for school leavers and criterion-referenced assessments have given grounds for optimism that some of the negative effects of failure might be mitigated by the promise of some concrete evidence of achievements at school for every child. However, proposals for nationwide testing at seven, eleven, fourteen and sixteen, as described in the DES Report, *Task Group on Assessment and Testing* (DES, 1988) are swinging the pendulum in the opposite direction, setting up the structures which produce and individualise 'failure', with all its attendant problems, from the earliest stages of education. These changes are likely to offer a powerful counter-thrust to attempts by individual teachers or schools to redress the balance of inequality of opportunity and so reduce the extent and severity of 'problem behaviour' in schools.

Together, the two 'frameworks' give substance to the claim made earlier that there is scope to improve the experience of schooling for all pupils, especially those identified as having 'behavioural problems'. They help to clarify the areas in which we believe intervention is both possible and likely to be effective. In the next section, we look at the kinds of changes which this process of questioning led us to attempt to introduce within the schools where we were currently working.

Part Three
Initiating Change

Situations vary, and we never fully know what implementation is or should look like until people in particular situations attempt to spell it out through use.

(Fullan, 1982, p. 79)

INTRODUCTION TO THE CASE STUDIES

The three 'case studies' drawn from our own work, which we present in this section, are not simply illustrative of theoretical points already made. They are qualitatively different because they show ideas developing *in and through practice*, in collaboration with colleagues and in response to the internal dynamics of the institution, and thus taking on a life and form unique to the particular circumstances. Indeed, logically, this section should have preceded the last, since it was through this experience, and reflecting on this experience, that the theoretical principles presented in the conclusion to Chapter 5 emerged.

Our 'case studies' are also intended to offer some insight into the complex, problematic nature of the development process itself. Ours was no ideal world where super-teachers achieve instant success in immaculate classrooms, where children never get bored or play up or ask when the 'real' work is going to begin. In our schools, as in most others, parents did not instantly welcome new teaching approaches, materials often ran out at the crucial moment. Heads were not always supportive of the developments we were undertaking and colleagues sometimes felt anxious that criticism of their own work was implied. We hope that writing about how our work evolved *within* and *in response to* the multitude of different pressures and stresses of teaching will help to convince readers that our ideas are relevant and applicable to a school world which they recognise, not just a set of pious ideals to be consigned to a dusty fate on the staff-room library shelf.

The following three chapters describe the development of a

'preventive' approach from three separate starting points. The first two are concerned with *prevention*, rather than *response*, i.e., they describe measures introduced to improve an aspect of classroom practice, or some feature of the organisation/curriculum, with a view to *preventing the emergence of problems* in the long term. Although they are, of course, a *response* to a perceived general problem, the initial and principal focus of activity and intervention is not an individual child. The third case study explores the possibility of combining responses to an individual child's difficulties with the process of improving relationships and learning experiences for the class as a whole. We shall examine in more detail the question of immediate responses to individual cases of 'problem behaviour', and how these may contribute to the process of improving the school's provision for all pupils, in our final section.

Case study 1 – Everest in plimsolls

> Few if any research traditions … have produced more defensible and clear results than that linking school failure to pupil deviance.
> (West, in Barton and Meighan, 1979)

This case study is principally concerned with the relationship between failure, problem behaviour and the curriculum. If children are moving from lesson to lesson feeling humiliated and frustrated by their inability to cope with the tasks set, it is not reasonable to expect that they will accept the situation with equanimity. Any attempt to remedy 'problem behaviour' must thus be tied into a concerted effort to improve their opportunities for successful involvement within the general curriculum. This raises the question of effective 'mixed-ability' teaching methods, of how to cater for the wide-ranging differences between pupils within the same teaching group.

ACTIVITY: QUESTIONING CLASSROOMS (see page 90)

- which of the features of the classroom environment were chosen as a focus of intervention in this case study?
- which other features were found to impinge on the success of the work and had to be dealt with along the way?
- which features were taken for granted/left unchanged, and what was the consequence of leaving them unexplored?

EVEREST IN PLIMSOLLS: A CASE STUDY IN CURRICULUM DEVELOPMENT

The door monitor swung on a dented brass doorknob, a large lump of luminous pink plastic circulating idly around in her mouth. She made no attempt to announce my approach to the chaotic inmates of her drab nineteenth-century classroom, judging no doubt that in my case such expenditure of energy would be futile. Instead, sizing me up with all the accumulated wisdom of her eleven years, she targeted her barb with painful precision right to the heart of my inmost fear. 'Can *you* control a *class*?' The scorn of her expression was more than matched by the incredulity of her tone; both left neither of us in any doubt as to her own opinion on the matter. She could tell just by looking at me that I did not have the sort of commanding presence that could quell the seething hubbub within at the twitch of a brow. Nor did she apparently sense in me that mysterious quality which enables some teachers to get even the most reluctant classes eating out of their hands within minutes. I was just another dud in a long succession of teachers who came and went with unrelenting regularity in those days of teacher shortage in the early 1970s.

And of course she was right. Offering up my inexperience into those children's merciless hands was, as she foresaw, like offering up a lamb for slaughter. Sold short yet again, they switched automatically into their familiar alternative gear, diverting their combined talents with infinite resourcefulness into the task of squeezing every last ounce of subversive potential from my efforts to teach them. And with upwards of 25 jostling for position as chief mischief-maker, I could not even console myself with the thought that the solution to my problems might lie in having the most troublesome elements removed. My only hope of reprieve was to let them teach me, little by little, what I needed to know to be able to teach them, until, finally, they let me survive to become a teacher.

The approach to tackling classroom problems, described in this case study, owes much to those early teaching experiences. They made it impossible not to see the relationship between children's behaviour and the quality of the learning environment the teacher provides. Years later, when I transferred into 'remedial' work and discovered how difficult it was to provide effective support for children from outside the mainstream, I began to realise the implications of this link for the organisation of special provision. If learning activities could be made more interesting, involving and accessible to *all*, then problems of any kind, whether learning difficulties, behavioural difficulties, or a combination of the two, would be less likely to arise. Our first focus of 'support' should thus be the *curriculum* rather than the *individual*. This case study describes the beginnings of my attempt to bring about that shift in emphasis. As well as addressing the question of *what kinds of changes* to traditional modes of secondary teaching might enable children to respond more positively and learn more effectively in their normal lessons, it raises a number of issues about the innovation *process* itself;

1. What happens when teachers, operating on an individual basis, try to introduce different classroom strategies in their

own teaching within an institution generally organised along traditional lines?

2. How can, or should, strategies, found to be effective with mixed-ability classes, be disseminated more widely among colleagues in the school?

3. How can learning support teachers, operating from outside the mainstream curriculum, bring about changes within the structure/organisation of special provision to enable them to pool resources with subject teachers to support children's learning more effectively in the classroom?

1. SIZING UP THE TASK

The school was a mixed, eight-form-entry urban comprehensive. In many respects, it was enlightened in its attitude to its less successful learners, holding as a matter of principle that children who needed special help should not be siphoned off into separate streams or special 'remedial' classes, but should be given any extra support they needed to be able to follow the mainstream curriculum along with their peers. As well as a strong pastoral system, generous resources were made available in the form of a remedial department and an on-site 'disruptive' unit to enable pupils identified as having literacy problems, behavioural problems or both to be withdrawn from classes for varying amounts of time to receive individual attention.

There is no doubt that this system provided a much-needed haven and source of support for pupils who were experiencing difficulties, but it had serious limitations. Quite apart from the difficulty of trying to promote literacy and good behaviour in isolation from the real contexts and purposes of the curriculum, it was not able to have any impact whatsoever on the kinds of educational experiences offered through the mainstream curriculum. Pupils and teachers were left without support for the majority of the week. Glimpses of worksheets used in lessons and tasks set for homework suggested that more direct support was urgently needed. Homework diaries sagged at times with detentions accumulated for failure to meet standards of work and behaviour. Was it so surprising, then, if some children responded to their sense of exclusion from the curriculum by disrupting lessons? Perhaps more surprising was that so few did give vent to their frustration by disruptive behaviour. It was more common to find children accepting the failure as their own and carrying around with them a burden of hopelessness and inferiority.

These observations are not intended to imply criticism of my colleagues' work. On the contrary, it was a 'good' school, a caring school. Teachers pressed pupils to work because they refused to write them off, hoping that the fading embers might, one day, miraculously rekindle. It seemed to me that we all stood to gain if subject teachers and I could work together to improve learning opportunities for these children instead of each of us battling on alone. To do so, however, would mean major changes in the concept and organisation of special provision in the school, over which, of course, as a newly appointed Scale 1 teacher, I had no control.

ACTIVITY

  (a) Before reading on, it might be useful for readers to consider the various options that were open to me at this point.
      (i) suggest possible courses of action I might have adopted in the particular circumstances outlined;
      (ii) consider the advantages/disadvantages of each one.
  (b) After reading the next section, consider the advantages/disadvantages of the particular course of action selected.

2. MAKING CONTACT

An opportunity arose when a subject teacher came to see me complaining about children being withdrawn from her lessons. They were getting further and further behind, and so were becoming increasingly difficult to teach. We worked out a plan in which I would use the content of her humanities lessons to develop reading activities for the pupils, so that work in the remedial department could be a continuation of normal classwork but specifically designed to take account of the children's reading development needs. Selling the idea to the children was predictably problematic, since they looked on my lessons as an 'escape' and were not about to relinquish the few perks that could be squeezed from their unenviable status as class 'thickoes' without a struggle. The response from the teachers was more positive. They began to enquire if the activities could also be made available in lessons for the 'less able' readers to use. I was doubtful. Clearly, this would be of help to inexperienced readers and their teachers, since it would provide those children with activities which they could accomplish successfully. On the other hand, I was not satisfied that feeding a set of learning materials into the classroom, to run parallel to the existing curriculum, was a solution compatible with the principle of 'mixed-ability' teaching. It seemed that if mixed-ability teaching was to be more than a disguised form of streaming or setting, then much more fundamental questions needed to be asked. Tackling the issue of what to do to help the minority with 'difficulties' in fact implied a thorough reappraisal of teaching methods and materials used with the entire class. Teaching approaches were needed which took individual differences into account from the start, not as an afterthought. The whole process of mixed-ability teaching, of how to set up classroom activities that would promote the active involvement and success of every child needed to be thought through again.

It would have been presumptuous to have raised these questions in relation to any practice other than my own. I approached the head of humanities and requested to take a class the following year, so that I would have the opportunity to explore the issues for myself. Senior management welcomed the move on the grounds that remedial staff needed to be recognised as competent classroom teachers. It posed no threat to my colleagues either in the humanities department or in my own department, since it left all existing structures intact. The only threat, in fact, though I had hardly begun to appreciate it at the time, was to myself. I was about as prepared as a novice climber in plimsolls at the foot of Mount Everest. It was folly, but up I went.

3. MIXED-ABILITY ISSUES

Mixed-ability teaching, according to HMI (DES, 1978c), 'calls for more sophisticated professional skills than does teaching in more traditional forms of organisation' (p. 61). It requires the adoption of 'teaching methods and modes of class management which are compatible with it' (p. 60).

ACTIVITY

(a) What are the 'problems' associated with mixed-ability teaching, which might require 'more sophisticated professional skills'.
(b) Make another list of classroom strategies, which you use yourself, or which you are aware of, which attempt to cater for the wide range of individual differences in a mixed-ability group.

OVERCOMING THE 'PROBLEMS'

It is ironic to note how little time has passed since schools were turning to mixed-ability grouping as a practical *solution* to classroom discipline problems presented by the middle and lower sets within systems of streaming and banding (Ball, 1981). Now it is widely argued that having differing 'abilities' in the same teaching group is the *cause* of discipline problems (with the '*solution*' to return to streaming or banding?) Among the 'problems' associated with teaching mixed-ability classes are:

- Pitching lessons at a level to suit everyone; how to ensure that the work is not too easy for some and too difficult for others.
- Pacing lessons right so that the children who learn or work slowly are not left behind, while others sit impatiently marking time.
- Matching the subject material to the interests and maturity levels of children who are at such widely differing stages of social and intellectual development.
- Enabling all children, not just the confident, more boisterous and vociferous learners but those who are shy or afraid to show themselves up, to be actively involved in lessons.

If satisfactory 'solutions' are not found for most of these, then the situation clearly has in-built potential for creating frustration and, eventually, disruption. Yet this definition of the 'problems' itself depends upon an assumption of whole-class teaching methods as the 'norm', i.e., the most effective and economic means of conducting the teaching/learning process with a class of 30 children. These methods are, in turn, based on the assumption that the teacher's function is to *pass on* a set of concepts, knowledge or skills *to* the learner. 'Mixed-ability' teaching presents problems, therefore, because it is impossible in the passing-on process to treat 30 learners as though they were one. It seemed to me that there was every reason to question the validity of whole-class teaching methods, not just for mixed-ability classes but for any group of 30 individuals. Apart from the fact that the sheer logistics of the formal situation preclude the active involvement of most of the learners most of the time, I could see no way in which presentation of ideas to a whole class could take account of 30 separate starting points, or tap the resources, knowledge and experience of 30 individuals who differed in a whole range of ways, not just in 'ability' (a category which is itself in need of critical scrutiny). No matter how skilful I might become at capturing and holding their attention, or at managing whole-class 'discussion', it was inevitable that some children would be excluded, and so problems would inevitably arise.

The alternatives to whole-class teaching methods frequently put forward, which involve differentiation or individualisation of tasks (DES, op. cit.), seemed equally unsatisfactory. While the intention of matching the task to the child is a worthy one, if underlying assumptions about teaching and learning remain unexplored, then the result may simply be that a workcard is used as a substitute teacher, to 'pass on' to learners individually what previously would have been taught through whole-class methods. From a practical standpoint, too, individualised approaches present major problems for the teacher, both in terms of pressure to produce different resources for different children to use, and in the management of learning in the classroom. Most of the teacher's time may be taken up with keeping the system ticking over rather than working with individuals and groups. And even if this problem can be resolved, trying to share out one's time fairly among 30 children during a lesson may mean that those who find it difficult to sustain concentration or to work independently for any length of time are left to struggle on unsupported for lengthy periods. Again, the potential for frustration, boredom and disruptive behaviour seemed to be built-in.

Looking for a 'solution' in terms of dismantling a mixed-ability class for teaching purposes into more 'homogeneous' component parts (which at its logical extreme meant, of course, into 30 separate individuals) seemed to run counter to the whole rationale of mixed-ability teaching. Why have children of differing 'abilities' working in the same class if you then set them to work apart? Whatever the limitations of whole-class teaching methods, they offer, at the very least, an experience shared with other human beings. Carefully graded materials to work on alone, no matter how interestingly or attractively presented, offer a poor substitute for the warmth and encouragement of a good teacher and the potential knock-on effect of enthusiasms generated from within the group as a whole.

It seemed to me that the approach I was looking for must lie somewhere between the two extremes, retaining the advantages of learning in a social context while allowing greater scope for each individual to take an active part. Breaking the class down into mixed-ability groups and setting them to work collaboratively seemed to offer a way forward. If, instead of treating teaching and learning as essentially an individual matter between teacher and child, the children could be encouraged to learn with and from each other, then the range of differences within a mixed-ability class could be transformed from an intractable problem into a positive asset. If the knowledge, experience and skills which the children bring with them to the lesson were valued and used as a resource for themselves and others, then the teacher would no longer be under pressure to be the fount of all wisdom, to try to teach 30 different individuals simultaneously or to provide individual teaching 30 times over.

Getting the children to work collaboratively would not be just another way of overcoming the 'problems' of the mixed-ability situation by promoting the 'abler' children to the role of substitute teacher for the 'less able' and justifying this on the grounds that the experience benefits both in different ways. It would reflect a view of teaching and learning which places the learner, not the teacher, at the centre and places maximum priority upon providing opportunities for all learners to make sense of the work on their own terms. One consequence of the change in emphasis would be to reduce the significance of those aspects of mixed-ability teaching previously found to be problematic, and thus, by implication, the potential for classroom disruption associated with them.

- Instead of having to sit quietly and listen most of the time, or compete with 30 others to answer the teacher's questions, everyone would be actively involved throughout the lesson; everyone would be able to contribute what they knew, to talk ideas through and engage in the kind of 'exploratory talk' (Barnes, 1977) now considered by many to be an essential part of learning. The potential for boredom and restlessness associated with excessively passive learning roles, would thus be reduced.

- If it is taken for granted that each learner will be bringing his or her own resources to bear on the task and making sense of the ideas in terms of what he/she already knows, then the problem of 'pitching' the lesson no longer has the same significance, since for each child the process and the outcome will necessarily be different. Pitching a task at the right level becomes a matter of designing a stimulus for learning in which everyone can take part, but which does not prescribe what the children say or learn. The potential for frustration, fear and resentment experienced by pupils unable to meet unrealistic demands could thus also be reduced.

- With groups working independently, and individuals within groups contributing in different ways, 'pacing' should no longer be a central concern. It was likely, in fact, that a group with several confident and knowledgeable children in it would take longer over a stimulus task because they kept finding new ideas to explore. Less confident learners, too, with the support of the group, need never get left behind. Groups could dictate their own pace of working, and no group would be held up from their work because another had not been listening, was experiencing difficulty, or was misbehaving. It would thus be less likely that pupils would be left with 'empty' time on their hands to fill, if they so chose, by distracting others.

- With poor readers always working in a supported situation, there was no need for them to be presented with drastically simplified texts. They could learn far more about reading by following a line of text alongside a competent reader, joining in the process of making meaning and seeing reading operating for real learning purposes in the classroom, than they could working alongside other non-competent readers in the contrived contexts of the reading room. On the other hand, the stimulus reading material could be kept relatively simple and therefore manageable by less confident readers, while still requiring pupils to grapple with quite complex ideas. The problems associated with poor readers feeling 'shown up' by being given simplified materials to use, or, alternatively, feeling helpless because they cannot read the class texts, could thus be potentially overcome.

- Encouraging children to work together, and validating their interests and experiences as a resource for classroom learning, would make it less likely that they would feel alienated from school knowledge and reject it as being of no relevance to their own concerns.

There were substantial grounds for supposing, therefore, that adopting collaborative learning methods as a general classroom strategy with my new class would not only create better conditions for learning but also mean that behaviour and learning problems, associated with more traditional forms of teaching, would, I hoped, be less likely to occur. The next question was how the humanities syllabus I was required to follow might be translated into collaborative learning activities.

4. ACTIVITIES FOR COLLABORATIVE LEARNING

Ideas for activities did not, of course, arrive in a timely flash of inspiration at the stat of the autumn term. They evolved slowly, through a continual process of revision and reworking, over a period of two years – and continue to evolve. Nevertheless, from the start, lessons (i.e., the standard secondary 'double period') took on a pattern which was to remain more or less constant throughout.

- They began with a short whole-class (or sometimes group) activity designed to arouse the children's curiosity, stimulate their interest or focus their attention on whatever topic was to be studied during the course of the lesson.
- Next, the class broke down into groups to work on a task, using some stimulus materials provided.
- When supplies permitted, there was then an opportunity to use resource books to check and confirm ideas, to find out answers to questions that had been raised, to pursue topics

further and extend understanding, or simply browse in accordance with individual interests and concerns.

- Finally, the conclusions and findings of the whole class would be pooled, and important points recorded in books as appropriate.

Planning a collaborative learning activity involved, essentially, taking apart the ideas for each topic in the syllabus and then thinking of an interesting way of presenting them to the children so that they could 'sort it all out' (Goodson, 1972) and 'actively reconstruct knowledge' for themselves.

ACTIVITY

How might you go about planning an activity which would get the children to explore together the following topic?

Original learning task

The lesson is part of a topic of work about adaptation and survival in the Arctic. There is a densely written worksheet available, explaining how, in times past, the Inuit learnt to use every part of the caribou and seal to provide for their basic needs. The explanation and diagrams are followed by a series of questions for the children to answer in written form by referring back to the text.

(a) How would you restructure this task so that, instead of being presented with ready-made ideas, the pupils have to 'sort it out' for themselves, drawing on their own resources?
(b) What problems would you envisage in terms of organisation and management?
(c) What would the teacher's function be while the children were carrying out the task?

(a) Restructuring the task

The components into which the information on the sheet can be broken down are:

(i) the concept of 'basic needs' (food, clothing, shelter, protection);
(ii) the concept of 'survival' as applied to the specific problems presented by Arctic conditions;
(iii) the concept of 'adaptation' in terms of using the available resources in the environment in order to provide basic needs;
(iv) an understanding of all the different parts of animals' bodies (hair, hide, bones, horns, flesh, innards, etc.) applied to seal and caribou in particular;

(v) understanding the potential for the various parts to be used in different ways to satisfy human needs.

All the children have some understanding and relevant knowledge relating to all of these, and the first activity is designed to encourage them to explore and formulate together the knowledge they already possess between them.

Activity 1: Jigsaw animals. Pairs of children working together might be given a picture of a seal or caribou cut into parts. They identify each part and how it might be useful to them if that was all they had available to stay alive. They might record their ideas on each part, before sticking them together to make a whole animal. Pairs could then compare ideas with another pair working on the same animal, or explain and justify their ideas to a pair working on a different animal.

By now the children should have explored the limits of what they already know, have begun to raise questions and be ready to extend their understanding further. The second activity focuses their thinking more specifically, requiring them to organise the ideas they have so far and apply them to a set of objects provided.

Activity 2: Seal or caribou? Two pairs of children, one with a caribou and one with a seal, are given a set of cards with pictures and a brief description of objects used by the Inuit. First they sort out those objects they consider to be essential to survival, justifying their views to one another, since everyone has to agree with the final decision. Then they divide up the chosen objects between them, according to whether they think they come from the seal or caribou, again giving reasons to justify their choice. Resource books would then be used to check ideas and find out more, as described earlier.

The same task can be presented to all the children in the group because it is designed in a way that each child can respond at his or her own level. There is nothing about the skills needed for the task which excludes any learner in the group, and every child can have the satisfaction of realising that they already possess information of relevance to what they have to do. At the same time, there is plenty of scope for the most sophisticated learners in the class to try to come to grips with quite complex ideas (Is a toy 'essential'; what if it is training children to hunt? Are items believed to ward off evil spirits or bring good luck in hunting essential? Are beliefs in spiritual things basic human needs? Where does the notion of basic survival end and the quality of human existence begin?, etc.).

The 'sorting-it-out' activities for a particular topic are not chosen purely for their motivational potential. They are selected because they seem accurately to reflect the conceptual structure of the ideas or to offer the best opportunity for getting the children to engage with the ideas and reconstruct them for themselves. Over two years, the repertoire came to include activities involving:

- *classifying* sets of pictures/information cards in particular ways;
- *sequencing/ordering/matching* sets of pictures and/or information cards;
- *examining* pictures to find common features/differences;
- *drawing* pictures/diagrams on the basis of information provided;
- *drawing* pictures/diagrams by *collating* own knowledge and information drawn from various sources;
- *interpreting* printed information as a mime or sketch;
- *extracting* key information from texts, *organising* it in some way and using it to form hypotheses, make judgements or draw conclusions;
- *choosing* between different courses of action operating different or conflicting sets of criteria;
- *simulating* situations;
- *predicting* missing information on the basis of information supplied through pictures or text;
- *linking* concepts through games such as 'Rummy', 'Happy Families', 'Connect 4', etc.;
- *following* a sequence of instructions (to make a game, carry out an activity) in order to build up an overall picture and draw conclusions.

(b) Making it work in practice

Of course it is easy to have ideas about getting children to work collaboratively in principle, and even to work out activities in theory. It is another matter entirely to make it work in practice, especially when desks are arranged in traditional lines facing the board, and classrooms are so small that the door only just squeezes shut behind the thirtieth child. I found it difficult to relinquish my position in the centre of the stage and still maintain the sense that I was in control. It was difficult, too, to judge just how much purposeful activity was going on amidst the buzz of everybody talking at once. Certainly, experimenting with unaccustomed teaching methods against a tide of expectations from children, parents and colleagues was a hazardous affair. Although failure and partial successes had to be expected as part of the fabric of urriculum development, I had not bargained for how exposed I vould feel when they happened. I felt that I could not risk losing redibility in the eyes of my colleagues if I was to have any hope of vorking collaboratively with them at a later stage. And since my bility to 'keep control' would inevitably be a central consideration n their judgement of my competence, I was continually torn etween the desire to experiment and explore all the possibilities n the one hand, and settling for the safer option, one I felt sure vould not get out of hand, on the other.

I had also failed to anticipate the resistance which the children vould put up to working in unorthodox ways, and how my own nsecurity would manage to communicate itself to the children and einforce their doubts. I had not realised how quickly they would ave developed expectations of what kind of work was the norm at econdary level, regardless of what they had been used to at their rimary schools. They treated what were intended to be 'open-nded' tasks as though they were 'closed', anxiously seeking my onfirmation that they had arrived at the 'right' answer; and while n the whole they enjoyed the activities, they regarded them as lightly frivolous and would no doubt have felt more comfortable vith routine written tasks.

During the course of that first experimental year, therefore, I iscovered, paradoxically, that my efforts to change traditional eaching methods in a way that would help reduce or prevent earning and behavioural difficulties had the effect, initially at east, of creating problems rather than resolving them. Experience nd careful analysis of classroom conditions were required if the otential advantages of collaborative learning were to be realised. y the time I began again with a new class the following year, I had earned enough from the previous year's efforts to iron out most of he initial difficulties. This meant:

- Negotiating teaching rooms with enough space for group discussions not to impinge on one another and force the noise level up unnecessarily, and where the desks were permanently arranged in groups not rows.
- Learning to streamline the organisation of the classroom using group leaders to hand out and check back equipment such as worksheets, cards, picture sets, etc., with the minimum of fuss.
- Discovering what kinds of activities worked best, how to time them right, how to get them off to a good start, how to anticipate and tackle any problems before they occurred.
- Learning about layout and presentation of materials, and how carefully instructions need to be phrased if children are to be able to follow them independently.

- Interspersing lessons involving intensive collaborative work with more relaxed periods when children could pursue their own interests independently, finish off work, browse through books or undertake personal writing related to what they had been learning. There was also a need to foster experiences shared with the class as a whole, for instance reading aloud to them stories, myths, legends connected with the topics we were studying.

Once the approach had become stabilised, a definite change was noticeable in the nature of relationships between myself and the class and between the pupils themselves. There was no longer a need for me to maintain a façade or 'distance' from the learners in order to be able to get 30 individuals to sit quietly and listen to me (or to each other) for extended periods of time. There was no longer a ready-made audience available for those with disruption or teacher-baiting in mind. And each individual was no longer in competition with the rest for my time, attention or recognition of effort or attainment. I could spend my time much more productively talking to children in their groups and establishing more personal and individual relationships than were ever possible with more formal methods. Of course, there were times when problems arose in a group, when pupils began to argue about people not taking part or not letting anyone else take part or disrupting the work of the group by being silly. But the difference now was that only that group was disturbed. I no longer had the dilemma of having to deal with it in public before the rest of the class could get on with their work. Other members of the group tended to put pressure on miscreants because they wanted to get on with the activities, and where this did not happen it was always possible to change the composition of groups to ensure a balance of children who would maintain the group's work.

If a child should show signs of distressed or troubled behaviour either before or during a lesson, which seemed to require private individual handling, it was always possible in this situation to give that child attention away from the group, safe in the knowledge that the rest of the class could get on on their own.

(c) My role

My understanding of my own role developed as circumstances freed me from preoccupation with organisation and management issues that had haunted my first year. Now that the groups had gathered their own momentum, I was able to sit down and work with each one for relatively lengthy periods, learning how to listen in to how they were tackling a task, to the sorts of issues they were concerned to explore, and to help them to take their thinking further. To begin with, I was almost afraid to join in their discussions for fear of recreating the situation where they were concerned not to think for themselves but to get the 'answer' from me. It took some time to begin to develop the knack of listening to someone's thought processes and intervening in such a way that learning was facilitated rather than inhibited.

By now, I was also freed sufficiently to take notice of some of those children who are easily overlooked in classrooms because they deliberately avoid drawing attention to themselves. There were those, firstly, who quietly opted out of group work, who were happy just to sit and let others get on with it without becoming involved at all. Then there were those who found collaborative learning too much to cope with because of the pressure which it put upon them socially, those who found it difficult to make relationships, who were isolated and whom everyone refused to work with. For the former group, I began to include activities which provided each member of the group with a different but complementary role, so that the task could not be completed unless everyone contributed. For the sake of the latter, I began to consider different kinds of activities, more flexible-sized groupings, more intimate settings that would foster their integration, drawing particularly on some of the ideas of developmental group work to promote trust, co-operation and positive relationships within the class. It was approaches of this kind which, had I continued the work into a third year, I would have wanted to develop further. However, my first priority now (as acting head of department) was to pursue contacts that were opening up with my humanities colleagues.

ACTIVITY

Before reading about my attempts to develop collaborative work with colleagues, readers might like to consider the following questions:

(a) What had been learned about effective mixed-ability teaching as a result of developing collaborative learning methods with my own class?
(b) How might I have used that experience to best effect in opening up discussions with colleagues?

5. THE SLIPPERY SLOPE

My work had reached a critical stage. So far, with a nod of approval from the head, I had been protected by the principle of autonomy as long as what I was doing stayed within the confines of my own classroom. If I was to begin to lay the foundations for what was to become, I hoped, my new role, then it was time to venture forth and open up exploratory discussions with colleagues. At this point, therefore, strategy was crucial. Two possibilities, in retrospect, presented themselves:

(i) I could use the insights gained from the work as a basis for continuing to explore, this time with colleagues, ways of adapting teaching methods and materials to meet all children's needs more effectively; or

(ii) I could try to persuade colleagues to think about alternative ways of organising learning in their classrooms by offering them activities to try out that I had used successfully myself, and explaining the principles behind them.

Had I been able to formulate these alternatives clearly to myself at the time, I would certainly have opted for the former course of action. As someone who claimed to value the *process* of learning, I would have noticed the contradiction involved in imposing the products of my own learning process on others. In the event, however, what I ended up doing was the second. Although I now see that it was a mistake, the ideas initially met with such a favourable response that I had no reason to question the strategy.

The teacher with whom I made initial contact was in charge of the first-year course. An experienced, well-respected teacher with a formal style, he welcomed my offer of working with him on the grounds that he felt he was being least successful with his 'less able' pupils. We agreed to meet during one free period a week, and began by simply talking through what he was planning to do in his lessons. We would identify places in the lesson where children might have difficulty and decide what to do at that point to help them. Then I began to offer short activities which I had specially prepared, to use for five or ten minutes during a lesson to help children sort out and clarify some of the ideas. When these went down well, and as the trust between us developed, I began to offer a collaborative learning activity I had already tried out, which fitted in with what he wanted to teach. We would talk the activities through beforehand, work together in the classroom while the children were carrying them out, and review what had happened afterwards. He was impressed by the children's response and wanted to try out more. Within half a term, he became a complete 'convert' to collaborative learning methods.

His enthusiasm spread to other people teaching first years. Teachers began to request samples of activities to try out. There was no time to talk them through and explain the principles behind them, but I did not want to discourage their interest. I knew the dangers of making it appear that I was the 'expert' and, in the process, making them feel that they lacked the very skills it was my intention to foster. At a meeting at the end of the year, it was agreed that the collaborative learning materials for each unit would be made available in the faculty room for anyone who wished to use them. I felt gratified that the work had been taken on with such a degree of enthusiasm, but uneasy about renouncing my own control over the material.

As it turned out, my misgivings proved to be well founded. The availability of the materials had exactly the *opposite* effect of that intended, inviting teachers to be less, not more, thoughtful about preparing their lessons to meet the needs of all the pupils in their classes. The unfortunate mystique which they began to acquire unwittingly down-graded the teachers' own expertise. The materials could not be an effective resource for mixed-ability teaching because the teachers did not 'own' them themselves. They had not been part of the process that had created them, so they did not feel able to adapt them to suit their own style or to meet their own teaching purposes. When problems arose, they found it difficult to modify what they were doing to sort the problems out. In some cases, this led to the rejection of the materials on the grounds that it was too difficult for inexperienced teachers to use and, ironically, caused unsettled classes to get out of control. Because the ideas had not emerged organically from the teachers' own collaborative endeavours, they felt no special commitment to supporting the work through its teething stages. And I, still fully timetabled in my traditional role, was powerless to support it either. Doubts about the materials began to be expressed that I was in no position to allay; criticisms voiced that it was not my place to answer.

So, for me, it was the slippery slope, with no help to call on from anywhere to break my fall. In the first flush of panic, I blamed the moment when I had allowed free access to the material, without proper induction into the underlying principles, for the resulting problems. It is only now that I realise there was a more fundamental flaw in my understanding of the process I was engaged in. Somewhere along the way, in the excitement of conquering my first small peak, I had lost sight of the purpose of the original exercise. This was to explore for myself possible alternative ways of working with 'mixed-ability' groups, unfettered by fears of trespassing on anyone else's territory. The ideas I came up with worked, eventually, for me because they embodied 'solutions' to the particular combination of questions that were my concern at the time. Unless those to whom these ideas were presented shared the same set of priorities, then they were not 'solutions' in any helpful sense at all. On the contrary, foisting them on colleagues as the 'new', 'improved' mixed-ability teaching methods was likely, at best, to be a distraction and at worst to undermine their confidence in finding solutions for themselves.

The problems of dissemination that arose were not due, therefore, as I previously supposed, to a lack of proper in-service training in the principles and use of the materials in the classroom, but to a basic misunderstanding of what it was that needed to be disseminated. What was valuable about the humanities work I had done, what should have been preserved from it to help me in my work with colleagues, was not the particular solutions I happened to have come up with myself, neither the materials nor the principles as such, but the *experience* of systematically and critically reflecting upon classroom practice and taking action to improve it. It was learning to make the ideas work, learning how to tackle the problems as they arose, and overcome them in a positive and constructive way that was the vital part. It was this aspect of the experience which I could bring to my work with colleagues, in order to support them effectively in finding their own solutions.

The experience as a whole showed that if the needs of children with learning or behavioural difficulties are to be taken into account and provided for in mainstream teaching, what will make the difference is not that their teachers are prepared to accept, on trust, ready-made packages of solutions, however expertly designed and scientifically tested, or to 'take on board' a set of principles, however sound. It is that they accept, as a matter of course, their professional responsibility for analysing their own practice and taking whatever action is open to them to make the curriculum more responsive to the children's needs. As support teachers, we can and should support them in that process. We can offer help in 'reading' classrooms, raising questions, identifying problems, exploring solutions; but our aim must always be to build a collaborative endeavour between two equals, a support which works not to diminish or remove, but to confirm and strengthen each teacher's basic responsibility for all the pupils in their care.

Afterword

This case study pinpointed *teaching methods* and *materials* as the main focus for enquiry and innovation. Formal whole-class teaching methods were identified as a major constraint on the possibility of enabling all pupils in a mixed-ability group to participate actively and experience success in learning. It was suggested that problems, including 'problem behaviour', which result from the non-participation or lack of success of certain pupils, might be alleviated if effective alternatives to whole-class teaching methods could be developed.

The success of changes in teaching methods and materials was found to be affected by other significant features of the learning environment, e.g.:

- the teacher's confidence and experience in using the approach;
- the pupils' expectations of the teacher and classroom activities;
- the physical proportions and layout of the room;
- general classroom organisation and management;
- the availability of resources.

They were also affected by factors external to this particular classroom, for example by the expectations and judgements of colleagues, by the influence of parents and pupils in other teaching groups.

Certain features of the learning context were either unconsciously taken for granted as unproblematic or were consciously accepted, for the present at least, as unchangeable, e.g.:

- curriculum content;
- pupils' ability to work collaboratively;
- teachers' assumptions about knowledge and the nature of the learning process;
- teachers' ability to create a climate in which pupils feel safe to contribute their own ideas and explore them with each other.

These created a set of in-built limitations for the potential development of the work. In particular, there were important consequences at the 'dissemination' stage when the methods and materials were extracted from the conditions and context which had supported and enabled them to 'work' effectively and were transported 'cold' into a whole range of different classrooms and different conditions.

The case study illustrates the 'disturbance' effect characteristic of innovation:

> Performance in change situations (however measured) worsens, even after the most beneficial changes, until everybody learns how to make the change work up to its potential.
>
> (Georgiades and Phillimore, 1975)

If this is not understood to be a natural part of the process, it may lead to the premature evaluation and possible rejection of the development on the grounds that it has not 'worked' in practice.

Teachers interested in researching any of these issues in relation to their own practice will find a list of resources to support the process in Appendix 2.

7

Case study 2 – rejecting the rational

Our second case study complements the work described in the previous chapter in two ways:

Firstly, at classroom level it takes as a central issue the nature and pattern of *classroom relationships* which were taken for granted in the first study. It explains why simply grafting collaborative learning materials and methods on to a classroom environment in which traditional patterns of authority and behaviour among teacher and pupils remain unchallenged and/or unchanged is unlikely to prove successful, and opens up the question of what alternatives to these traditional patterns might be developed.

Secondly, it takes up where the previous study left off in relation to the process of change. Aware of the limitations of the 'hero innovator' approach (Georgiades and Phillimore, in Easen, 1985), it illustrates just how far it is possible to go in this particular context, building up a base of support among colleagues, before the point is reached where no further development can take place without some more fundamental changes being introduced.

ACTIVITY

(a) Which of the elements of the framework 'Questioning Schools' (page 92) were identified by this teacher as the focus for intervention?

(b) What strategies did she adopt in order to make space to work within the existing structures?

(c) In what ways did the existing structures impede the development of the work and how might they be overcome?

Counselling and pastoral care which aims to help individuals adjust to classroom demands will do nothing to tackle underlying tensions in school and classroom climate ... Neither full-time withdrawal from the classroom nor special help will do anything to tackle factors within the classroom which might have contributed to, if not caused the learning adjustment difficulties that made withdrawal necessary.
(Galloway, 1985)

1. JO – A 'TYPICAL' DISRUPTIVE PUPIL

Jo has now left school and is quite capably making her own way in the world. Yet her school record shows that her years of secondary schooling were characterised by persistent, unresolved antagonism and conflict with her teachers. None of the set procedures laid down by the school to deal with such problems, or the additional resources made available to help Jo, seem to have had any effect in improving her behaviour.

ACTIVITY

The purpose of this activity is to illustrate the case of a 'typical' pupil referred to an on-site 'disruptive' unit.

  (i) While reading the case study notes, make a list of all the individuals who have been involved in dealing with Jo, and the types of intervention that have been tried.
  (ii) After reading the case study notes, consider the following questions:
      (a) If you were Jo's *tutor*, what would you try to do to improve matters?
      (b) If you were Jo's *year head*, what strategies would you suggest classroom teachers use when teaching Jo?
      (c) If you were the *unit teacher*, how would you try to deal with the nineteen points of referral, and what could you do to help classroom teachers and the tutor group?
  (iii) Are there any contradictions in your answers to the three questions above?

NB: even with well-kept records such as this, there are frequently gaps. Departmental and tutor reports, for example, do not always find their way into the main file. This activity is not intended to imply criticism of the care taken in maintaining this record.

Notes based on Jo's school record

First year
Trouble began very early on in her secondary career. After a term in the first year, the tutor group she was in was defined as 'difficult' and Jo was identified as one of the principal culprits. She was moved into a different tutor group.

Summer term
In May of her first year, her new tutor expressed concern about her attitudes to work and her behaviour towards staff, and she was put on report to the year head. The report had to be signed by each member of staff as a record of her attendance, achievement and co-operation, and was checked by her tutor and year head at

the end of each day. It was hoped that for Jo, as for many pupils, the extra attention built into the report system, the opportunities for praise and the incentive to behave which it provided (in order to escape immediate detentions) would be sufficient in itself to remedy the problem. Unfortunately, that was not the case. Her record shows that towards the end of May, she was excluded for three days for 'failure to comply with the conditions of the report'. When she returned to school, the strategy of putting her on report to the year head was again tried.

Second year
Problems clearly continued, and during the Christmas term of her second year, she was referred on to the deputy head. The reasons for her being on report were:

- persistent disruption of lessons;
- basic failure to work in class;
- ignoring homework assignments;
- truancy and lateness;
- rudeness, loud shouting, refusal to work;
- complete flouting of authority;
- lying.

Spring term
She remained on report to the deputy head until the end of December, but on her return in January was transferred back to year head's report. By the end of January she was again back on report to the deputy head. At the end of March she was excluded for failure to comply with the conditions of the deputy head's report.

At this stage, it was decided to make a referral to the on-site unit. For this to happen, it was necessary to make contact with Jo's parent and to collect information from all members of staff teaching her about the kinds of problems Jo was presenting in lessons. Nineteen points were mentioned by her teachers as reasons for her referral:

1. Loud disruption
2. Non-stop talking across the room
3. Very little work both in class and at home
4. Unpopular with many pupils and staff
5. Limited concentration
6. Interferes with other pupils either by taking their equipment or physically interfering with them
7. No sense of responsibility
8. No sanctions seem to have any effect
9. Does not seem to understand her work, but general view is that she does not think about it

10. Demands to be the centre of attention and instigates conversations (usually) by shouting
11. Will apologise on occasions, but never reform
12. Has truanted from various lessons, including PE
13. Appalling presentation of work
14. Failure to attend detentions
15. Physically restless all the time
16. Rude
17. No attempt to improve standards of work
18. Impertinent
19. Poor integration with other pupils

A placement in the school's on-site 'disruptive' unit was agreed, followed by the suggestion of referral to the Schools Psychological Service.

After this, there is a gap in the records. The suggested referral to the SPS does not seem to have been followed up. Passing reference to a stay at an off-site centre during this period indicates that Jo's placement in the on-site unit had little impact upon her behaviour in lessons.

Third year
The story is taken up again in her third year. In May, there was a three-day exclusion for abusive language. This was followed in June by another unit placement for maths. In the middle of June, a letter was sent home about her truanting fifteen sessions in one month.

July
Two letters dated the same day in early July inform Jo's parent, firstly, of a three-day exclusion, and secondly, of a ten-day suspension. Both these letters refer to an incident where there was defiant behaviour to a senior member of staff.

The file continues to her fifth year. More exclusions occurred, but the main problem at this stage was truancy.

A 'typical' pupil?

The past six years' experience of working with 'disruptive' pupils in comprehensive schools suggests that Jo's case is typical. Most pupils presenting problems of this kind do remain within mainstream schooling throughout their school careers (or at least they remain on the school's roll, once chronic truancy has set in).

Of course, there are some pupils who may be offered on-site provision for reasons other than disrupting lessons, for example those who are withdrawn or truanting, or who have experienced one or more of life's traumas, such as the death of a close relative. There will also be pupils who are involved with drugs, or who have a temper which is so unpredictable that they are a danger to themselves and everybody else. For these pupils, often the victims of family or society abuse, on-site provision will be the first staging post before outside agencies intervene or the school expels them. However, out of the 40 to 50 pupils the unit would cater for in any year, only one or two pupils fall into this category and *some years there will be none*.

The reason that so few cases of this kind are identified is not the low overall incidence of such problems, but the fact that most of the pupils involved go to considerable lengths to avoid being noticed, so that if or when a crisis occurs and we do find out about them, it is often too late to tackle the problem constructively from within the school's resources. For these unknown members of our society, the best we can hope to do is to create opportunities to talk about such issues and design an education that includes health and children's rights. But schools are educational institutions, they cannot take on all the problems of the world. The most we can hope for as teachers is the knowledge that we have acted as responsible adults in that we have alerted other professions to the pupils' plight as soon as we have become aware of it. (More on this subject in our final chapter.)

For the most part, though, our bread-and-butter work is concerned with the 'Jo's of this world. This chapter is about pupils such as Jo and the systems schools set up for dealing with their behaviour.

Relying on the rational?

It has been a common thread to my teaching experience that teachers often look for explanations for a pupil's behaviour that extend away from the school and into the home. In Jo's case, however, looking for outside explanations for her behaviour draws a blank. Is it her family? Is it poverty? Is it the way she lives? The answer to all these questions, duly reported by the Education Welfare service, is not really. The most we can say is that Jo comes from a single-parent family. However, in an inner-city school single-parent families are not uncommon even among teachers, so this hook offers no clue as to why Jo, who comes from a happy and secure family, should be disrupting lessons.

Jo's first placement in the unit coincided with the moment when, after four years as a 'remedial' teacher, I was taking up my first post as a teacher in an on-site 'disruptive pupils' provision. Such referrals were common enough, and my first reaction to them was apprehension. What could I hope to do with a person to whom 'no sanctions apply'? I certainly did not think to challenge any of the assumptions in the referral. Now, years later, when Jo has left school to live as normal a life as any of us, it makes me laugh to remember how apprehensive I felt looking at the nineteen points on her referral form. Of course, I'm not denying that Jo was a difficult pupil in the main school, but in the unit she was completely different. She showed no sign of the anti-social behaviour which had led to her referral and conducted her social relationships with teachers and other pupils in a relaxed and friendly manner. Admittedly, she continued to reject formal academic work, even in the unit, but when arguments occurred over this, she remained calm; she did not swear at us or swing from the light bulbs. She just saw no relevance in having a fat folder of work, so the folder remained thin. In my experience most pupils who end up having on-site provision made for them do not exhibit intolerable behaviour while in the unit. But few of them transfer their good behaviour back to the classroom or corridors. Many are lost to exclusions and suspensions for incidents that occur during break, lunchtime or en route to another part of the building.

It is this Jekyll and Hyde existence that makes it so difficult for unit teachers, on the receiving end of the conveyor belt referral system, to find anything to work on with the pupils so that the effort has some carry-over into the hurly burly of mainstream school life. Reading the case study notes about Jo may have raised some questions in your mind about what exactly was going wrong and about the strategies the school was adopting to deal with it. For instance, is her truancy anything to do with difficulties in learning (see Point 9 on the referral list)? And how exactly is the report system supposed to connect up with the support provided in the unit? Questions such as these certainly do need to be asked. However, they do not really go to the heart of the problem. At the time I received Jo's referral, I was so enmeshed in the school's particular system for dealing with problem behaviour that I could not immediately see the more fundamental questions which needed to be asked. Were I to be back in that position now, with all the wisdom of hindsight, I should want to respond to her referral form in the following way:

A letter to a good school

Dear School,

You are well respected in the Education Authority for your efficient organisation, your sound teaching practices, your good exam results. You have a well-thought-of Special Needs department and separate on-site provision for disruptive pupils. You have a carefully thought out and water-tight system for dealing with troublesome behaviour, which is recognised and meticulously followed by the majority of staff. If a pupil gets into trouble in a lesson, the Head of Department nearly always sorts it out in the first instance. If the trouble persists, the pupil will go on report either to his/her tutor or to the Head of Department. If the trouble appears to be occurring across several subject areas, the pupil goes on report to the Year Head. If there is no response to being on report to the Head of Year, the pupil will be put on report to the Deputy Head responsible for that year group. Referrals to on-site provision, off-site provision or the Schools Psychological Service, which may or may not happen at the Head of Year stage, are authorised, processed and monitored under the vigilant care of the Deputy Head Pastoral.

In these days when the terminology of industry and technology is increasingly being adopted by schools (e.g., 'line management'), you already have all the 'procedures' in place. In fact, you have had for years. You like the system because it is *rational*. It all fits logically together. It makes sense. The only problem is that computers and production line systems either work or they become garbled and stop. To repair them is just a matter of time and knowhow. You have to replace all the broken parts or work out the logic. But teachers and pupils are not like this. They may well be logical, but it is unlikely that they will remain passive long enough for complicated responses to a situation to be 'unpackaged'. Have you ever thought that disruptive behaviour between pupils and teachers, which gets worse instead of better with schools' efforts to deal with it, much like industrial sabotage, is an attempt at *rejecting the rational*?

Yours sincerely,
A teacher

Rejecting the rational

I am not arguing that these systems are wrong. I prefer them to the chaos that would ensue if they did not exist. My point is simply that they disregard important personal, idiosyncratic and emotional dimensions of individuals' behaviour, and so we should not be surprised if a pupil becomes indignant and rejects them. Most teachers will no doubt recognise the pupil who arrives claiming that such and such a member of staff is going to lose all his/her teeth by the end of the week, either at the hands of the pupil or of a body-building member of the family. This, in my view, is often caused by the pupil being handed on up the system to a teacher who has little knowledge, or only negative knowledge, of the child. To whom the child is passed on next is predetermined by the system, not by a careful consideration of who might be best able to offer constructive help, given the particular set of circumstances relating to a particular child. For the pupil on the receiving end of the report/referral system, the process is fragmented, impersonal and often deeply alienating. Unlike jars of pickle, which can be neatly and uniformly ordered, pupils are complex, chaotic individuals whose needs cannot conveniently be encompassed within a rational, ordered system. Unlike those pickle jars, pupils have feelings.

This is the first important point underlying the criticism Galloway makes of the withdrawal approach to dealing with 'problem behaviour' quoted at the beginning of this chapter: once a pupil becomes troublesome to the school, the tendency is for the pupil to be dealt with outside the classroom situation. From the point of view of both the pupils and teachers between whom a difficulty has arisen, this confuses the issue because the 'problem' is not tackled *in situ* and a loss of control is experienced by both parties. The difficulties between them thus remain unresolved, setting further problems in store for the future since the pupil who is withdrawn from a lesson inevitably has to rejoin the class at a later date.

This contradiction may help to explain the lack of success of units such as ours in reducing the level of difficulty in schools. Our unit was modelled upon what was considered to be good practice and was well respected both within the school and outside. Yet, despite the best of intentions of many staff involved, it did not draw teachers into addressing the fundamental issue of how they or their classrooms could change, either to prevent disruption or to make the re-entry of the separated pupil an easier and more optimistic occasion. The question was what needed to be done if these issues were to be directly addressed, and whether I, from my present position, could be instrumental in bringing any changes about?

2. FINDING AN OPENING

Addressing the question of teachers' knowledge of behavioural problems, Hargreaves (1980) says:

> We should not pretend that elaborate systems of pastoral care will solve many behaviour problems ... [they] ... take the expertise away from teachers.

I found myself caught up in one of these elaborate systems of pastoral care. At the time, it was not so easy to see what alternatives there might be. The impetus to turn my attention to the classroom came in two bursts:

Firstly, an educational psychologist recommended that we look at how another team had developed work in classrooms, with recourse to withdrawal only one afternoon a week to run a social skills group. Although the technique did not appeal to those of our colleagues with whom it was discussed – no doubt precisely because it would displace the rational referral system – its effect on us was significant, opening our eyes to a different approach to 'disruptive' pupils. Here was a system where virtually all the work was done in the classroom. The key to this and any other classroom-based system seemed to be the quality of the observation which preceded and accompanied any intervention. However, we had doubts about the individualised behaviour checklists (Stott, op. cit.) that were being used. A clip-board, stop-watch and schedule might enhance our status, but what did they imply in terms of the nature of our involvement in classrooms?

This line of thought led us to make a distinction between:

- support in the classroom where the main focus of activity and intervention is still the individual pupil; and
- support in the classroom, which takes into account all that is happening, including curriculum, teaching styles, group dynamics, etc.

Secondly, I attended a course on group work methods: 'Developmental Work with Tutorial Groups'. This course convinced me that working with *groups* rather than with *individuals* was likely to be the most effective strategy in dealing with problem behaviour. I was sent on the course partly because I was a tutor in a particular year group, and partly because it was thought that the approaches might be of some use in the unit. Despite this clear message that my role in the school was essentially regarded as a *pastoral* one, the insights which I gained from the course about the notion of pastoral curricula persuaded me that issues as important as health, relationships, examination preparation, study skills, etc., should not be confined to 'tutorial work', to be dealt with by the tutor in the limited time available (see, for example, Button, 1981). Furthermore, the methods recommended as appropriate to the pastoral curriculum: creating an atmosphere of trust, working with different pupils in the class, ensuring that every pupil makes a contribution to the work of the whole group, fostering co-operation, etc., were approaches that would be useful to all classrooms and to all learning activities, not just to 'tutorial' time.

To my first argument, about the effects of the rational academic/

pastoral divide on pupils in difficulty, can thus now be added a second, also echoed in the quotation with which this chapter began: that the academic/pastoral divide is having the effect of funnelling into a marginal place in pupils' experience of schooling, issues and methods which should, in fact, pervade every classroom as necessary conditions for pupils' successful engagement with the academic curriculum. So when, on my return, a hiccup fortuitously occurred in the referral system, I found myself able to recognise and exploit the opportunity it offered to work with pupils and teachers in the classroom.

The situation which created the hiccup was as follows. Collaborative learning methods were being tried out by a number of humanities teachers, supported by the special needs department, with the aim of enhancing and improving the learning opportunities and achievement of all children. The unit had not so far been involved because, as explained earlier, it was perceived as having a predominantly pastoral role, and thus had no foothold for influence or change within the academic system. Considerable progress had been made in the development of appropriate *materials*, and the general approach seemed to be compatible with the kinds of ideas I was beginning to formulate myself. However, little consideration seemed to be given to how to create the right sort of classroom climate and foster pupils' co-operative skills so that they could use the collaborative materials effectively. A pupil was referred to the unit from one of the classes experiencing particular difficulty, and the referral was soon followed by a despairing plea for some help with the group as a whole. The head of department, whose role it was to deal with difficult pupils or groups within the rational referral system, decided to dispense with set procedures and enlist my help with the group directly in the classroom. Using the unit pupil as a justification for my involvement in the classroom, an *ad hoc* arrangement was arrived at between the class teacher, the head of department and myself to try out group work methods in order to reduce the incidence of problem behaviour among pupils in the class.

My early experiences of working with the class confirmed the suspicion that working with groups, rather than concentrating upon individuals, was likely to be the more effective strategy. Peer group relationships can be a powerful force for good if harnessed towards educational and social goals. If not, they can generate hostility and anxiety which actively undermine teachers' educational aims. In this case, it was evident that the behaviour of the pupil referred to the unit was no better or worse than the rest of the class. Even if support in the unit helped to solve his 'problems', another pupil would be certain to take his place. Fresh from my course, I could see that if the behaviour of these pupils was to be improved, consideration needed to be given first as to how to *enable pupils to work effectively in groups*. Specifically, thought needed to be given to:

- the structure and timing of activities so that what is wanted from the pupils is clear from the start;
- organising the room in such a way that groups can easily transfer from a small-group activity to the large group for feedback about the lesson;
- setting up a contract to establish the ground rules for working in groups and questioning the work with pupils.

The request for help came at the end of the year, so we had only a few weeks in which to begin to develop the work. An accidental administrative solution was found for the 'problem' presented by this difficult class, which was disbanded because of a need to reduce from eight forms to seven. Nevertheless, it had provided me with a route into the classroom, and I had discovered that a number of humanities and English teachers were as keen as I was to explore new ideas. We agreed that while collaborative learning was desirable in principle, the ability to work collaboratively was not a skill which could be taken for granted. An understanding of group processes was essential if we were to foster pupils' co-operative skills and create a classroom climate supportive of all pupils, in which problem behaviour would be less likely to occur.

3. CREATING A POSITIVE CLASSROOM CLIMATE

The idea that the 'climate' of the classroom has an important effect on pupils' achievements and behaviour is now widely acknowledged both in theory and in practice (e.g., Hopson and Scally, 1981). In addition, there is a substantial literature which suggests that whether the classroom climate is positive or negative is, to a considerable extent, under the teacher's control.

> The concept of 'climate' summarises the group processes that are worked out by the teacher in interaction with students, and between students in the classroom. Climate is *what* the classroom activity is in carrying out educational goals; it is *how* the curriculum and learning materials are actually used through human exchange; and it *is* the styles of relating among members in the classroom group.
>
> (Schmuck and Schmuck, 1979)

The case study which follows is an example of how we tried to **merge the methods and processes of the 'pastoral' curriculum with** the topic 'Survival', used with second years in their English lessons. This meant, in effect, that when we were planning lessons, we gave consideration to how activities might be structured so as to promote group development goals, e.g.:

- *a sense of belonging* (I am accepted and trusted as a member of this group)
- *a sense of achievement* (I have achieved something worth while for myself and my contribution to the work of the group is valued)
- *a sense of shared influence* (I help to decide what goes on in this classroom, my opinion counts, I take responsibility for my own learning and behaviour)

Case study: project survival

Outline of the original topic

The pupils are told, or create together, a story about their tutor group being stranded (in the desert/mountains/jungle) and they have to survive. They read extracts from *Lord of the Flies* and other gory tales of people surviving in the jungle or mountains, being injured and eating one another, etc. They are asked to do some problem solving, for example how to make a fire, collect water, make a shelter. They have to keep a diary about what happens.

Potential for development of group skills

Notions of interdependence, co-operation, trust and group goals are integral to the context of this topic, which thus, by its very nature, provides an ideal opportunity to develop group work skills. One of the tasks we developed was as follows:

ACTIVITY

What opportunities does this classroom task provide for promoting:

    (a) a sense of belonging?
    (b) a sense of achievement?
    (c) a sense of shared influence?

Survival in the desert:

Pupils are given a list of items (pictures and words) to prioritise in terms of their usefulness for survival in the desert. The items are:

- whisky
- pistol
- air map
- edible animals

- torch
- plastic raincoat
- sunglasses
- first aid kit
- salt tablets
- compass
- penknife
- water
- one top coat
- book
- mirror
- parachute

… per person

In groups of four, they argue out what their group's priorities are going to be. All the groups then come together and describe how the decisions were made and how each member felt about the decisions.

Tasks and groups

The tasks are structured but open-ended. They are designed to require co-operation, working towards group goals. The nature of each task determines the size of group and the style of individual or group working, for example:

- working in pairs
- working in fours
- reporting back to the main group (circle)
- brainstorm
- working alone for a short time

Reflecting on group work skills

After carrying out the task, pupils are encouraged to consider aspects of the work of the group, for example:

- listening to one another
- working together
- friendship
- conflict
- ground rules for discussion
- rules for classroom organisation/behaviour
- effectiveness of planning (e.g., preparing for a visitor's session)

Evaluation

It is important that this work is carefully structured and thought through before one goes into the classroom, and that it is evaluated afterwards. We encouraged pupils to make comments on the work they had been doing after each session. They would be asked to identify activities they had enjoyed, aspects of the work they had found difficult, whether they felt all group members had made a contribution, etc. Sometimes we would put big sheets of paper up on the walls with statements about the work and ask pupils to tick the ones they agreed with, e.g.:

- this work helped me to talk to people I don't usually talk to
- this work helped me to think about other people in my tutor group
- I felt that I contributed to this work
- I feel pleased about the way my group worked

(For descriptions of these and other activities, see Button, L. (1981) *Group Tutoring for the Form Teacher*.)

Co-operation and achievement

It might be felt that activities such as these are a *digression* from the serious pursuit of educational goals, and so introducing them with a view to reducing levels of problem behaviour amounts to a watering down of standards for potentially high academic achievers. I would want to argue, first, that social goals, such as promoting tolerance, support and understanding between pupils, are hardly insignificant in themselves. Co-operative learning methods are reported to be having 'impressive results' in terms of 'promoting friendship choices and pro-social patterns of interaction between pupils of different sex, race, and achievement levels' (Slavin, 1983). Secondly, I would want to draw on the considerable body of evidence now available (as, for example, summarised by Johnson, Johnson et al., 1984), suggesting that achievement defined in the traditional intellectual/cognitive sense *is enhanced in all forms of learning tasks* when co-operative rather than individualised methods are used. The reasons advanced to explain this suggest that co-operative learning methods help to promote:

- development of higher quality cognitive strategies
- discussion and controversy, which leads to improved understanding
- improved long-term retention, because ideas are continually restated and reformulated in new ways through discussion
- peer academic support
- enrichment of ideas through exchanges between pupils of different background, achievement levels, experiences
- increased motivation for learning
- improved self-esteem
- better attitudes to, and relationships with, staff, which in turn affect attitudes to learning

While the validity of these claims for the benefit of co-operative learning methods has elsewhere been questioned (e.g., Bennett, 1985), there is clearly a case to be made that co-operative approaches have the potential to enhance and improve the quality of learning for all pupils. Although as yet there has been little experience of using such approaches systematically within the general curriculum, there is every reason to expand such work and develop our understanding of how to realise its potential in practice.

Furthermore, since the publication of the Hargreaves Report (ILEA, 1984), we have been working with a broader definition of 'achievement', in which the ability to co-operate, to communicate, to learn in a social context as well as alone is recognised not just as a *means* to achievement, but as an *aspect of achievement* itself. This report gave a welcome impetus to our work, not just because it gave official sanction to a broader definition of achievement, but because of its emphasis on the need for 'active learning modes' and its refusal to draw any firm distinction between the 'academic' and the 'pastoral' curriculum.

Since that time, developmental psychology has taken the argument one stage further, firmly reinstating *interaction* at the heart of the learning process (Bruner and Haste, 1987). The implication is that a classroom where silence is hallowed and interaction suppressed is, by definition, the *least conducive* climate for learning.

4. REASSERTING THE RATIONAL

This work in classrooms was, for me, the most significant aspect of the developments which took place over two years. Slowly but surely we were altering the unit from a reactive to a preventive model. The teachers and pupils we worked with seemed happy with the movement. We received increasing requests for help. For the most part, we were not threatening. However, the school never formalised the move from unit to classroom. Although I succeeded in obtaining the support of two heads of department and a senior teacher for the approach I was adopting, and was allowed 'time out' from the unit for two hours a week to work in classes, it was never established as a principle that my role should include in-class work, nor were the reasons for it appreciated, and so the work in classrooms remained simply a prolonged hiccup as far as the school's rational system was concerned.

In view of this, the school's response to my growing experience of working with groups was perhaps predictable. I was invited to contribute to the development of a *tutorial* programme, beginning in the first year. Again, the message came through loud and clear that my role in the school was a pastoral one. Searching for the silver lining, I realised that accepting to work within this official definition of my role still allowed me, indirectly, to further the aims of in-class support. To have official sanction from the school (which, in turn, made possible the allocation of some INSET time) was a definite plus compared to the reluctant tolerance of my time spent in the classroom. And tutors, after all, are also subject teachers. Many of them teach their own tutor groups. There was a chance, therefore, that methods tried out with my support during tutorial time might subsequently be carried over into their subject teaching. Similarly, tutor groups are mostly taught together in the first three years. So any positive effects that might be brought about as a result of using group work methods (e.g., improved relationships between pupils, more trust, co-operative skills, reduction or better management of conflict) had a good chance of carrying over into their normal lessons.

Working on the tutorial programme meant that I was included in year meetings for that year. Sometimes we organised them as workshops, to introduce activities that tutors could try with their groups, and give tutors a sense of what their value was and what the experience was like for the pupils. It is essential that developments such as these should not be seen as just another *scheme of work* that should be followed to the letter. Each teacher should be able to adapt and change the activities to suit their own teaching styles and their group's needs. We encouraged the teachers involved to express both positive and negative feelings about the work. As when we worked with children, it was held as a matter of principle that time should be allocated for participants to reflect explicitly and critically upon the activities they carried out. Through the criticism, we were able to evolve and develop new ways of working.

For me, the most significant and ironic feature of the criticisms was that they focused on the feasibility of carrying out work of this nature in the limited tutorial time available. Although the methods were unfamiliar and sometimes threatening, most teachers were prepared to try them out if they had some support, but *not* in the pressured setting of twenty-minute morning registrations. Presented in this way, they just seemed like an added burden to an already over-crowded administrative schedule, instead of a constructive way of using the time. Sometimes, too, they seemed like an intrusion of structure into one of the few times of the school day when informal and relaxed interchanges between teachers and pupil were, at least in principle, possible. Ironically, therefore, although the school was satisfied to categorise the methods and my involvement in them as appropriate to a *tutorial* programme, many of the tutors implementing them soon saw the illogicality of trying to fit them in as extras, realising that they were only operable in practice if they were introduced as and when appropriate in normal teaching times. On the negative side, though, it was by no means certain that all or any of the tutors I worked with would take the initiative of transferring the methods to their own teaching. In allowing the methods to be presented for use in tutorial time, but in circumstances that were less than favourable, I had run the risk that, since clearly their potential could not be fully realised, they would be rejected *in toto* rather than being transferred to the classroom context to be merged with the academic curriculum, as I had originally intended. It has to be recognised that, in most cases, for want of time and more active support, this is what happened.

A second important outcome of the overall developments, including the collaborative work which the special needs department had been extending into different subject areas, was that a network gradually built up of colleagues interested in, and to some extent committed to, the way in which we were working. We organised workshops for staff to attend in free periods, on topics such as responding to provocative behaviour, adapting curriculum materials to make them more accessible, responding positively to children's work. A lot of support now existed across departments in the school, but all our efforts were fragmented and unsystematic. We still had no official recognition of any change in role, and the two special needs departments were still structurally and administratively separate. It was time to attempt to win official acceptance for the principles underlying our new style of working. If the work was to develop further and more coherently, there needed to be a whole-school policy based upon the principle of teachers and support staff *working together* to try to improve the experience of schooling for pupils currently experiencing difficulties and, indeed, ultimately for all pupils. Now that we had the 1981 Education Act to reinforce the notion that meeting special educational needs is a whole-school responsibility, and especially since we were able to offer a ready-made list of volunteer members, the proposal to set up a working party received official sanction and it was duly timetabled into the year's diary of meetings.

5. RESTORING THE RATIONAL

Setting up this working party was the culmination of work that had now been going on for more than four years. The moment of truth had arrived. Either the school as a whole would take on the idea that problem behaviour (and learning difficulties) needed to be tackled in the context of the curriculum and everyday classroom experiences, or it would not. The unit could not simultaneously be *both* part of the structure designed to keep things ticking over nicely at their present stage of development *and* instrumental in bringing current practices under critical scrutiny in order to improve the school's provision for its less successful pupils. We had gone as far as we could go without changing institutional structures. Something had to give.

> The inherent threat of any innovation is that it may change the pattern beyond recognition and be interpreted as destruction resulting in chaos.
>
> (Shostak, 1983)

Unfortunately for us, but perhaps predictably given the climate of cuts, accountability and low teacher morale, it was the safe option that prevailed. A new head of unit was appointed to maintain and actively develop the unit in its traditional role. Since the school had never formalised any of the changes that had occurred, the suggestion that this was a move in reverse could arguably be dismissed. Nevertheless, a choice was made.

To end on a positive note, it should be recognised that collaborative learning materials are still being used in the school long after we have all moved on. The pastoral curriculum is still being developed. Whether the school will break the academic/pastoral divide which the two special educational needs departments found themselves caught in and formally marry the two, only time will tell.

AFTERWORD

That our efforts to establish preventive modes of working were, in the end, unsuccessful is not so surprising in the circumstances. A housemaster interviewed by Shostak (1983) explains the problem as follows:

> Once you start lifting up stones like that ... y'know you're into really serious sorts of problems aren't you, and the ramifications of it for all of us are very serious ... you know, if you were to reflect on the messages that ... these kids, I think ... more and more beginning to tell, then they're very serious. Very serious indeed. They throw into doubt the whole purpose of what these schools are here for and what we're sending most of our pupils here for in our present society anyway.

A disruptive unit can help to ensure that everything functions as well as possible while keeping those 'stones' firmly in place, or it can help to prise up the stones and support the process of dealing with whatever is lurking underneath. The implication of the approach we were attempting to introduce into our school was that stones would be lifted. The school chose to keep them firmly in place. Given that it was already held in high regard as a successful school, it had good reason to decide to leave well alone. But once the example of other schools becomes known, and it becomes clear that the kinds of approaches to tackling 'problem behaviour', for which we failed in this instance to win acceptance, not only do not lead to a breakdown of order, but function effectively to reduce the incidence of disruption (see for example Appendix 3), schools such as ours may be prepared to think again.

8

Case study 3 – The cock-eyed optimist

Our third case study focuses upon work carried out in a junior school classroom. It takes up a point raised in a study carried out as part of the ORACLE project (Ashton, in Simon and Willcocks, 1981), which draws attention to the need for teachers to plan strategies to promote the *positive* behaviour they desire from children in the classroom, rather than simply reacting to *negative* behaviour as and when it occurs. It describes activities which were developed specifically to help children co-operate and work more effectively together, as a basis for introducing them to a more challenging curriculum.

As well as contributing a primary dimension to our discussion of preventive approaches, this chapter raises two important issues which have not, so far, been addressed in any detail:

- the role of in-service courses in supporting individual teachers in carrying out the process of *critical self-questioning*;
- the role of parents in creating or limiting the possibilities for curriculum change.

ACTIVITY

1. What are the characteristics of in-service courses which have been of most use to you in terms of offering direct, practical support/ideas for solving classroom problems and improving practice?
2. How would you respond to parents who express anxiety that changes you are introducing are detrimental to their children's education?
3. How do/would you enlist the co-operation and, if possible, active support of parents for curriculum developments you are undertaking?

During my fifteen years of teaching in various sorts of primary schools and classrooms, 'INSET' has played an important part in my professional development. Keeping up to date and looking for new ideas has meant attending courses and events at the local teachers' centres and at other institutions. These activities have included the usual range of organised events such as guest lectures, workshops and conferences as well as some off-the-cuff gatherings of enthusiastic individuals. The gatherings, more than the other events, were likely to be concerned with materials and ideas for day-to-day use in the classroom. Sometimes that meant a development from scratch with only our own ideas and experience from which to work, but on other occasions it would be to analyse and interpret commercially produced materials.

One typically cold, wet evening, I attended a workshop-type session run by the local authority and led by a lecturer from the local polytechnic. Interest in the topic, 'Behavioural Difficulties' was demonstrated by the overwhelming demand for the course which was to be run in seven sessions over a term. The content was to include an emphasis on the following areas:

1. Case analysis
2. Development of appropriate strategies
3. Trial interventions
4. Evaluations
5. Modifications
6. Professional support
7. Group support

Although I did not immediately realise it, the course was to give me a firm theoretical and practical framework for the approaches and materials I developed over the next six years. Because teachers so often describe INSET activities in this area as unsatisfactory, it is worth considering why this particular course was considered so successful by the people who attended. Some of the reasons appear to be characteristic elements of good INSET in this field.

1. **The course took into account realistic situations**
   Teachers are often placed in the apparently impossible position of having to manage large groups of children and at the same time cater for many of them on an individual basis. Many times I have heard colleagues say, 'That's all very well, but what can I do with the other 32 children while I am dealing with that one?' This course was able to provide some insights into how to deal with that situation!
2. **The course created supportive, self-help groups**
   As the weeks went by there grew a fellowship which was to last for many years. The group would meet in the centre before the start of each session for coffee and a chat, to exchange notes and observations. This exchange became an important aspect of the activity as it gave us a chance to discuss, listen to colleagues and to learn that we were each not alone in our difficulties.

3. **We were able to rehearse and to extend the presentations made to the group**
   Before presenting a case, it helped greatly to talk it through first in an informal setting, almost like a rehearsal, with other members of the group. This was possible because of the growing sense of fellowship described above. At the same time, members of the group occasionally met informally in one another's schools, to see how someone had arranged a class or managed particular materials. This gave a context which is often missing in discussions or courses which take place away from the participants' usual working environment.

4. **We were actively listened to in a relaxed atmosphere**
   As the weeks progressed everyone had the chance to be listened to in a relaxed, secure environment. Together, we used the same strategies that we were to use in the classroom, 'catch them being good' and 'positive cognitive interventions'. Again, we had the opportunity to share experiences and ideas and to discover that others have similar problems.

5. **The course offered practical and constructive ways forward**
   The first session provided a framework of observations which could be put into action the next day. Most teachers attend courses to improve their own practice, to learn new techniques and to up-date the theory relating to their practice. From many discussions with colleagues I know that they, like me, wish to leave a course feeling that they have got at least one thing from it that they did not know before and/or something that can be applied in the classroom. However, the most important aspect for many of us attending this particular course was the relief we felt when another experienced professional said, 'Yes, you are doing the right thing; you could try X, Y or Z to improve that, but keep up the good work!'

As the weeks progressed the members of the group were each involved in observing and evaluating their own classroom practice and trying to improve methods and techniques which could motivate the learner and place greater emphasis on cognitive participation through attention-gaining and sustaining activities. This had implications for all of us in that we were not just evaluating what we were doing, but also how we were behaving as learners ourselves. Because learning is an active process and capable of changing one's perceptions or of heightening one's awareness of particular matters, it can disrupt the existing frameworks we use for making sense of our worlds. This happened to me when I decided to reorganise a familiar pattern.

My observations of my own practice led me to query the type of task I was presenting to the children. Were they really problem-solving situations which allowed the children to discuss, question, reason and think? What I saw of the limited extent to which the children could actually work with one another led me to doubt whether the tasks were achieving what I wanted. In order to facilitate that type of task, *talk* had to be legitimised and materials developed which would require the children to contribute their thoughts and opinions. If possible, I wanted them to become more actively involved in their own process of learning. For this to take place, talk had to become a valuable and therefore valued feature of what happened in the room. The process of using language and the language used in the tasks had to contribute to the development of a *shared language experience* which would enhance the ways in which each pupil could perceive him or herself and also in which he or she could respond to other pupils.

According to Montgomery (1981) 'Process approaches to teaching and learning should cause the pupils to "engage brain", think about the subject matter and relate it to their previous experience and knowledge'. In theory, engaging the children in this manner should help to lessen the tension which builds up through frustration and non-contributory learning, and help children with particular learning difficulties to spend at least a portion of the day engaged in questioning, thinking, reasoning and discussion.

Figure 8.1 *A model of modern pedagogy* (from Montgomery, 1981)

'What we must fit the child for is the ability to understand and use information, to problem pose, to be flexible in their thinking, to imagine and to have well developed social skills to facilitate the understanding and cooperation of others' (Stonier, 1979). If this was the way forward, how was I going to involve all the children with materials in a way that required them to contribute their thoughts and opinions and collaborate with others? Not an easy task with those 32 children in the class!

THE SCHOOL CONTEXT
ONE AND ALL!

The junior school was situated in a residential suburban area and, because of the foreign embassies located nearby, had a substantial intake of children from other countries. I was a new appointment and had come from an environment where children were encouraged to work in groups and to be involved in their own learning. This school was more formally organised and the children followed set textbooks. I was informed that they did do topic work in groups on Tuesday afternoons and that the teachers were being encouraged to use a more integrated approach to teaching and learning. I was appointed as the special needs co-ordinator throughout the school and year leader for the three second-year junior classes. Of the 32 children in my class, three were being seen by the Schools' Psychological Service, four had language difficulties and two had significant medical conditions. In addition to these there was Simon.

For the first two weeks of September Simon appeared to settle well and to enjoy being in the class, although he made little effort to talk or play with his peers or they with him. Soon after that settling-in period, and for no apparent reason, Simon began to kick and scream the minute it was time to go home, and to repeat the performance in the morning when it was time to come into school. The only way I found to cope with this situation was to hold him firmly and talk in a quiet voice to him.

I looked back through Simon's records to when he entered nursery at the age of three and noted that he was admitted 'full time' for 'domestic reasons'. The teacher had recorded that at first Simon had settled well, but after about three weeks had shown signs of becoming 'difficult'. He had increasing difficulty in being separated from Mum when she brought him to the nursery, but also difficulty separating from the nursery to go home. When Simon was old enough he transferred to the reception class and at first 'settled well'. Six weeks after, the teacher responsible for Simon was finding him 'very difficult'. She described his as 'extremely stubborn, defiant, sullen, cross and rude'. It was also said that his moods would swing erratically, from being bright and cheerful, helpful and eager to please, to sullen, cross and defiant. It appears that these mood swings were difficult for Simon to cope with as he did not know whether to laugh, cry, be grumpy or rude. He often ended up being some combination of them all! At the time it was noted that Simon was very pale and thin and it was said that his life at home was unstable. Mum was on her own and a new baby was expected. It appeared that the pattern and circumstances of Simon's behaviour had become well established and quite repetitive over the next few years.

The behaviour persisted in my classroom for several weeks, but with the help and support of my colleagues and other children Simon gradually became able to come and go in a more peaceful manner. A month later, Simon had another baby brother at home and again Mum was having to cope on her own. During November, Simon began to complain of hunger and to show other signs of stress. I became concerned about his general physical well-being and so a case conference was held. Everyone, teachers, social workers, child guidance experts and doctors, agreed that the family needed practical support. It was decided that Mum should be offered help to do the shopping and some household chores for an unspecified period.

During the next few weeks Simon became a little more stable in his behaviour and I decided to use this opportunity to observe his behaviour more thoroughly.

ACTIVITY

Think of a child who causes you particular concern and try to answer these three questions:

1. What behaviour from that child concerns you most?
2. How could you systematically observe the child's behaviour?
   (i.e., What techniques and approaches do you know of, which would give you the information you needed with sufficient accuracy and detail?)
3. How would you use the information you obtained?

We considered three styles of observation available to us, diary description, time sampling and event sampling.

Diary description involves an attempt to record everything that occurs during the period of observation. Different media, including writing, audio or video recording, can be used in this kind of exercise, but it is time consuming and dependent upon some selectivity on the observer's part. That may be an advantage if it is borne in mind that the recorded material, because it can only be a partial record, may say as much about the interests and concerns of the observer as it does about the total experience of the observed.

An example of a simple time-sampling schedule is used by Chazan and his colleagues in the Swansea Assessment Schedules (Chazan et al., 1983). Their behaviour recording sheet demonstrates the main components of such a schedule, a time scale, a description of the behaviour and a description of the context. The time scale, which need not be regular, does have to be frequent enough to produce the required profile of the child; the descriptions of behaviour have to be accurate and useful; the context has to be described with a relevant degree of detail. Decisions about each of these components are critical to the exercise. In their case study of 'Brian', Yule and colleagues report that his teacher was asked to observe his behaviour only between 11 a.m. and 12.00 noon at only five-minute intervals. His behaviour was described only as *on* or *off task*, but the thirteen observations each day for three weeks provided a sufficient baseline from which his current behaviour and future improvements could be assessed (Yule et al., 1984).

Event sampling, used by Lawrence et al. (1984) to determine the number of disruptive incidents in a secondary school, requires a record to be kept of each occurrence of a defined type of behaviour in a given period of time. Lawrence provided a quite open definition of the behaviour 'incidents of disruption' in a quite long period – two weeks. In all, 101 incidents were reported, although Lawrence concludes that because of faulty recording – a risk in this kind of exercise – there may be an underestimate of the actual incidence. Yule (op. cit.) reports the case of Jane whose behaviour was observed for twenty minutes each day, during which each occurrence of anti-social behaviour was recorded. Anti-social was more specifically defined in terms of pushing or pinching other children, passing provocative comments and repeating what others said.

Teachers wishing to use any of these techniques are recommended to investigate them in more detail and to consider carefully which of them suits the problem they are facing. In Simon's case, we kept a diary for a period and allied this with an intense time-sampling observation through one class session. For that period, because we were sharing the exercise, we were able to observe Simon and to record the observation in ten-second cycles: ten seconds of observation, ten seconds of recording.

After the observations had been collected together, a pattern emerged in which it appeared that:

1. Simon had considerable difficulty in coping with any kind of change whether it was from one task to the next or from one room to the next.

2. His self-esteem seemed to be at a very low ebb.
3. Other children did not want to include him in any activities.
4. Parents, teachers and other adults were critical or embarrassed when he displayed unacceptable behaviour.
5. Adults and children simply did not know how to respond to him.

I therefore decided that there were a number of things, some of which had general application and some of which concerned only Simon, that I needed to do in the classroom. These were:

1. To try to improve all the children's self-images, while paying particular attention to Simon.
2. To make a list of activities which Simon could do well and which he enjoyed; these were, my observations had shown mainly visual–spatial activities, including drawings and jigsaws.
3. To make a collection of work done by Simon over a period of time, to use as a diagnostic tool.
4. To draw up a negotiated behaviour contract with Simon. wanted a reward for Simon's good behaviour when change occurred and so our eventual agreement was that at the end of each task or when we changed rooms, I would hold his hand for the short time until the new activity began.
5. To praise and use a smile to reinforce:
   (i) quiet co-operative behaviour;
   (ii) success in completing a small task.

Over the next few weeks I tried (with every smile I could muster to put my plan of action into practice! The other children in the class seemed to appreciate and benefit from the change, but Simon continued to disrupt and generally shout over everyone else, both during discussion time and story time. I tried to improve the children's discussion skills and introduced a few collaborative activities. This raised even more questions about organisation and presentation: who should sit where and with whom? Should there be more structure? Should all the quiet children sit together for discussion? How could Simon be included?

INSET to support the process

The answers to problems often crop up partly by accident and partly by design, and so it was in this case. Although I hoped that the course on Oral Problem Solving which I was about to attend would enhance that area of work in my classroom, I was unaware that it would provide me with a number of strategies for approaching the problems of Simon's behaviour. During the week which followed the course I listed all the problems and successes I had encountered in those first crude sessions on problem solving. Some of the problems were more predictable than others, but the range was remarkable:

1. The children were not used to working together to find a common solution.
2. The children's handwriting skills appeared to be deteriorating.
3. The children had great difficulty in actively listening to one another.
4. The materials were not open-ended enough to integrate all the children's varying backgrounds.
5. The noise level was higher.
6. The tables seemed to be getting in the way of constructive discussions.
7. Some children dominated the discussion.

At this point I contacted the course leader, who had run the Oral Problem Solving course, and invited her to work in the classroom with me and the children. Over the next term we developed materials for activities which took into account the children's developmental levels and their inability to listen and to co-operate with one another. All the activities were based on the belief that good relationships depend on efficient communication, a co-operative atmosphere and affirmation of the value of each individual (*Ways and Means*, 1985).

I invited the two other teachers who worked with the same age range to join me in preparing and using the materials in their classrooms. It was agreed that the first session should be run by the course leader and the classroom teacher would be able to watch. This was an invaluable experience as it gave an opportunity to observe the children at work impartially. The topic was to be 'Friendly Classrooms' and the children were given an agenda from the beginning.

AGENDA
1. Establishing the rules
2. Getting to know you
3. Friendly animals
4. Passing the message
5. Evaluation

Agenda-setting had a twofold effect. Firstly, it helped the children to get a flavour of what the morning held for them.

Secondly, there was a certain amount of material to be got through and if some activities were taking longer than expected or being enjoyed too much to leave, then there would need to be some form of negotiation between each other about whether to stop or to continue. This had further implications as it raised the question of how to prepare the children so that they could negotiate.

The most important task for all of us was the review and evaluation which took place at the end of each session. This continual review, over the weeks, enabled each of us to create a 'window' on our ability to listen and create effective opportunities for learning in many different situations.

ACTIVITY

A cluster evaluation of your last teaching session

You will need about twenty pieces of paper around 4 cm square.

Try to recall your last teaching session and as you recall the events of that lesson, write them on a piece of paper and number them in the order you recall them, e.g. talking 1, reading 2 and so on. When you have sufficient items, usually around twenty, sort them in your own way into sets or clusters. Think about the relationship between the activities in each set and why you put those particular items in that set. Give each set a label or title. See if you can see any relationships between the sets. After you have done this, consider the following questions:

1. What were my expectations of that teaching session?
2. What was I thinking about when I put the sets together?
3. Did I have the main points of the session in one set and if so which set?
4. How many activities were initiated by me and how many by the pupils?
5. Did I think of any items and then not record them? If so, why did I reject them?
6. Were my expectations achieved and how do I know the answer to this question?

When you have completed the task you should have some insight into what you considered to be the most important feature of that session. Your sets should heighten your awareness of your own teaching skills and highlight areas you considered to be important or unimportant. Further insight can be gained by asking the pupils to repeat the exercise for the same session so that your perceptions can be compared with theirs.

Perhaps the most complex aspect of teaching is that of acting as facilitator to children's learning. If the materials provided are too structured, they remove the need to develop personal skills and judgement. However, an approach which is too open-ended may make children feel vulnerable if they have no experience of exploring situations and being encouraged to come to different conclusions in a secure atmosphere. As experienced teachers know, each child comes to the human or material resources in the classroom with their own experiences, beliefs, values and skills which establish expectations and, ultimately, determine the quality of the strategies for learning adopted by the child.

During our sessions, no attempt was made to dictate the course of events. Instead, the pupils were encouraged, first, to discover how and why they reacted to certain influences, and then to respond to problems in a way which would make constructive solutions more likely. A record was made of all the different responses and why they were made. Over the next few weeks the children began to realise that the insights they were gaining could be applied in various areas of their own lives and, beyond that, even to international affairs.

Our evaluation of the initial sessions led us to conclude that the ability of the children to co-operate – or not – was a significant restraint on what could be done in the classroom. Our next session was therefore on 'co-operation' and the agenda was as follows:

AGENDA

1. **Labels and goods**   An activity in which children are asked to share anything nice which has happened to them or something good which they have done recently. Older children usually prefer to think of someone outside their close circle of family and friends, whom they particularly admire or respect and to record the reason for this regard.

2. **The maligned wolf**   An example of empathising or putting oneself in someone else's shoes. It is the story of Little Red Riding Hood as told by the wolf from the wolf's point of view.

3. **A trust walk**   An exercise to encourage discussion of the relationship between trust and responsibility.

4. **The warm iceberg**   A diagram built up on a flannel board, which the children talk about before producing pictures which illustrate co-operation, communication and valuing each other.

The children responded particularly well to the idea of the maligned wolf and, after some negotiation, it was agreed that they could concentrate on this topic and develop it in different ways. Some enacted the story again, others chose another well-known story and wrote about it from an unusual point of view. It was interesting that children who had not been acknowledged before were now being incorporated into the groups. I noticed that Simon was being asked to give his opinion about a design for the front cover of a book which one group was making. Although we all knew Simon was good at drawing, nobody had realised how good because he usually scribbled on his drawings before anyone could appreciate them.

Involving parents

As the term progressed we gathered information about children, groups and interactions between adults and children as well as between particular children. We amassed a large selection of materials, equipment, ideas, reactions and, most important, evaluations. One of the indirect, unplanned feedbacks which confirmed that the children were discussing what was going on in school came from parents. One or two were worried that there was too much talk going on and not enough writing. There was only one way to overcome this misconception and that was to invite the parents into the sessions. A letter was sent home saying that any parent who wished to take part in the sessions would be welcome. Initially there were three, and meetings were held on a Friday afternoon to talk through the process with them. At first the parents were apprehensive about:

(a) its value;
(b) their ability to join in.

However, inviting the parents was, for all concerned, one of the most valuable decisions made at this period. As time went on, it became clear that the exercise was:

1. Giving the opportunity to create a shared language between all the participants.
2. Disseminating classroom practice and demystifying activities.
3. Giving parents the opportunity to participate in a session and to contribute in a practical way.
4. Allowing the children to see their parents' views being valued by others and allowing the parents to see their children's views being valued.
5. Giving all parties a framework to use when difficulties arose.
6. Providing a positive model of interactions between children, parents and teachers.

The sessions on co-operation took place one morning a week and everyone involved was soon talking about how well the children were applying their experiences from them in other parts of the school. The following example of this occurred when the lessons learned from a listening activity were transferred to an outside difficulty. In class, a situation had been devised between myself and a parent, in which I appeared to have had a nasty bump on the head caused by accidentally knocking myself on a cupboard door which had been left open. We enacted a scene in which my friend (the parent helper) came by to offer advice. The children had to identify as many different responses as possible and to label them. The children then set up their own examples from their own experience. The following is an illustration of how the exercise developed.

My Operation

Statement: I have had an operation and I still feel poorly.

Responses:
- I have had one of those and you never seem to get better. Mine still hurts me. (*Doom and gloom*)
- Well, if you had not eaten so many sweets, it would not have happened. (*Tut … tut …*)
- I don't like talking about operations. They make me feel sick. (*Damping down*)
- You told me about that before. Shall we talk about something more pleasant? (*Diversion*)

Some time later, two children from the class were walking down the path towards the school from the playground where they had seen another child trying to explain to an adult why he was where he was in the playground. In the conversation they overheard, the child was only able to say:

Child: 'But Miss I was only …'
          'But I …'

The children concluded that the boy should be allowed his turn to put his case in what had otherwise become, to use one of the new phrases they had picked up, 'a non-listening situation'.

Because the pupils, parents and teachers were building up a framework for working through a problem, we all found that we could use it in many different ways. The approach was flexible enough to be used in curriculum-based problem solving, classroom management, or relationships around the school and all the participants expressed opinions that the material was beneficial because it

- improved self-esteem;
- established an atmosphere in which people could put their point of view and learn to listen to others;
- fulfilled a prerequisite for collaborative activities;
- enabled children to express feelings and to accept criticism more easily;
- reduced aggression and other behavioural problems;
- allowed pupils to work on materials at their own level;
- created equal opportunities for all.

It is not possible to be certain which factors had the most influence in Simon's successful integration into the classroom and acceptance by his classmates. Perhaps the improvements in their mechanical, thinking and social skills were as much to do with the additional attention provided by the helping parents as the particular strategies we were using. However, in the few years following our original, small start, I developed a lasting partnership with the Kingston Friends Workshop Group (see Bibliography) which was founded to help young people to deal with the conflicts and problems they experience. The group's material, created by contributors from many walks of life, follows similar principles to those described above. It can be adapted for use in a variety of contexts, including business, education and politics, where the participants need to consider how they can respond to problems in ways which make constructive solutions more likely than destructive ones. The success of these approaches in the hands of other colleagues is convincing evidence that although we cannot presume that children have the skills to work together in ways that we find acceptable, the curriculum can be the vehicle through which those skills are introduced and reinforced.

AFTERWORD

This case study has shown that even with quite young children it is possible for relationships to become the focus of interest, discussion and development, for children to become more aware of the choices open to them in the way they behave towards one another, and to talk about the feelings generated by different responses. Following the specially designed 'workshop' activities, the children were helped to transfer this awareness to their normal classroom interactions, and were encouraged to monitor their own progress in resolving conflict and managing their relationships more effectively.

Such approaches have a particular significance for children with special educational needs. Those whose behaviour gives cause for concern need, more than most, a supportive, accepting classroom climate where negative feelings and hostilities are generally at a minimum, and where everyone possesses some understanding of how to manage those which do arise. According to a recent research study (Croll and Moses, 1985), children can expect to spend, at most, only 3.2 per cent of their class time receiving individual attention from the teacher. Left to work individually for the greater part of their day, children identified by their teachers as having behavioural difficulties spent twice as much time distracted from what they were supposed to be doing as other children. Thus, although all children potentially stand to gain from a classroom which actively encourages learning together and helping one another, children with behavioural difficulties would seem likely to gain most. If the resources of every child in the group can be pooled to support others' learning and thus complement the scarce resource of teacher time, children who lack confidence, concentration or motivation may be helped to sustain interest and effort during the periods when the teacher inevitably must be involved with others. This cannot be achieved, however, simply with good intentions. Time has to be spent helping the children *learn to co-operate* and to help one another, and to review and evaluate their own success in doing so. Once a basis of understanding has been achieved, they can then gradually be encouraged to apply their skills in solving together problems presented by a range of challenging curriculum tasks designed to enhance the quality of their learning (see, for example, the recommendation for small-group learning and the limitations of its current effectiveness in Bennett *et al.*, 1984).

Since the work described in the case study was carried out, the value of the approaches used has been widely acknowledged. They have been developed for use in a range of different contexts: primary and secondary schools (including sixth forms), work with the young unemployed, parent–children workshops and work with young ex-offenders. Their potential as a set of tools for *preventing* problem behaviour has been recognised by the Institute for the Study and Treatment of Delinquency, which has recently made funding available for further research and development.

If we'd known then...
Managing the process of change

> ... the sheer complexity of the process of implementation has, as it were, a sociological mind of its own which frequently defies management even when all parties have the best of intentions.
>
> (Fullan, 1982, p. 79)

The individual experiences described in this part of the book make it abundantly clear that the 'preventive' approach to tackling 'problem behaviour', presented in this book, offers no quick or easy panacea. It is one thing to identify features of our work in schools which, if modified or developed in some way, might help to inhibit the emergence of 'problem behaviour'. It is quite another to be able to carry modifications through successfully and sustain them in practice. It requires considerable understanding and skill relating to the process of innovation and change, which, at the outset of the work described, we certainly did not possess and, to a considerable extent, were unaware of. And even if such initiatives are carried through successfully, the pace of change is such that it will clearly be some time before improvements are able to have a significant effect upon the total experience of schooling of any individual child. In this chapter, we take up the former point concerning the lessons to be learnt about managing the process of change. In our final section we will take up the question of responding to individual difficulties meanwhile, and how these responses may themselves contribute to the overall development process.

It is important to note, firstly, that while we may have had cause to temper our initial 'ecstatic celebration' (Whitty, 1975) of the possibilities for individual teachers to bring about change in schools, nevertheless nothing in the experience has undermined our basic conviction about how 'problem behaviour' should be addressed. In spite of our lack of experience and explicit knowledge of how to manage the process of innovation, our 'case studies' have shown that progress can be made in improving the learning climate of classrooms so that pupils become more actively involved in the work and difficulties are reduced. Colleagues can be involved and productive partnerships developed; existing structures can be bent into supportive postures. What we have learnt is not that the approach itself is ill advised or impracticable, but that we need, firstly, to be more realistic in our assessment of the changes that can be undertaken with a good chance of success, and, secondly, to develop our expertise in understanding and managing the process of change more effectively. We must learn how to lay firmer foundations for future developments, and how to direct our available energies and resources in the most fruitful way possible.

In retrospect, many of the 'lessons' learned from our experience seem so obvious that it is surprising that we were not able to anticipate them at the time. Certainly, since the work described in this section began, there has been a general heightening of awareness of the processes of staff development and change, due, no doubt, in part to the shift towards more school-focused in-service training and to the development of 'whole-school' policy statements on various issues, which have necessitated negotiation with the entire staff. With GRIST and the introduction of statutory staff development days, it seems likely that priority will continue to be given to improving expertise in this important area.

ACTIVITY

What specific lessons about managing the process of 'school improvement' can be learnt from the 'case studies'?
  (a) Identify one 'lesson' from each 'case study'?
  (b) Which 'lesson' do you regard as most relevant to your own experience/situation?

SEVEN LESSONS FROM THE CASE STUDIES

As we look briefly at seven 'lessons' drawn from our experience, we make reference to sources which readers may find useful in pursuing these points further themselves. We then draw some more general conclusions, as a prelude to considering what the next stage of development might be.

First lesson

Explore fully the resources and constraints of the particular circumstances in which change is to be introduced, and plan any initiative to use the resources to maximum effect.

At the outset, we had very limited appreciation of just how difficult it is to introduce new ideas within existing practices. We tended to assume that if an idea was 'good' and could be shown to 'work' then it would automatically be welcomed by colleagues Fullan (op. cit.), in *the Meaning of Educational Change*, illustrates th extreme naivety of such views. This book provides so man important insights into the overall process of change that it shoul be essential reading for teachers attempting innovation at any leve Defining educational change as a 'dynamic process of interactin variables over time', he analyses in depth the range of factors whic contribute to successful innovations, both from within school an from outside. Bines (1986) uses a sociological approach to analys current attempts to develop more integrated approaches to speci educational provision. She explores the interaction of differen elements of the 'context of change', showing how they may limit th possibilities for change. The analysis helps to explain *why* th process is likely to be problematic, and thus helps us to make realistic appraisal of what can be achieved within our own set o circumstances.

Second lesson

Seek the active involvement and collaboration of at least one other perso when embarking on any initiative, rather than trying to 'go it alone'.

In their popular article, 'The Myth of the Hero Innovator' Georgiades and Phillimore (in Easen, 1985) point out that 'organisa tions such as schools ... will, like dragons, eat hero-innovators fo breakfast'. Our experience confirms the need for a group o like-minded people (or at the very least one other person) workin together to sustain and support each other through difficul patches, and to help withstand institutional pressures that ma jeopardise the work. As well as mutual support, collaborative wor with other teachers provides the opportunity for continual stimulu and exchange of ideas which, for adults as much as for children, i an essential part of any active learning process.

Third lesson

Actively seek institutional support and sanction for any initiatives.

Most success was achieved in those areas where support of som kind was forthcoming from the senior management. Th importance of such support (e.g., at deputy head level) was als emphasised by Georgiades and Phillimore. Obtaining status an official sanction for the work within the school, with someone in position of power to defend and promote it, makes it possible t argue for preferential treatment (e.g., in timetabling, extra resour es, free times, etc.) that may be crucial to the maintenance and successful outcome of the work. It also means that we can inform other colleagues officially about the work in progress, and by involving them, if only indirectly, help to allay potential fears or suspicions about the nature of the work and its implications for others.

Fourth lesson

Work initially with a self-selected group of colleagues.

A theme which runs through the literature, and is borne out by our experience, is the need to begin developments in those areas which seem most amenable to change. Hanko (1985) stresses the importance of involving volunteers – people who have a commitment to the task; who have chosen to participate because they recognise that they have something to gain from it personally or professionally. We found that dissemination of ideas and the development of practice was, in all cases, most effective with colleagues who had elected to participate and who understood, or were sympathetic to, the aims of the work. This basic commitment means that when the inevitable problems arise, they can be tackled in a spirit of openness and mutual support, rather than criticism and defensiveness.

Fifth lesson

Expect, and understand the reasons for, resistance; respect and respond sensitively to colleagues' points of view.

There is a need to recognise that conflict and disagreement are fundamental to successful change. Each individual member of staff has to undergo a process of bringing meaning to educational developments on her/his own terms. Knowing the kinds of responses to expect and understanding the reasons for them helps to defuse the feeling that any hostility or criticism is in any sense directed towards individuals, either personally or professionally. We can thus be less defensive and more prepared to listen to those who have very real doubts and fears about the consequences of developments for their own work. Helpful references on this point include:

- *Making School-Centred INSET Work*, P. Easen (1985), dealing with formal work with colleagues, through a series of meetings/structured activities. The group leader's guide is particularly useful on skills for managing groups.

- *Special Educational Needs & Human Resource Managemen* T. Bowers (ed.) (1987). Looks at the 'human factors' relating t the process of innovation in schools, with regard to changes i provision for children with special educational needs. Th chapter 'Mainstream Support Work' analyses the skil required of a support teacher to introduce and implemer successfully 'partnerships' between special education an mainstream teachers.
- 'Helping Colleagues Cope – A Consultant Role for the Rem dial Teacher', C. Smith, in *New Directions in Remedial Educatior* (1985), dealing with interpersonal skills in collaborative wor with colleagues.
- *I'm OK – You're OK*, T. Harris (1965). Analyses the differer forces at work in the interactions between people, and show how to identify what goes wrong when communication break down.

Sixth lesson

Consult as fully as possible with colleagues not immediately involved.

Consultation is essential if we are to win the support c colleagues. In *School-Based Staff Development Activities* (Oldroyc Smith and Lee, 1984) the point is firmly made that initiatives ar most likely to be successful if they are related to teachers' perceive needs, not imposed from the outside. This creates a problem for th approach proposed in this book because the way teachers perceiv their 'needs' in relation to children in difficulty has, up until now tended to be in terms of the provision of specialist, individua attention outside the classroom. It is to be expected, quit reasonably, that they will resist moves to impose an alternativ approach, if they have not been properly consulted or had th opportunity to appreciate why such changes may be of benefit bot to themselves and to the children (see, for example, a study of loca authority changes in provision by Gipps and Goldstein, 1987 Consultation creates the opportunity for colleagues to express thei views and for us to explain ours. The form of any changes can thu be negotiated jointly, and other teachers enabled to take ove ownership of the ideas and developments themselves.

A second point relating to consultation is that a group carryin out development work must be careful not to become isolated. Th need for mutual support may make those working together undul self-protective, inward-looking and ultimately elitist (those wh have 'seen the light', compared to the common herd), and so cut i off from the educational context which it hopes, ultimately, t nfluence. What is then rationalised as 'institutional resistance' may ictually be a problem of the group's own making. To avoid this happening, we believe, in retrospect, that it is important to keep group membership open, actively encouraging colleagues to join the group and talking openly and informally with as many of the non-participating staff as possible.

Seventh lesson

Enlist the involvement and co-operation of pupils, and ensure that they, as well as staff, receive support through the process.

Pupils may be a strong conservative force, putting up resistance to any changes in routine practices if they do not understand the teacher's reasons for introducing changes or see any reason to value them positively. Ruddock (in Hopkins and Wideen, 1984) argues that in our concern to support teachers, we should not forget that pupils, too, need support if they are to 'move out of the comfortable cradle of convention and accept a period of negotiation and exploration' (p. 66). She proposes four 'hypotheses' for teachers to consider in order to help pupils adjust to any fundamental changes that are envisaged in pedagogy or in the organisation of school life.

1. Provide access to concrete representations (e.g., videos of other pupils working in the manner intended).
2. Develop mutual commitment to the work in order to counter the pull of existing conventions.
3. Negotiate with pupils procedures for management of class control in new teaching situations.
4. Remain alert to the need to communicate with pupils about the nature of the innovation.

General conclusions

Taking the implications of these seven lessons together, the single most important outcome of our experience is the realisation that the process of school improvement cannot be carried out solely at the level of individual initiative. Whereas, at the outset, we were convinced that only grass-roots initiatives, undertaken on the basis of individual interest and commitment, were capable of bringing about real and lasting change, we have come to realise that the overall process is too important and too risky to be left to random initiatives which may or may not be successful. Although individual initiatives may be an important, indeed an essential, starting point, much effort and good will may be spent in vain if individuals, left to their own devices, find they lack necessary skills, succumb to institutional pressures or simply run out of steam. If initiatives are to survive and to contribute to a long-term programme of school improvement, they need to be supported by the institution and co-ordinated into a coherent whole. That means, in effect, that they need to be organised into a '*whole-school approach*', which would be given status, sanction and support through an official '*whole-school policy*'. While, previously, we viewed 'whole-school policies' with some scepticism, having seen what happened to 'Language Across The Curriculum' once the 'policy' documents were written, our experience has served to highlight ways in which such a policy, far from being a mere paper exercise, might play a crucial role in supporting and sustaining developments such as those described in our case studies. Having a whole-school policy means that decisions can be made with reference to an established set of principles, and that practice which conflicts with those principles can be challenged. It enables a case to be made for modifications to organisational structures to support particular initiatives, and it enables roles and responsibilities to be clarified so that overlaps do not give rise to unnecessary conflict or duplication of effort.

Of course, the idea of a 'whole-school approach', supported by a 'whole-school policy' in relation to special educational provision is not itself new. It is now more than a decade since the Warnock Committee (DES, 1978a) proposed that responsibility for pupils with special educational needs, including those whose behaviour causes concern, should be *shared* by the entire staff of a school rather than *passed on* to specialist staff or *divided among* specialist staff and mainstream teachers, as has been the case up until now. But what is generally meant by a 'whole-school approach' is by no means necessarily synonymous with the approach to tackling 'problem behaviour' taken in this book. The formal definition above tells us only *where* responsibility is located, not *what* exactly that responsibility entails. In our final section, we look at the *nature* of that 'shared responsibility' within a 'preventive' approach, and at the process which needs to be undergone in order for those responsibilities to become accepted individually and collectively as an essential feature of routine professional practice. We consider the question of *how to move beyond* the stage of unco-ordinated individual initiatives, to build a more constructive and firmly founded 'whole-school approach', in which preventing and meeting special educational needs in general, and 'problem behaviour' in particular, become an integral part of the process of improving the quality of education for all. We look at the kinds of individual support which will be needed to supplement that process, and at particular kinds of problems which may call for specialist help, either for the children themselves or for the teachers working with them at school.

Part Four
Towards a Whole-School Approach

10

Questioning classrooms, questioning schools

So far, our interpretation of a preventive approach has tended to equate *intervention* with *change*, as though carrying out the process of 'critical self-questioning' would automatically lead teachers into 'initiatives' of the kind described in the previous section. Having seen how demanding the task of innovation is, and how fragile its achievements, it is obvious that a 'whole-school approach' cannot be built solely upon a basis of initiatives of this kind. It would not be reasonable or even desirable for all teachers to be routinely engaged in 'projects' of this nature, and certainly not to have such work imposed upon them. Change may create only an illusion of progress, while undermining both pupils' security and teachers' effectiveness. Innovation must have a place, but if a 'whole-school approach' is to be a realistic possibility, with *all* teachers acknowledging and sharing their 'preventive' responsibilities, these must be defined in a form which can permeate our teaching activities at every level; a *mode of approach* to professional work which can become a permanent feature of our practice, rather than a sudden burst of innovatory zeal which, once over, may simply subside without a trace.

In this final part, we attempt to define this basic *'mode of approach'* and use it both to clarify the process of development of a 'whole-school approach', and to help answer the urgent, practical question of what we should be doing *tomorrow* about those children in our classes whose behaviour is causing us concern, those who cannot wait for the hoped-for benefits of preventive measures. We need to consider how to respond positively to their needs, and in a manner consistent with preventive principles, while ensuring that the educational needs and welfare of the other children are also safeguarded. We also need to consider the support that should be available to help teachers in their efforts, and what relief should be provided for teachers and pupils locked into negative patterns of interaction for which no immediate solution can be found. As we indicated at the outset, our intention is not to conclude by providing a set of definitive answers, but to elaborate further the set of procedures already introduced in

Chapter 5, through which teachers and schools can evolve their own solutions.

BASIC PREVENTIVE PRINCIPLES

The key issue is *how we go about* tackling 'problem behaviour', not the scope or permanence of any particular strategy we choose to adopt. Taking action to inhibit the emergence of problems or to respond constructively to an existing problem can just as well refer to the sort of routine planning and moment-by-moment transitory interactions with individual children which make up the major part of our teaching day, as to more major changes in classroom practice, or, in wider aspect, the organisation and curriculum of our schools.

Preventive strategies can be distinguished from other ways of responding to 'problem behaviour' by means of three characteristics:

1. They focus on the *whole context* in which 'problem behaviour' occurs, not just upon the pupil or pupils.
2. They seek to *make adjustments* within that context which will help to prevent problem behaviour from occurring or recurring.
3. The adjustments are directed towards *accommodating the needs believed to lie behind the behaviour*, rather than simply trying to suppress or control it.

PREVENTION OR CONTROL?

ACTIVITY

(a) Dinner-time ancillary staff are complaining about the numbers of pupils involved in fighting in the playground. Staff meet together informally to discuss what to do.
(b) You catch a child sucking paper pellets and firing them up a biro tube to stick on the classroom ceiling.

In each case:

1. Suggest one or more possible strategies which are directed simply towards eliminating the unwanted behaviour.
2. Suggest one or more possible strategies for dealing with these situations, that are consistent with preventive principles.
3. On what basis would you decide between the two sorts of intervention?

Adopting a 'preventive' approach does not necessarily mean ignoring the behaviour itself and only attending to what are believed to be its underlying causes. In both the above instances, some direct intervention to stop the behaviour and show disapproval is no doubt necessary. Children cannot be left to fight on while teachers debate how such incidents may be prevented in the future. Nor can gross infringements of accepted rules of classroom behaviour be seen to be disregarded if the teacher hopes to retain credibility with colleagues and the confidence and respect of the other children. However, within a 'preventive' approach, the use of 'control' methods to establish or regain order will lead to an investigation of possible *underlying reasons* for the behaviour, and a consideration of steps which might be taken to prevent the need for such methods in the future. In the above examples, teachers might take into account possible contributory causes such as:

Playground incident

- too little space for too many children
  too much unstructured time
- lack of constructive play equipment

Classroom incident

- work too easy/too difficult
- work fails to interest child
- child doesn't understand what to do
- peer group influence on child's behaviour

and possible preventive strategies such as:

Playground incident

- staggered dinner times
- providing alternative indoor playtime activities
- providing play equipment

Classroom incident

- ensuring tasks are appropriate
- providing a choice of activities
- explaining task individually
- attending to group dynamics

in contrast to:

Playground incident

- telling off/punishing those who fight
- warning the whole school about playground behaviour

Classroom incident

- telling off the child
- giving lines/punishment
- warning the whole class to deter others from copying

GENERAL DEFINITION OF SHARED 'RESPONSIBILITY'

The *responsibility* to be shared by all teachers, individually and collectively, in responding to problem behaviour can thus be defined according to two principles of procedure:

1. To select *'preventive'* in preference to *'control'* strategies wherever and whenever such a direct choice is possible.
2. If 'control' strategies are judged necessary as part of an initial response, to examine the circumstances in which the need arose and, if possible, identify measures which might be taken to *prevent* such circumstances arising in the future.

Together, these define a *'mode of approach'* to 'problem behaviour', which can be applied as a permanent and integral feature of professional work both at classroom level and in the wider context of the whole school.

QUESTIONING CLASSROOMS

From this more down-to-earth reformulation of principles associated with a 'preventive' approach, it will be obvious that all teachers not only can, but already do, use what we are calling 'preventive strategies' automatically in the planning and moment-by-moment management of their teaching. In planning lessons, we try to anticipate our pupils' needs and as far as possible make provision for them. During lessons, we are continually interpreting our pupils' behaviour and, within limits, making adjustments to our lesson plans, methods, organisation and behaviour to accommodate what we judge to be the needs underlying their behaviour. What we are proposing, therefore, does not require teachers to introduce changes in their practice in the sense of adopting new or different strategies and skills, but simply to give *new emphasis* to strategies and skills which are *already part of their repertoire*. Tackling 'problem behaviour' constructively means making a conscious and deliberate choice to apply strategies, which we use successfully and as a matter of course with the majority of children, to those children who need them the most but who, because of the threat to classroom order which their behaviour presents, are least likely to receive them.

ACTIVITY

A child scribbles on her work, tears out the page and throws it in the bin

1. Would you consider this to be 'problem behaviour'? How would you decide?

2. If you decide that it is 'problem behaviour', would you:
    (a) Ignore it, but take some other action to help the child?
    (b) Reprimand the child?
    (c) Admonish the child, but take some other action to help the child as well?

On what basis would you decide on the best course of action to adopt?

We noted in Chapter 4 that whether a particular classroom event or series of events is interpreted by the teacher as 'problem behaviour' depends upon a whole range of factors. These include:

- our perceptions of and knowledge of the child, our previous experience with her and with pupils whom we judge to be similar;
- our views about the nature of the learning process, which define what we regard as appropriate and inappropriate learning behaviour;
- the set of values which we draw upon to create the informal rule system which we operate in our classroom, which defines appropriate and inappropriate social behaviour;
- the general ethos of the school, expectations of parents and colleagues, which influence our behaviour and judgements.

If our judgement is that this is *not* 'problem behaviour', we have no difficulty in responding in a manner consistent with preventive principles. There is no conflict to resolve between our dual responsibilities for *education* and *control*, so in our role as educator we treat the behaviour simply as a sign that some sort of difficulty has arisen in the child's work and automatically we offer any assistance that may be required in overcoming it.

If we decide that it *is* 'problem behaviour', then we are faced with a choice between a 'preventive' strategy (i.e., one which addresses the underlying needs), a 'control' strategy (i.e., simply trying to suppress the behaviour by the imposition of our authority), or a combination of the two. Which option we select is likely to depend, for example, upon:

- *How much threat* to classroom order we feel is posed by the behaviour (and this will depend also upon our relationship with the rest of the class, how this particular lesson is going, how much pressure we are under, etc.).
- *How successful* we have been in the past in responding to this particular child's behaviour, and hence how optimistic we feel about being able to resolve the problem this time through preventive measures.

Of course, most of the time we make these decisions automatically and intuitively because there simply is not time for analysis and deliberation. However, that does not mean that the processes involved cannot be made explicit, or that we cannot afterwards submit our decisions to critical scrutiny and ask ourselves what other choices might have been available to us that, consciously or unconsciously, we chose to ignore.

THE 'PREVENTIVE' DILEMMA

In the case described above, very little threat is posed to classroom order, and most teachers would no doubt prefer to try to find out what the problem is and offer assistance rather than wade in with a public reprimand (although some might feel that some sort of public show of disapproval should be made to deter other children from copying the behaviour themselves). It is when we are confronted by 'problem behaviour' which threatens to disrupt the lesson seriously, to jeopardise the safety, well-being and educational interests of other pupils, that whether to adopt a preventive approach presents the most difficult dilemma. If the behaviour of one or more individuals appears to be consuming a disproportionate amount of our time and energy and undermining our relationship with the rest of the class, simply suppressing or eliminating that behaviour becomes a necessary condition for us to be able to fulfil our educational responsibilities towards the other children. Since it seems that we cannot simultaneously serve the educational interests of both groups, we find ourselves forced into a compromise which justifies adopting purely disciplinary measures towards certain pupils in order to preserve the educational opportunities of the majority towards whom we feel an equal if not greater responsibility.

A vicious circle of self-fulfilling expectation can thus become set up, with teachers, on the one hand, pre-disposed to expect 'problem behaviour' from certain pupils, automatically adopting 'control' strategies in dealing with them and feeling justified in doing so; and pupils, on the other hand, anticipating that they will not get help from teachers and feeling that they are being 'picked on' for misdemeanours which other pupils are allowed to get away with. This, in turn, has repercussions for the educational opportunities of the whole class, since in planning our lessons we are likely to select activities more for their control than for their educational potential. Simply to suppress unwanted behaviour without exploring how the underlying needs or problems may be resolved merely condemns us to a fruitless, increasingly stressful and time-wasting cycle of action and reaction with the pupils concerned, which can only lead to worse confrontation as the pupils get older and are prepared to challenge the teacher's right to exercise authority over them. A more constructive alternative is to explore systematically what the underlying problems may be, which of them we are in a position to do something about and what scope there may be for remedying or alleviating the difficulties from within the resources of our classroom. To do so need not mean promoting the interests of the troublesome few at the expense of the more deserving majority. If it is the case, as we have argued earlier, that the needs of the few are frequently symptomatic of the needs of all, when we make the difficult choice in favour of a 'preventive' response, we are not just opening up an educational opportunity for that particular pupil, but potentially opening up an opportunity to fulfil more effectively our responsibilities towards all pupils.

ANALYSING PROBLEM BEHAVIOUR

A 'preventive approach' requires us to tackle problems which do not respond to our usual repertoire of strategies, by *looking again* more closely at those strategies to see if there may be possibilities which we are excluding without realising it, or ways in which we might extend or adapt our existing provision to accommodate the child's needs that we have not yet thought of. This process of analysis will have three stages:

1. *The classroom context*: how adequate is the provision we are making for the child and which features of the immediate classroom context may be contributing to the problem?
2. *The child*: what do we know, or need to know, about this particular child which may help us to understand both the contribution which the child is making to the dynamics of the problem situation and what needs to be done to avoid it?
3. *Preventive strategies*: having evolved a working hypothesis about the nature of the child's needs, what classroom strategies can we adopt to accommodate them?

. The classroom context

For the first part of the analysis, we need to be aware of the full range of factors identified in Chapter 5 (see page 90) which may help to generate or sustain positive or negative responses among pupils.

ACTIVITY

(a) Think of a way in which each of these features of the learning context might have a negative effect on a particular child's behaviour:

> teacher's attitudes and behaviour
> the attitudes and behaviour of other children
> the child's perceptions of school/the teacher
> the child's perceptions of the lesson content
> the child's understanding of the task (or lack of it)
> the teaching methods/materials
> the classroom language used
> the physical conditions
> classroom organisation/management

(b) Which of the contributory factors you have identified do you think would be easiest to adjust? Do you think that making adjustments in those areas would make a substantial difference to a particular child's behaviour?

In the examples below, we have concentrated upon the relationship between the learning environment and *disruptive* behaviour. It should, of course, be made clear that the same set of procedures would be just as applicable if we were trying to understand and respond positively to children whose behaviour concerns us because it is withdrawn or bizarre, even though it does not disrupt.

Contributory factors within the classroom learning environment	*Possible effects which may lead to 'problem behaviour'*
(i) *the teacher's behaviour, e.g.:*	
• teacher finds it very hard to like child	• child senses unfavourable perception and acts accordingly
• teacher feels threatened by the child and reacts aggressively when provoked	• child responds aggressively/defensively to teacher
• most of the attention teacher gives to child is negative/critical	• child learns that the most effective way of getting attention is to misbehave
(ii) *the other children's behaviour, e.g.:*	
• they enjoy it and encourage the child to play teacher up	• child feels driven to live up to peer-group expectations
• child is rejected by group	• child feels hostile and reacts aggressively to teacher and other children

- they use child to express hostility on their behalf
- 'problem behaviour' is sustained by other children

(iii) *the child's perceptions of school/teacher, e.g.:*
- child seems to experience school as an alien, hostile place
- fear/insecurity may create a defensive/aggressive response
- child refuses to accept the legitimacy of teacher's authority
- deliberately sets out to show overt rejection of teacher's authority/total refusal to co-operate
- child seems to come to lessons anticipating trouble
- expectations may be self-fulfilling

(iv) *the lesson content, e.g.:*
- the content of lesson is rejected by child as boring/pointless
- refusal to work, boredom/resentment/frustration
- the content of lesson does not enable child to contribute ideas from own knowledge/experience
- feels disaffected/alienated from tasks set

(v) *the child's understanding of task, e.g.:*
- child often seems confused/bewildered by instructions
- may disguise lack of understanding by work-avoidance tactics/disruptive behaviour
- child doesn't understand concepts
- boredom/frustration/resentment
- child doesn't have literacy skills to understand the printed material
- fear of failure, of looking stupid/of getting into trouble for not doing work, etc.

(vi) *teaching methods/materials, e.g.:*
- child does not enjoy activities set
- rejection of tasks/lack of effort/boredom/resentment
- work is too easy/difficult
- boredom/fear of failure/frustration
- children are expected to sit still and listen for lengthy periods
- restlessness/diversionary tactics with ready-made captive audience

(vii) *classroom language, e.g.:*
- language demands of task are beyond child's existing resources
- bewilderment/frustration

- technical/specialist language is impeding understanding
- standard English is the only accepted form of communication

- sense of exclusion from learning

- sense of exclusion/alienation/devaluing of own language/dialect

(viii) *physical conditions, e.g.:*

- the room is too hot/cold/stuffy
- the room is too small/overcrowded
- child is not within teacher's sight or within easy access of help from teacher

- discomfort/irritability

- child distracts others or is easily distracted
- takes advantage of physical limitations of room to find opportunities for mischief

(ix) *classroom organisation/management, e.g.:*

- child is not clear about rules in operation at a particular moment
- child has too much or too little time to complete work

- frequent interruptions to flow of lesson (pupils arriving late, books to hand out, equipment to set up, etc.)

- may infringe rules inadvertently

- gets bored with empty time to fill/gets behind and gives up
- takes advantage of interruptions to mess about

Of course, establishing a likely relationship between particular features of the learning context and 'problem behaviour' does not necessarily help us to know what to do to resolve the problem constructively. We may suspect that part of the reason why a child is presenting problems is because he/she is bored or cannot do the work, but we are not necessarily any closer to knowing *how* to engage the child's interest or provide work at an appropriate level within a class with wide-ranging differences of maturity and intellectual development. However, this analytical process does help us to be more aware of the extent to which the problem does not simply lie with the child, but is, at least in part, a *teaching* problem of how to make more appropriate provision for the child. It makes it more likely, therefore, if our initial efforts at developing preventive strategies do not meet with success, that we will continue to **see the problem as** *our* **responsibility and seek outside help for** ourselves in tackling it, rather than simply seeking outside help for the child.

Looking critically at the whole classroom context helps to bring home to us just how unlikely it will be that a child will be able to 'reform' if only punitive measures are used, and all the other features of the environment remain the same. It also raises the question of what *right* we have to expect obedience and acceptable behaviour from pupils if we are not, for whatever reason, able to offer them the basic educational conditions which are *their* right:

- learning activities which hold intrinsic interest for the child or, at the very least, whose point/value is made clear;
- learning activities set at an appropriate intellectual/cognitive level;
- lessons which are thoroughly planned and effectively managed;
- teacher authority exercised fairly and consistently, with respect for pupils' autonomy and sensitivity towards their feelings.

2. The child

For the second stage of the analysis, we need to consider personal factors unique to the child and his/her experiences in and outside school, which may help us to understand both why the behaviour is occurring and what might be done to avoid it.

ACTIVITY

Which of the following kinds of information do you think would be of most help to you in understanding the nature of the problem and tackling it successfully?

- the child's home circumstances;
- the child's previous school history/records;
- how the child's brothers/sisters got on/are getting on at school;
- any physical impairment affecting child (e.g., sight, hearing);
- the child's self-image, and the image which he/she wants to present in public;
- any outside interests: sports, hobbies, etc., which the child regularly engages in;
- the child's own perception of the problem and the reasons for it;
- types of activities which the child particularly enjoys/becomes engrossed in;
- types of activities which the child is particularly good at;
- types of situations which seem to trigger problem behaviour and kinds of responses which seem to be effective in dealing with it;
- other teachers with whom/lessons in which child gets on well;

- classmates with whom child works well/not well;
- any wider features of the child's experience of schooling outside the classroom (e.g., bullying) which may be affecting his/her behaviour.

Choose two kinds of information which you regard as particularly significant and say how that information could be used to construct preventive strategies.

Any of these may provide insights into the underlying causes of the 'problem behaviour' associated with a particular child and help to identify strategies to tackle it constructively. Of most immediate and direct use, however, are likely to be those which focus directly upon *school situations*:

- If we can identify *contexts* and *types of activities* in our own lessons, and find out from other teachers about circumstances which seem to produce positive or negative responses from the child, then we can compare the two sorts of situations and try to identify the significant features which distinguish them as a basis for planning more effective approaches.

- If we taken into account *the child's own perspective* on the problem, we may come to understand the logic of what appears, from the teacher's perspective, to be pointless, destructive or anarchic behaviour. Werthman (1965), for example, studying the behaviour of delinquent gang members in the USA, found that behaviour which looked like a revolt against authority and a rejection of the aims and values of the school was, in fact, governed by a set of implicit criteria consistent with the aims and values of schooling and with which most teachers would be in agreement. Such insights may help to overcome initial pessimism that there is any point in trying to 'get through' to certain pupils through preventive measures, since they highlight the common ground, and thus the potential for successful negotiation between teachers and pupils.

Knowledge of stressful family circumstances may help the teacher feel more sympathetic and comfortable in relation to the discipline problems presented by a particular pupil, because it offers an explanation for the difficulties that are occurring. However, although this is a step in the right direction, such information is not usually of a sort that can be of any direct or immediate use in knowing how to tackle 'problem behaviour' constructively. The danger is always that focusing on circumstances outside of school will deflect our attention away from features of schooling which we are in a position to influence directly. We would agree with Watkins and Wagner (1987) that:

... the starting point ... is the classroom and an analysis of classroom situations, i.e. lessons. When necessary, this approach moves out to take in factors from the wider system, i.e. the family.

'When necessary' is clarified as follows:

- when there is little variation across situations;
- when there does not seem to be any discernible pay-off for the behaviour in the immediate situation;
- when it is known that parental involvement has been important in the past for similar sorts of difficulties in school.

(p. 125)

3. Preventive strategies

Combining the insights gained from the first two stages of analysis, we can create a 'working hypothesis' about the nature of the needs being expressed in the 'problem behaviour' to guide the development of appropriate strategies. In accordance with preventive principles, these will involve making some kind of *adjustment to the learning context* to accommodate the needs identified. What type of adjustment will depend partly upon what is judged appropriate and partly upon what appears to be feasible in the circumstances:

(i) *Individual or whole-class?*

- making an adjustment which affects just that one child (e.g., changing the child's seat to join a more supportive group); or
- making an adjustment which affects the entire class (e.g., creating mixed-ability groups instead of ability groupings);

and:

(ii) *Temporary or permanent?*

- making a temporary adjustment to alleviate an immediate problem (e.g., offering a child who is bored an alternative activity); or
- making an adjustment that will become a permanent feature of the learning environment (e.g., offering a choice of modes of presenting work so that children with literacy difficulties are not limited to writing alone).

ACTIVITY

Outlined below are two 'cases' of problem behaviour.

- what kind of on-the-spot, individual preventive strategies can you think of to try to accommodate the children's needs?

- can you think of any whole-class, permanent strategies which, if you were to adopt them, might enrich the learning environment for everyone?

BEN

Interrupts lesson with continuous sequence of minor irritations – does no work – never reforms when told off

Worst when: has whole class as captive audience, e.g., whole-class teaching, also during follow-up work when teacher is busy with others.

Best when: listening to a story, watching a film or video, drawing.

Background: family travellers, now settled. Has only attended school regularly since last year. Only just learning to read and write.

Working hypothesis: has adopted role of 'class clown' as a positive solution to threatening situation where he is bound to fail.

LOUISE

'Able', but makes no effort at all to do work set. Insolent, sneers at teacher, aggressive when told off.

Worst when: teachers react defensively/aggressively to provocation.

Best when: teachers joke with her and refuse to get hooked into a confrontation. Responds when teachers firm but not punitive.

Background: taken into local authority care, suspected abuse, lives in local children's home.

Working hypothesis: is 'testing' out teachers to see if they will set limits to her behaviour but without rejecting her as a person.

Short-term strategies

Both these examples present problems for on-the-spot, short-term intervention. Teachers cannot easily change the patterns of responses they make to pupils such as Louise under provocation, nor is it easy to provide a constructive alternative for pupils such as Ben without some fundamental rethinking of the classroom strategies in use.

In Louise's case, the teacher will, no doubt, take steps to avoid confrontation by observing some basic guidelines, e.g.:

- avoid reprimanding her in public;
- avoid the use of threats;
- negotiate the rules of behaviour with pupils;
- make requests rather than issue imperatives;
- offer alternatives and choices;
- look for ways out of escalating conflict, which allow both sides to save face.

It will also be important to seek opportunities to build a more positive relationship with the child, e.g.:

- emphasising the things she does right rather than those she does wrong;
- talking to her individually before/after or during lessons, making a point of smiling and acknowledging her in corridors, etc.

Ben, on the other hand, presents little threat, but is likely to remain locked into his chosen role unless he is presented with the opportunity to be actively and constructively involved in lessons, to find intrinsic interest in and gain some sense of achievement from the work. Recognising that a lesson may present limited opportunities for him to *change* his behaviour is an important first step. The teacher will feel more tolerant of his irritating behaviour, and more prepared to give him time and attention. Prior to each lesson, it will be necessary to consider what Ben will actually be able to *do*, and plan appropriate on-the-spot strategies to help him over likely difficulties, e.g.:

- individual help with reading instructions/worksheets;
- a choice of tasks, not necessarily always involving reading and writing;
- a participative role to play during 'whole-class' teaching sessions (e.g., helping with equipment, etc.);
- giving him organising responsibilities within the classroom (e.g., handing out books, etc.).

Limitations of short-term strategies. We use an individual, temporary response much of the time because of the demands and pressures of our teaching day, and also because, on occasions, a permanent general response would be inappropriate. However, even a sensitively chosen individual response may be resented or rejected by the child if the effect is to be singled out or 'shown up' as different; and a purely temporary response, while alleviating the situation on this occasion, leaves the needs unmet in the long term, and therefore likely to recur in 'problem behaviour' on another occasion. Both from the child's point of view, therefore, and from the point of view of the long-term preventive aim, it is preferable, whenever possible, to respond in a way which will not only produce a more positive response from a particular child on a permanent basis, but potentially improve the conditions for learning for other children too, perhaps for the entire class.

Long-term strategies

Both these pupils' needs present us with an opportunity, if we are in a position to exploit it, of extending and improving aspects of the curriculum on behalf of all pupils. Working out how to tackle the problem with Ben might, for example, cause us to bring under scrutiny:

- the amount of time spent with teacher talking and children listening;
- the educational value of, and reasons for, writing activities we set;
- the importance which we give to imaginative work/reading aloud to pupils;
- the nature of pupil groupings/limitations of pupils working individually;
- the range/choice of activities and outcomes for pupils' learning;
- how to tap more effectively, and make links with, the knowledge/experience which all pupils bring to the lesson;

any of which might lead to developments in our teaching from which all could benefit.

Similarly, Hanko (1985) has presented a convincing case for the benefits of a curricular response for pupils such as Louise, the origin of whose difficulties, it might be argued, lie outside the school context. She describes how, through their discussion groups:

> Teachers became more alert to the opportunities in the general educational programme to design learning experiences which could help children deal with the problems in their lives better (while respecting the problems as private), to feel better about themselves and to widen their understanding of themselves, their world and the possibilities and limitations of choice which are open to them.
>
> (p. 87)

A curricular response to Louise's 'problem behaviour' might thus lead us to examine the potential of our own subject content/ methods/activities for:

- engaging pupils' own experiences/life situations and feelings;
- allowing pupils to explore the part emotion plays in people's lives;
- allowing pupils to explore the nature of relationships;
- allowing pupils to explore how people behave in the face of obstacles and pressure.

To extend and develop such opportunities, Hanko argues, is not just of benefit to particular 'problem' pupils, but a means of enriching the curriculum for all:

> Any child's special need can be seen as expressing more strongly the need of all and as forming a significant part of those 'basic themes which give form to life and learning' (Bruner, 1968) and which therefore ought to form a significant part of the curriculum content.
>
> (p. 95)

Adjustments made to our classroom practice, to respond positively to an individual child's behaviour, are thus more than just interim measures to be taken while we wait for the long-term improvements to the organisation and curricula of our schools to take effect. They are essential ingredients of that long-term developmental process itself. Ben and Louise's behaviour gives us occasion to question our practice, highlighting possibilities for change in organisation and pedagogy which, elsewhere, are being recommended as good educational practice for all children. The process of tackling their ostensibly special, individual problems thus feeds into the overall preventive process, helping to ensure that the measures we take to 'improve the curriculum and organisation of our school' are rooted in 'needs' identified through practice and, consequently, more likely to be effective in inhibiting the emergence of 'problem behaviour' in the long term.

Beyond the individual classroom

There are, of course, limits to what any individual teacher can achieve working alone.

Firstly, the effectiveness of each teacher's efforts depends upon the extent to which preventive principles and some consistency of approaches are being operated by *all* the teachers with whom a particular child comes into contact. Arrangements need to be made to enable teachers to co-operate with one another and co-ordinate their strategies for working with individual children.

Secondly, teachers need, and have a right to expect, *support* in carrying out their preventive responsibilities. The process of classroom enquiry can be carried out alone, but is greatly enhanced by the support of a colleague (preferably one who is engaged in similar process in his or her own classroom, so that the support can be reciprocal). Working with each other in this way can facilitate the process of making explicit, and reflecting upon, the decisions judgements and choices implicit in our classroom actions, helping us to see the familiar with new eyes and rediscover possibilities which are being ignored in our current practice (Winter, 1986). Some flexibility thus needs to be built into the timetable so that opportunities for collaborative teaching can be structured into the teaching week.

Thirdly, applying preventive principles will inevitably bring to our attention issues which we are not in a position to resolve ourselves which have implications for the wider curriculum and organisation of our department, year group or the whole school. The insight gained from our classroom practice must be fed into the process of policy and decision-making through the exercise of our *collective* responsibilities at whole-school level.

2. QUESTIONING SCHOOLS

Our collective responsibilities within a whole-school 'preventive' approach require us to apply the same basic principles of procedure to issues of policy and organisation beyond the confines of any one classroom:

Addressing the problems

To *implement the process of critical self-questioning* at whole-school level (see page 92) as an automatic feature of any response the school makes to 'problem behaviour', of individuals or groups, i.e.:

- *Assert as a matter of policy* the need to tackle 'problem behaviour' via a systematic programme of school improvement, and thus *reconnect officially* the process of responding to 'problem behaviour' to the general educational process.
- *Take action* to improve aspects of schooling known to exert an influence on pupils' behaviour, but which lie outside the control of any individual teacher.

Supporting staff

To create the formal and informal structures required to support teachers in carrying out their individual and collective responsibilities:

- *Foster an ethos of mutual support* and shared problem-solving among staff, as a context in which any teacher experiencing difficulties can seek help without fear of censure.
- *Build opportunities for teamwork* into the timetable: discussion, co-operative teaching, joint curriculum planning, etc.
- *Sponsor staff development projects* which help build teachers' confidence and skills in finding solutions to problems from within the resources of their own classroom/curriculum.
- *Ensure that any additional resources available or specialist services* called upon are used in conjunction with, and as a means of supporting, the operation of preventive principles at classroom and 'whole-school level', not as a substitute for them.

DEVELOPING A WHOLE-SCHOOL APPROACH

From these principles, it will be clear that our 'blueprint' for the development of a 'whole-school approach' is neither an outline of virtuous aims nor a prescribed list of desirable outcomes. It is a framework and set of procedures for questioning existing individual and institutional practices, which enable each teacher and school to evolve their own solutions according to their unique circumstances. (In Appendix 3, we have reproduced examples from one school's set of solutions which Galloway (1985) reported to be reducing failure and disruption with good effect.)

The process of developing a 'whole-school approach' can begin, without any ceremony or challenge to existing structures, with a small number of like-minded teachers exploring, within the autonomy of their own classrooms, the emphasis which they are already giving to preventive strategies in their work, discovering for themselves the potential for tackling 'problem behaviour' through the systematic (and if possible collaborative) application of preventive principles. Many sources of practical support, particularly in the 'action-research' field, are available for teachers embarking on their own process of classroom enquiry (see our Appendix 1). Insights gained from this work can then be fed into the discussions of existing curriculum planning groups, working parties, INSET projects, etc., to begin to re-establish the link between 'problem behaviour' and the curriculum. In this way, small groups of teachers acting on their own initiative (and without necessarily engaging in developmental work of the proportions described in Part Three), can make quite substantial progress without disturbing, or being hampered by, the school's existing structures.

FUNCTIONS OF A WHOLE-SCHOOL POLICY

A 'whole-school policy' does not become crucial until these early developments reach the point where they can go no further without institutional support, or without some more fundamental changes being made to aspects of the school's organisational and curricular structure, which can only be authorised at senior management level. A policy has four functions at this stage:

1. To provide official acknowledgement of, and sanction for, the developments taking place at grass-roots level.
2. To make explicit the principles upon which such developments are based.
3. To provide a justification and lever for changes to be made within existing structures to make way for future developments.
4. To provide an overview of developments so far and, as far as possible, to co-ordinate and rationalise them.

To be able to fulfil these functions, two kinds of statements are required to make up the policy document:

1. A *statement of principle*: the nature of whole-school responsibility defined in accordance with preventive principles.
2. A *statement of intent*: how the staff intend to carry out their individual and collective responsibilities (e.g., additional resources, posts of responsibility, function of support staff, specialist help from outside agencies, etc.).

Of course, a 'whole-school policy' cannot be conjured out of the air just at the moment when it becomes needed. The process of its development, through consultation and collaboration between staff, needs to have been going on simultaneously with, and as part of, the early stages of developing the 'whole-school approach'. This process inevitably takes time. Real commitment to shared responsibility based upon preventive principles can only come from teachers' practical involvement in the process of applying those principles in their own practice, and assessing for themselves their effectiveness in terms of alleviating difficulties, reducing stress and increasing job satisfaction. That is why formulating a policy in advance and seeking to obtain the agreement of the majority of staff is unlikely to prove an effective strategy. The relationship that we envisage between 'whole-school policy' and 'whole-school approach' is not a mechanical putting into practice of a ready-made set of principles in a once-and-for-all document. It is a *dynamic relationship* in which the beginnings of a 'whole-school approach' create the conditions which make agreement on a 'whole-school policy' both necessary and possible and the existence of the policy, in turn, makes possible the further development of the 'whole-school approach'.

THE ROLE OF THE SPECIAL NEEDS DEPARTMENT

Teachers with specific responsibility for special educational needs are well placed to be both catalysts and active agents of these processes. Whether school-based or peripatetic, they can provide a source of collaborative support for teachers carrying through the process of 'critical self-questioning', helping to explore effective preventive strategies for tackling 'problem behaviour'. Of course, such collaborative work also creates the potential for conflict, so teaching partnerships need to be carefully chosen. The teacher whose classroom is, as it were, under investigation, must feel safe with the second teacher, as well as having a strong personal investment in what can be learnt from their collaborative work. The second teacher must have the skills to be able to participate in and facilitate a genuine process of enquiry rather than trying to impose his/her own solutions. If this can be achieved, then collaborative teaching and in-class support can open up possibilities for the development of preventive strategies which might otherwise remain unexplored.

However, it is clearly impossible for special needs teachers to undertake this degree of collaborative involvement with more than a few teachers at any one time. There are complementary ways in which the collaborative and consultative processes, which are integral to the development of a 'whole-school approach' and which must inevitably precede the formulation of a 'whole-school policy', can be carried out on a wider, if less in-depth scale:

- Organising workshops for colleagues on features of the classroom context which may give rise to 'problem behaviour', in response to needs arising directly from collaborative enquiry work (and based upon mutual sharing, not passing-on of expertise).
- Teaching one or more mainstream classes in order to become part of subject teams and become involved in curriculum planning (as well, of course, as having their own classroom 'context' in which to explore preventive strategies).
- Setting up support networks/groups to enable teachers to share and talk through problems together.
- Being involved in curricular initiatives.

- Being involved in existing working parties/setting up a working-party on 'problem behaviour'.
- Setting up liaison networks with designated persons with responsibility for special educational needs in each subject area of the school.
- Being involved in any overall policy of decision-making bodies of the school.
- Providing in-class support as a means of relieving pressure on teachers and building up trust that will lay the basis for possible future collaborative work.

Perspectives for the future

The special needs department is, of course, only one potential source of support for a 'whole-school approach' to 'problem behaviour' based upon preventive principles. For a variety of reasons, teachers with responsibility for special educational needs may be unable or unwilling to take on a leading role in implementing such developments. In practice, the initial impetus may come from any area or level of the school organisation. Opportunities for collaborative teaching can be organised, given sufficient flexibility within the timetable, between colleagues in the same department, or colleagues in different departments, who share a common commitment to the principles of classroom practice we have outlined. If anyone in senior management shares a similar commitment, it may be possible for INSET resources to be specifically allocated to facilitate co-teaching arrangements. Certainly the extent of development of a 'preventive' approach is likely to depend on the opportunities that can be created formally or informally for teachers to share ideas with one another, and upon the eventual commitment of resources and redefinition of teachers' conditions of service to enable the process of school improvement to become part and parcel of the job, rather than something additional to be fitted into teachers' goodwill time after school hours.

> The more teachers experience the rewards of interaction the more they will use the criterion of professional contact and development – satisfaction from the intellectual and practical benefits of helping, getting help, and sharing with other teachers – as a measure of whether to become involved in innovation.
>
> (Fullan, op. cit., p. 122)

The most important point to bear in mind is that a 'whole-school approach' is a developmental process which cannot miraculously be brought into being by a worthy statement of intent, or by imposition upon colleagues unconvinced of its potential benefits to their own professional work. Given the range of ideologies and practices represented in any one school, and the difficulty of introducing any kind of change, the aim of a 'whole-school approach' is not to create the ideal of a unified staff all pulling together towards a set of agreed goals, but, more realistically, to get the principle of tackling 'problem behaviour' through preventive strategies accepted and operating in practice as widely as possible through the school. Every teacher who adopts this mode of approach takes the development one step forward: the process of tackling 'problem behaviour' becomes not time wasted, but time well spent, feeding back into the self-reviewing, self-renewing process of improving comprehensive education as a whole.

11

Psalm CXXI

I will lift up mine eyes unto the hills from whence cometh my help.

Because the approaches advocated so far in this book cannot solve all the problems associated with behaviour in schools, two fundamental questions about additional help and support need to be considered.

1. under what circumstances, and
2. in what forms should it be available?

These are not questions about *whether* help should be sought but about *when* and *how* the decision can be made and in what forms help can be provided without undermining professional responsibility.

UNDER WHAT CIRCUMSTANCES?

Given the varied interpretations placed on similar behaviour in different contexts, a question about the circumstances in which additional help should be available is especially difficult to answer. There is some behaviour (examples from our experience in mainstream schools include suicide attempts or faeces smearing) which everyone would accept as justifying some sort of additional help. In these extreme, and possibly more frightening, instances the question is not *whether* additional help is justified but *what* is required. However, the less frightening and less disruptive the behaviour is, the more difficult it is to decide whether teachers in a primary or secondary school ought to deal with it using only their own skills and generally available resources. Eventually, this line of consideration comes round to what, with given resources, constitutes the proper limitations of either a teacher in a classroom or of a school as a whole. The diversity of opinion about that makes it impossible to provide definitive criteria for the circumstances in which something additional to the teachers' or the schools' usual resources is justified.

There is, anyway, a common, continuing assumption that help and support are synonymous with taking the problem – often the pupil – away. In the absence of clear criteria for determining when help is justified, teachers are drawn into a form of barter whenever they raise a difficulty with a colleague or a support service. Because the model of 'experts' capable of taking over and 'solving' problems has left a substantial legacy, the barter is to establish 'what will *you* do about this problem', rather than 'what can *I* do about this problem'. As a result, both colleagues in school and external support services are often drawn into the following sort of Catch-22:

Unwanted behaviour from teachers should not be encouraged;
Constantly trying to pass on problems is unwanted behaviour;
Constantly trying to pass on problems creates a fuss;
A fuss attracts attention and help;
Attention and help justify making the fuss;
Unwanted behaviour is justified.

There is an alternative approach to these difficulties, based on the strategies outlined in the previous chapter and, strangely enough, on teachers' rather than pupils' behaviour. Using this approach it is possible to identify three circumstances in which recourse to help from a colleague or a service is not only justified but is the proper, next stage:

1. As a result of following the preventive approach, the teacher has evolved a working hypothesis about the nature of the problem ... but is uncertain what strategy to pursue.
2. As a result of following the preventive approach, the teacher has evolved a working hypothesis about the nature of the problem and has pursued various strategies ... but without success.
3. Despite following the preventive approach, the teacher has not been able to achieve any useful insight into the nature of the problem ... and so has no constructive strategy to pursue.

IN WHAT FORM?

Although there are no perfect solutions, there are ways of providing help and support to teachers, which attempt to encompass the principles and avoid the pitfalls described above (Coulby and Harper, 1985; Hanko, 1985; Lawrence, 1984; Booth and Coulby, 1987). These approaches involve,

... taking [the school's] problems as it sees them, resourcing the school with knowledge about what to do and helping the school evaluate what the effects of any change have been ... 'empowerment' – giving to schools the capacity to go for change and to get personal growth that can result from successful personal and institutional change.

(Galloway, 1987)

This commitment to the enhancement of skills requires a change in the expectations of both the teachers who make requests for help and of those to whom the requests are made. Teachers need to accept that

- requests for help do not have to be a late resort when removal of a pupil seems to be the only viable option; and
- someone who agrees to help them with a problem is not necessarily offering to take it over.

Their colleagues, or others to whom they might turn, need to accept that

- if the teacher says there is a problem then there is, by definition, a problem, even if others might perceive it somewhat differently from the teacher;
- a problem cannot be taken over, owned or removed unless it is quite clear that the teacher who has raised it is unable to make any more progress.

The worst dilemmas inherent in the relative nature of particular difficulties can be avoided if it is generally accepted, first, that teachers can define when there is a problem, although not necessarily what the problem is, and, second, that what constitutes a problem will vary among teachers. The worst paradoxes of support systems – undermining teachers while appearing to solve their problems – can be avoided if teachers' problems can be taken at face value as a problem of some kind to be worked at, at least in the first instance, co-operatively. What kind of systems doing what kind of work could do this?

SYSTEMS OF SUPPORT

Systems of support include school-based and other LEA services as well as social service, health and voluntary agencies.

School-based services

In the previous chapter we proposed that any 'whole-school approach' would need eventually to be supported by a 'whole-school policy', including *statements of principle* and of intent. This is the basis for our view about the nature of school-based services. When designated staff have particular responsibilities in this field, this should be as an internally coherent and integral part of a school's commitment to improving the quality of its pupils and staff's experience. This is a matter of providing a service based on prevention and collaboration rather than being a service based on reaction and specialisation.

An internally coherent service could be developed by any school using the strategies outlined in the previous chapter to promote a staff-development programme concerned with the general quality of classroom activity, the general support and help given by staff to one another and the particular help which would be available when problems persist. This applies equally to primary or secondary schools, but we have already noted the extent to which the latter can commit resources to troubleshooting pastoral systems or withdrawal units under one guise or another. Where this is thought necessary, it can take place within a framework which contributes more or less to a preventive, collaborative approach. Every effort which diminishes that approach is counterproductive.

Schools also need to identify the most effective ways of organising their liaison with external services, particularly when these have a more co-operative function. We have had personal experience of the difficulty external services can have in identifying the correct member of staff with whom to liaise and of the confusion which can arise when decisions are made by staff without the authority to execute them. The Fish Committee noted that:

> ... some but not all schools could readily tell us how many pupils were at that moment receiving their education off the main premises or how many visits the educational psychologist had made this year and to what purpose.
>
> (para. 2.7.69, ILEA, 1985)

The committee went on to note with concern how the staff who carried specialist responsibilities inside schools often had limited contact with the personnel representing external agencies, sometimes because external contact had to be directed by a head or deputy headteacher. It makes no sense to create a hiatus by denying the individual with special responsibility suitable access to the external services. If more than one person shares responsibility, for example, a head of unit and five heads of year, there is a strong case for rationalising contact so that best use is made of the school's external service's time.

LEA external services

Implications for existing services

The developments we are proposing for schools require corresponding development of the services established by local authorities to support and help teachers. Their structure and methods have to be compatible with the overall aim of supporting teachers and pupils through an initial focus on the general curriculum and organisation of a school, with the potential to provide increased assistance when necessary. What does that mean in reality?

Two important, general points have to be made about the services currently operated by education authorities. The first is that although the level and distribution of resources will put a ceiling on what can be achieved, the commencement of change need not be held up by any general shortage of resources. In some areas the ceiling will be much lower than in others and it has to be recognised that resources currently deployed in one approach cannot normally be redirected overnight. This lesson is being learnt repeatedly as teachers are asked to take on teamwork and consultative roles for which neither their training nor their experience has prepared them. Nevertheless, planning and recruitment policies can take into account service development and begin to move in new directions within the majority of authorities where some kind of service already exists.

Secondly, external services need to be coherent and comprehensible to their customers in primary and secondary schools. We have already noted how the development of these services was a response to perceived demand from schools expressed through different branches of the education service. As a result, within a single area, teachers allocated to individual pupils, peripatetic teachers, units of all sizes or shape and special schools can be variously responsible to special educational needs advisers, educational psychologists, divisional education officers, special education officers, education welfare officers and headteacher management groups. In some cases, where the 1981 Act has led to an increase in the number of teachers allocated to individual pupils, often with statements, it is unclear to whom those teachers are responsible and how or whether they should liaise with other services.

Confusion also has drawbacks for the pupils who, in the absence of rational, systematic methods for working with external services, may be slotted into the external system at points which are less to do with the particular character of their difficulties than with their teachers' knowledge of local provision. This might not be an insuperable problem when external services operate as a co-operative coherent enterprise. When they do not, the pupils' eventual placement and career will often be determined as much by their point of entry to the external services as by any objective or assessed criteria.

Whatever the dedication and skill of its individual parts, a system, or lack of system, with this kind of structure cannot supply a unified service. However, since variety in the delivery of services to schools and pupils is desirable, it has to be asked whether a single teaching service could offer variety with coherence? The answer is that it could, both by removing current anomalies and by being better placed to provide the kind of support and help which is consistent with a preventive, co-operative approach. However, as with the development of policy within schools, it is not always possible to move at a dramatic stroke from one system to another, but nor does every improvement have to wait until an entire new system is implemented.

ACTIVITY

Think of one way in which each of the following individuals could, on their own initiative, improve their liaison with colleagues in other external services to provide a more coherent service to the primary and secondary schools with which they are working.

A part-time unattached teacher allocated to support for four mornings a week.

A pupil said to have behavioural problems in a primary school.

A teacher in a unit for pupils with behavioural problems, which currently takes twelve children full time from local secondary schools.

The headteacher of a special school for children with emotional and behavioural difficulties, who wishes to collaborate with local schools so that pupils at her school can attend those schools part time.

There are some LEA services which would not be part of the unified teaching service but which need to be correspondingly coherent because part of their work is also directly concerned with behavioural problems in schools. These would include the schools psychological services and educational welfare services whose involvement would require methods of consultation and joint planning within an LEA framework. Another group of LEA activities including, for example, language support units or similar Section 11 funded work, as well as arrangements for teachers' in-service development, have an indirect affect on the ability of teachers to prevent or respond to behavioural difficulties. In particular, methods used by the former are increasingly similar to those advocated for special educational needs support work and their efficiency will affect teachers' views about those methods. At some point liaison with all these agencies would need to be a priority for a developing unified teaching service.

The new model at work

Although local circumstances, including the quality and quantity of services currently available, will have their effect on the form which new services can take, three features should be common to all LEA unified teaching services.

1. Pupils should remain on the roll of the referring school.
2. The work of the unified teaching service should be organised by contract with schools.
3. Facilities should be available to allow a small number of pupils to spend time away from the referring school.

Keeping pupils on the roll of the referring school erodes the institutional boundaries which require pupils to be categorised as 'yours' or 'ours'. It is a simple, technical but effective way of signalling that the initial function of the external service is to help and support schools with problems, rather than to take them over. It also maintains a school's links with the pupil, at least at an administrative level and often at an operational level.

The use of contracts by a unified teaching service is designed to make the referral system a more reciprocal and less linear process than has been the case. The service would do its own assessment of each referred problem and then, if appropriate, agree a contract with the referring school. The nature of the contract would depend in part on the negotiation between the service and the school and in part on resource constraints, but otherwise the range of potential contracts is as wide as local needs demand. For example, a school which reports difficulties with its third year could be offered help, if it had not already been done, to identify the nature of the difficulty with more precision. An exercise could be mounted in the school to identify which individuals, groups and behaviour, at which time, were causing problems. The exercise would be an end in itself, but would also demonstrate observation techniques to staff and be a basis for further negotiation.

In the further negotiation the head of the unified teaching service would make a response based on the relationship between the school and the service's perception of the problem. Again the range of responses is wide. Some professional development of staff in pupil management or in responding to behavioural problems could be undertaken by the service. Some additional teaching resources could be provided for a fixed period at the school, for support in the classroom or, if necessary, to run some kind of withdrawn group. Whatever strategy is used, it would be on the basis of a clear contract with identified purposes for fixed periods.

The head of the unified teaching service, responsible for the management of its resources, would be in a position to monitor demands on the service and to provide an annual or termly account of overall use and of use by particular schools. In some cases this would enable the service to identify schools making unusually large or small demands and to make some assessment of why. The model also enables staff within the service to maintain their links with schools and to vary their work. They may, from time to time, be leading INSET, working in classrooms or running a small group. In many local authorities there is concern about the career development of the relatively young teachers recruited into their expanding support services and units in the 1970s. There is every indication that it is difficult for those teachers to move on from positions which have provided them with wide experience but are seen as being outside the mainstream. If the value of that experience is to be recognised, as well as new teachers of quality recruited to the services in future, the work will have to be commensurately attractive.

The third feature of our unified teaching service is that facilities should be available to allow a small number of pupils to spend time away from the referring school. Schools can improve, but we do not know of any system which enables them to educate every child in the local community. As many pupils as possible should have the advantage and pleasure of schooling with their peers, but for a tiny number, smaller than at present, we cannot imagine how that can be done. To reach this position in general, or in a particular case, through a process which presumes that a school is responsible for the community it serves and that at each stage of consideration a pupil should remain with or as close as possible to his or her peers, is quite different to reaching it on the presumption that, at each stage, the proper course of action is to identify the specialist, and increasingly separate, service which can solve the problem.

Provision for this within the unified teaching service would retain the advantages of scale which are available to staff and pupils in small establishments without recreating their isolation. The placement and replacement of pupils can be more responsive and flexible because of the unified services' continuous contact with local schools; pupils remaining on a school roll would hold a mainstream place by right and their 'replacement' into school could be co-ordinated with the services' outreach work there. Pupils who stay longer in out-of-school facilities need a balance between the continuity and care of a smaller establishment and the stimulation of activities and relationships in a larger group. A service within which staff can perform different roles, and which is constantly in touch with mainstream curriculum development, is better placed to achieve that balance.

We have referred directly to statutory assessments conducted under Section 5 of the 1981 Act or to the production of 'statements' which may follow them. The particular conduct of those assessments does not differ significantly for children with emotional or behavioural difficulties, although some local authorities may seek advice from social workers or psychiatric services if they think a child might have emotional or behavioural difficulties. We do not want to give much space to considering what criteria should apply to determine whether a statutory assessment is necessary in a particular case. Many of the pupils about whom we are now writing have educational needs requiring careful, and possibly multi-disciplinary, assessment; many of them will require additional and perhaps even specialist help. It is a matter for the local authority whether that assessment needs to take place under the auspices of Section 5 or whether it should be arranged in some other way. And it is a matter for the authority to decide whether access to services and provision, or to which parts of them, can only be obtained with a statement. We have limited ourselves to describing the services needed.

The approach we have outlined offers continuity and coherence across and throughout staff-development programmes, school-based provision and out-of-school facilities. Its advantages, in our experience, in theory and in practice, are already identified (Coulby, 1985; Lloyd-Smith, 1985; Steed, 1985), but its wider implementation requires a sense of commitment which eludes a currently dispirited education service. To a degree, the development of that commitment requires an increased knowledge among teachers of the possibilities for constructive change and that, in turn, requires corresponding INSET programmes. We have made passing reference to the INSET work which LEA services, including the unified teaching service, can pursue. We now turn to that in more detail, before discussing other services outside the LEA.

Options for INSET: the Professional Development of Teachers

Two elements of an LEA's INSET programme are particularly relevant in this context: first, the general professional development of its staff and, second, particular INSET activities concerned with behavioural problems.

Each LEA's overall package for staff development reflects expectations about the general work of teachers, the extent to which they are responsible for the problems they encounter and about how they should respond. If this reflection is not planned, it will probably occur differentially around the package. Accordingly, any local authority with a commitment to meeting children's educational needs as far as possible in their primary and secondary schools, will need to ensure that the philosophy and practices to achieve that are demonstrated throughout its general staff-development programme.

The second element, INSET activities concerned with behavioural problems, does introduce a degree of specialism. Schools will expect to be given advice on how to respond to pupils who are persistently or exceptionally difficult and this will sometimes require staff-development programmes with particular objectives. Some of these programmes may be concerned with the skills required by all teachers, for example, in managing classrooms. More specialist elements may be directed at enhancing the skills of a smaller number of teachers in, again for example, matters of personal relationships, school organisation and administration, with specific reference to behavioural problems.

A particular concern for INSET activities in this field is the increasing store being set by the ability of teachers to create a negotiated, contractual response to problems of behaviour. It cannot be presumed that the necessary skills of assessment and negotiation are generally available and, therefore, discussion and investigation which attempt to answer questions about problems can be, in their own right, a valuable form of staff-development exercise. In the changing model of support, external services, somewhat outside the day-to-day demands of a school and yet prepared to participate in them, are in an ideal position to help teachers with this kind of activity. If teachers can express their intimate knowledge of and feeling for a problem, and if outsiders can help them focus that knowledge and feeling, then there are the ingredients for a purposeful, innovative response.

Lawrence, Steed and Young (1984) provide an example of the potential for staff development through this type of exercise when they describe some of the unpredicted outcomes of their school-based research into the incidence of behavioural problems as a powerful form of INSET.

> It provided the mechanism for involving and training staff in schools in research procedure and in particular, in procedures for looking at problems of children's behaviour in the whole context of the school... it was possible in the limited time available to dispel anxieties and doubts and to act as a catalyst in bringing together the concern and vast resourcefulness of the staff in dealing with difficulties.

Their research, asking teachers to report and discuss incidents of disruption, created an opportunity for teachers, who were usually confined to discussing problems with colleagues or superiors about whose judgements they were anxious, to discuss their problems and fears in a non-judgemental context. So strong was the reaction and feeling expressed by teachers to the research team that the latter found themselves unintentionally cast in the role of teacher counsellors.

Although general curricular or managerial developments might follow a close examination of a school's response to behavioural problems, staff-development programmes, with a particular emphasis on behavioural problems, are a more obvious consequence. It is important in these programmes to avoid the temptation to drift towards the deficit model. Arguing the case that the traditionally individualistic and contradictory psychodynamic and behaviourist approaches can be usefully synthesised, Hanko (1985) writes that teachers can develop 'constructive educational relationships' in the belief that children's behaviour, unless biophysically determined, expresses something for the child, arising from need and expectation rooted in the past, while something in the present coincides with those needs and expectations and helps to activate or maintain the behaviour. Without making a commitment to any particular agency or technique, Hanko writes that the fundamental skills and principles for 'supporters' working with groups of teachers are that they should:

- not see themselves in an exclusive expert role;
- be prepared to learn from the teachers whom they aim to support;
- not supplant, but supplement teachers' expertise and knowledge;
- understand the institutional realities of schools they hope to help;
- accept the teachers' views of their difficulties as being of paramount importance and essential starting points;
- not encourage watered-down applications of clinical expertise, but mobilise the teachers' own skills and inner resources;
- help teachers to recognise the signs of stress and its different manifestations.

Similar principles have also appeared in 'packages' now available for teachers (e.g., Chisholm et al., 1986). One of these (Grunsell, 1985) provides a sort of distance consultancy through a series of carefully constructed exercises presented in a booklet. In a distance learning style, the precise content and timing of each exercise is given in detail. In answer to his own question, 'What do these materials offer?' Grunsell writes (our italics):

In the pressured life of school there is very little time for teachers to talk to each other about problems relating to disruption and to look together for solutions. Their prime objective, therefore, must be to make the most efficient use possible of the time available to them. These materials are designed to provide teacher groups with a tool to achieve that aim. They contain structured discussion exercises to help groups work as rapidly as possible towards their own solutions. *They do not offer any ready made answers.*

...In each case the sequence of activity points users to a way through from individual perception to a shared understanding of the issues under discussion and a consensus view of the steps required to translate talk into action.

The underlying philosophy of the approach favoured by Hanko and Grunsell, among others, is that there are no ready-made answers, that clinical perspectives are not a readily transferable solution and that teachers have an unrealised capacity to deal satisfactorily with many of the problems they currently fear. These presumptions are both a strength and a weakness. Their strength is that they lead directly to a model of in-service staff development which encompasses the best methods of professional autonomy with task-orientated application and assessment of new ideas *in situ*. Their weakness is that they run contrary to so much of what teachers expect of experts in the behavioural field – that they can teach the answer to the problem. Bill Gillham (1984), a tutor of educational psychologists, reflected on work he had done in the non-expert style by writing:

How undramatic this level of detail is! And how far remote from the traditional preoccupations of psychologists and psychiatrists ... has it much to do with really disturbed children?

This undramatic, apparently understated approach to problems is, on the face of it, so novel and unconvincing that many teachers cannot give it credibility. However, its theoretical attraction is already obtaining practical vindication and credibility in the hands of the practitioners we quote above.

It has, finally, to be acknowledged that staff-development programmes do require a commitment of time and energy, and occasionally additional resources. This may limit the rate of change in schools but does not prevent a start being made. One of us has written elsewhere about the imaginative use of current resource levels in a response to behavioural difficulties and much the same approach is required in the INSET field (Mongon, 1986). Given a commitment to create change in this area, a school can examine its use of time, from the relatively small but precious amounts given over to staff or departmental meetings, through to its priorities for seeking staff secondments.

Services outside the LEAs

Although the LEAs cannot control the work of other services, their contribution to helping and supporting schools with problems should, ideally, be compatible with their own. Key elements of that support will come from health authorities, social services and voluntary agencies.

Health authorities

Although the role of doctors in the treatment of behavioural problems raises issues about the medicalisation of social problems, teachers should be aware of the role which health authority personnel can play. Given their responsibility for primary health care and child health surveillance, *general practitioners* may be the first professionals to whom families (or even teachers) under stress from behavioural problems take their concerns. *Health visitors* for pre-school children and *school nurses*, at a later point, obtain a view of children which can complement that of the teachers. *Specialists in community medicine (child health)* are an essential link between the health services for young people and education authorities. In many areas this person will be responsible for providing or co-ordinating the medical advice provided when a child's needs are being assessed under Section 5 of the 1981 Education Act. *Child psychiatrists* work in a variety of settings including hospitals and child guidance units and although their work is largely confined to more severe cases, some of the children involved will continue to attend school.

In some instances, the presence of physical symptoms, whether organic or not, will, in their own right, justify the intervention of medical services, in others the role of medical services may be ambiguous or negotiable. In all these circumstances the quality of communication between busy people and the management of professional boundaries will both be central concerns. Medical staff cannot be expected to acknowledge the education service's approach to problems unless it is clearly articulated to them and professionally executed. Schools and LEAs should have both the clear lines of responsibility for communications with outside agents and the confidence in their professionalism which promote constructive liaison.

The difficulties of a tiny number of children are so chronic and extreme that the specialist help they require can only be provided in a hospital setting which offers a sufficient degree of security and care

These children will not usually attend local schools, although teachers working in those facilities should be encouraged to maintain contact with mainstream developments.

Social services

Although there is some variety in practice, it is rare for schools to refer pupils directly to social services departments. On the other hand, recent public anxiety about child abuse or neglect appears to have drawn social workers into increased monitoring of children and, consequently, into increased contact with their teachers.

For some young people, who are 'at risk' in one way or another, social services departments make some kind of provision. For example, one-third of the young people taken into care enter residential provision and of these some continue to attend schools, while some receive their education on the premises of their children's home. It cannot, in any individual instance, be presumed that a young person will have difficulties at school because they are in care, but a number of those in residential accommodation are likely to experience emotional difficulties, with implications in all areas of their lives.

Young people on the verges of delinquency may voluntarily, or by order of a court, attend an intermediate treatment centre, usually run by the social services department. The term 'intermediate' denotes its position as an intended preventive measure somewhere just ahead of giving a young person a criminal record. The use of the word 'treatment' has been criticised as inappropriate for the wide, but often ill-co-ordinated, variety of activities which pass under this title.

Given their wide-ranging involvement in the welfare of young people, it is important for social services departments to consider and consult on the educational needs of the young people for whom they are responsible, both institutionally as well as on the individual basis derived from being *in loco parentis*. They must also provide for the professional support and development of teachers employed, sometimes by the social services rather than the education department, to provide education on social services premises. As a result of the overlapping responsibilities between the two departments, Holditch (1985) identifies the central issue between education and social services as one of effective communication where two groups are each playing both a professional and a parenting role in relation to one child. Holditch recognises that the two are often quick to blame one another or quick to hand over the problem to the other group.

- 'It is impossible to get social services/the school to do anything.'

- 'We didn't do anything because we thought it was an issue fo the school/social services to sort out.'

are statements we have heard many times from teachers or socia workers. Holditch's hypothesis is also borne out in Covill et al.' summary of their case study:

> Her teachers were not prepared for the depth of J's disturbance They were never shown any of the numerous assessments of her They made no attempt to contact her mother, although she continued to be a dominant influence on J's emotional life assuming social services would do this. They also had littl contact with J's social worker. Social Services, while admittin that J could be disruptive felt that all would be improved by a mer change of school. Thus, instead of trying to work with the school they undermined its attempts to cope with J by constantl applying for a transfer. *J's case illustrates an unhappy breakdown i communication.*
>
> (Covill et al., 1984; our emphasis

Voluntary sector

The Warnock Committee (DES, 1978a) recognised the value c voluntary work and identified three trends in its development:

1. There had been an increasing trend for voluntary organisa tions to specialise. Fewer of them had a general concern wit handicap and disability, more focused their attention on particular condition.
2. Voluntary organisations were more involved in the provisio of services, including schools.
3. They were increasingly active as pressure groups.

Despite this, there are no organisations in the field of emotiona and behavioural difficulties, comparable to national agencies suc as the Spastics Society or the National Deaf Children's Societ which play an important role as pressure groups in other fields There is, however, an organisation for professionals in this field formed when the Association of Workers for Maladjusted Childre and the Association for Therapeutic Education amalgamated in th early 1980s to form a single, multi-disciplinary group.

In the area of provision there is a stronger voluntary presenc running units for behavioural difficulties (ILEA, 1986; Ling et al 1984) and a number of special schools. In the early 1980s, fc example, prior to the abolition of categories, approximately 10 pe cent of the special schools for the maladjusted identified in the DE tatistics (DES, 1984) were in the non-maintained sector. Usually, upils are placed in these units or schools by an LEA following its ssessment procedures. However, the Warnock Report expressed oncern about the ability of local authority officers to monitor lacements in independent schools and recommended some trengthening of their formal and informal accountability. In the onger term there is a growing interest in the consequences for the oluntary and private sectors of new legislation. Given local nancial management, schools might be tempted to 'go it alone' if sing outside services meant incurring additional cost. Alternavely, independent provision may prove attractive to schools repared to pay a price for the removal of their 'worst' problems. here are already indications that in the absence of effective public ector 'community care' for the adult mentally handicapped, ndependent groups have been encouraged to make provision, but a financial and perhaps humanitarian price.

upport in practice

rug abuse

chools should have the name and telephone number of an uthorised contact for drug-related problems – *does your school have ne and do you know it?* – but since their intervention in identified ases is usually too late, their best efforts are directed at prevention. rom the work of organisations like Kaleidoscope, a community roject helping youngsters at risk of drug abuse, they can identify ıe most productive strategies.

Workers at Kaleidoscope have noted common elements in cases ıey have studied.

- The young person was often out late at night, maybe in touch with other users. The parents may also take drugs or alcohol.
- There were signs of serious alienation from parents, school or other stable peer-group relationships.
- There were poor prospects of the young person being successful in the ways for which parents had hoped.
- The young person cannot identify with the religious or social expectations of the family.
- There is no easily accessible ally.

(Kaleidoscope, 1986)

Pressure on teachers to consider ways in which they can identify ıd intervene in suspected cases of drug abuse has resulted in them sing a variety of approaches including some supported by the 'ealth Education Council (1985). *Drug Misuse and the Young* (DHSS,

1985) is a booklet directing teachers to look for the signs whic
would indicate 'young people at risk'. Specific counselling pro
grammes are less popular than they were in the early 1970s, bu
pastoral systems and personal social education courses hav
increased. Useful though these are, it is often too late when the sign
they describe, or respond to, are noticeable. On the other hand, th
Kaleidoscope team identified

- the need for *a significant person*
- alienation
- the lack of access to an ally

as the factors most significantly associated with drug abuse.
teacher is often a transient ally.

ACTIVITY

Reflection

Thinking back to your own childhood, note down answers to th
following questions:

Who was your ally?
Who was the person you turned to when things went wrong?
Name the qualities that person had to help you.

In order to deal with the problems of rejection and alienatio
vulnerable young people need to explore techniques for analysir
conflicts and suggesting alternative solutions. The Kaleidoscop
approach is to help young people address their need to 'blank ou
rather than deal only with the mechanics of drug taking.

> We know from experience that if a person becomes involved in other
> activities and finds new interests this dependency on drugs will
> decrease. We also know that if a person does not find a new way of
> life, simply withdrawing from drugs will only leave the individual
> vulnerable to further drug abuse, alcoholism or some other form of
> escape.
>
> (Kaleidoscope, 1986)

ACTIVITY

Group activity
Coping systems and routine

Materials: Paper and pencil; chart and felt-tip pens or blackboard ar
chalk

Write down on a piece of paper the strategy/strategies you use to che
yourself up. One person writes everybody's items on a flip chart for all
share. The final list usually contains some of the following items:

Sport
Change of scene
Food ⎫
Drink ⎭ (substance)
Laughter
Activity – model railway/knitting/stamp collecting
Time out – bath/shower/sleep
Shopping
Visit a friend – ally

The project has found that helping young people to become aware of their own coping systems, developing a wider range of desirable strategies and putting young people in reach of them is an effective way of providing comfort before a young person seeks a potentially destructive solution. Helping them to create options and make informed decisions about their own lives creates flexibility. At Kaleidoscope, it has also been observed that when young people are seriously insecure they are unable to benefit as easily from verbal assistance. Schools should note that, initially, they need to be 'affirmed by an environment' which offers a pleasant and trusting atmosphere.

The evidence from work of this kind suggests two important lessons for schools. First, responsibility for preventing or responding to drug abuse has to be shared with other statutory and voluntary organisations in the neighbourhood. Second, their best response to a drugs problem may have less to do with specialist responses to behavioural difficulties or with timetabled activities and more to do with the general quality of personal relationships between young people and adults – the available ally – and with the general environment of the school.

Child abuse

Child abuse is a problem to which teachers must be alert and responsive, although the causes are rarely in school and the response inevitably requires the intervention of outside agencies. To a considerable degree the main problem is handed over to another group of workers, but schools will continue to work with and to care for the children involved. How is that best done?

Despite the current national concern about its extent and the need to support children who find themselves the victims of abuse, it is probable that the majority of instances of sexual abuse will not come to light during a child's schooldays. Nevertheless, there are occasions when teachers suspect that a child is being abused and the cause of suspicion varies greatly. Bruises or marks may suggest non-accidental injury; sexual abuse may be suspected when a child shows emotional extremes or refuses to be touched. Messages and statements from children about abuse can crop up anywhere, through the spoken word, 'A friend of mine says...' or through play, 'What are the dollies doing?'. But these are also part and parcel of growing up and the distinction between normality and oppression is not always easy to recognise.

An overriding responsibility for teachers who suspect abuse is to keep an accurate and factual account of what they are told or what they observe. School records sometimes contain old, unsubstantiated but avoidable conjecture which pursues a family through their children's careers. If Linda comes to school with bruises on her legs it is a matter of fact to write '29.02.88   Linda came to school with bruises on her legs'. It is not a matter of fact to write 'Linda has been hit again' on the evidence of bruises alone. It is a matter of fact to write '29.02.88   The social worker, John Marsden, told me that Linda may be the victim of abuse'. It is not a matter of fact to write '29.02.88   Linda is a victim of abuse'.

But an accurate account is only one of the means to an end which teachers and schools simply cannot fulfil on their own. At some point it is essential that an outside agency is called upon to offer the casework which a school is not equipped to provide. The decision to request help or not is, in itself, a major one with which teachers will need support or guidance, and the presence of a nominated person, a member of staff with particular experience and possibly training, is especially helpful in this respect. Many local authorities now have an agreed procedure for schools and this, typically, involves a chain of reference through a nominated person at the school to a designated officer in the education welfare service, and if necessary, on to the social services department. Throughout this chain the hidden, though sometimes more explicit, agenda is the pressure on staff. Individual cases will have to press themselves into the priorities which a school, an education welfare service and a social services department set against a background of insufficient time and other resources.

If the social services department does implement its casework pattern of medical examination and case conference, a school or teacher could reasonably expect to participate when they had a useful contribution to make. This would be greatly affected by the quality of the work and observation they had done in the past. In the meantime, and whatever the outcome of the investigation, the child may continue to attend the school. There is then a need for the school to be kept informed of what is happening so that its responses can be consistent with those of the other professionals involved. The main task of the school would be to support the child through the difficulties surrounding him or her, although it would be wrong to assume that there would always be a significant presenting problem at school. In many cases nothing more would be needed than the continuity and care provided by good schools with a sensitive consideration for the pressures which might be generated by the peculiar circumstances. In some other cases, where unacceptable behaviour is the child's response to the stress, it is important for teachers to work their way through the strategies we describe in earlier chapters, to ensure that if extra help is necessary in school, it is obtained promptly.

Child abuse illustrates a circumstance in which a school may be properly using the support of an outside agency – the social services department – when a child's behaviour is causing only concern to the school. Despite the low-level of difficulty caused, there is an overwhelming recognition that the risk to children demands a response beyond its resources.

Conclusion

The services we have described in this chapter are a paradox in the way that they can represent both the best and the worst elements of educational practice. They are capable of providing teachers with supportive expertise and of developing teachers' own expertise to deal with problems; they are equally capable of undermining and deskilling teachers who feel less and less confident in their own ability to address difficulties. They are capable of providing pupils with the differentiated programmes to which they are all entitled; they are equally capable of pushing children into divided areas of the education service and depriving them of opportunities offered to their peers. As a structure, they are capable of moving in opposite directions depending on the approaches and processes with which they are programmed. We have outlined approaches for external services which we think are compatible with the general approach we outlined earlier and which we therefore think will offer the best opportunities to pupils and teachers alike.

Appendix 1 Questioning classrooms

These are some resources which may be of use to readers who are seeking to understand and take action to prevent or alleviate 'problem behaviour' in their own classrooms.

TEXTS PROVIDING A GENERAL FRAMEWORK TO GUIDE THE PROCESS OF CLASSROOM ENQUIRY

Good, T. L. and Brophy, J. E. (1987) *Looking in Classrooms* (4th ed). New York: Harper & Row.
  Adopts a firm preventive stance. Provides extensive summary of research carried out to date into classroom processes and draws out implications for teachers attempting to appraise critically and develop their own practice.
Gray, J. and Richer, J. (1988) *Classroom Responses to Disruptive Behaviour*. London: Macmillan.
  Offers detailed practical support for teachers wishing to investigate the reasons for disruptive behaviour and critically examine the strategies they use in responding to it. Contains a major section on anticipation and prevention.
Hopkins, D. (1985) *The Teacher's Guide to Classroom Research*. Milton Keynes: Open University Press.
  Describes four stages of classroom research process, which it suggests are simply 'organised common sense'. Offers detailed advice on carrying out systematic classroom enquiry, with descriptions, examples and critique of methods for gathering and analysing data.
Hoyson, J. (1985) *Inquiring into the Teaching Process*. Ontario: Institute for Studies in Education.
  Offers an analytical procedure to 'stimulate action and reflection' based on four kinds of information gathering: the teacher's frames of reference, the teacher's actions, pupils' actions, pupils' covert experiences.
Montgomery, D. (1984) *Managing Behaviour Problems in Schools*. Kingston, Surrey: Kingston Polytechnic.

A useful handbook for school-based in-service training, heightening awareness of the process approach to teaching as well as presenting many varied strategies for looking at behaviour.

Open University (1980) *Curriculum in Action: Practical Classroom Evaluation*. (A continuing education pack for teachers). P533. Milton Keynes: Open University.

Provides a simple framework for analysing and evaluating what is happening in our classrooms and what the children are learning, based around six questions.

Pollard, A. and Tann, S. (1987) *Reflective Teaching in the Primary School*. London: Cassell.

Provides a series of practical activities designed to help teachers reflect upon and develop their own practice. Includes chapters on classroom organisation and management, the curriculum, developing relationships, discipline, etc.

ASPECTS OF CLASSROOM CONTEXT WHICH MAY BE LINKED WITH PUPILS' DIFFICULTIES, AND STRATEGIES FOR PREVENTION

Teachers' attitudes and behaviour towards pupils

Caspari, I. (1976) *Troublesome Children in Class*. London: Routledge & Kegan Paul.

A very practical, readable book. Particularly useful here for exploring the role of emotions (of teachers and pupils) in the dynamics of classroom behaviour, and strategies for dealing with them positively to create a safer, more secure classroom environment.

Hargreaves, D. H., Hestor, S. K. and Mellor, F. J. (1975) *Deviance in Classrooms*. London: Routledge & Kegan Paul.

Explores how, without realising it, teachers may be treating pupils they perceive as deviant differently from others; how the ways in which we respond to deviance can have the effect of provoking further misbehaviour and confirming the child in his/her identity as deviant. Draws some positive implications for what teachers can actually *do* to prevent this happening as far as possible.

Nash, R. (1973) *Classrooms Observed*. London: Routledge & Kegan Paul.

Explores the relationship between teachers' favourable/unfavourable perceptions of pupils and the pupils' achievements/behaviour.

(*Looking in Classrooms* and *Reflective Teaching in the Primary School* are also useful sources of positive assistance for teachers in exploring their attitudes/possible unwitting differential treatment of pupils, and strategies for monitoring their own behaviour.)

Pupils' attitudes and behaviour towards one another

Button, L. (1981) *Group Tutoring for the Form Tutor*. London: Hodder & Stoughton.
  Clear presentation, very easy to use. Provides a series of activities (role play, discussion, participation in groups, receiving visitors, etc. as outlined in Chapter 7) which can be adapted for use in curricular areas to promote a positive group identity.

Hopson, B. and Scally, M. (1981) *Lifeskills Teaching*. Maidenhead: McGraw-Hill.
  Can be used by teachers working individually or together on in-service courses. Argues that education should be expansive not restrictive, stimulating not boring, peaceful not aggressive, accentuating strengths not highlighting weaknesses, etc., and provides detailed help in creating a positive climate for learning, understanding how groups operate and managing group work.

Kingston Friends Workshop Group (1985) *Ways and Means*. Kingston, Surrey.
  A practical handbook for teachers dealing with relationships (as described in Chapter 8). Activities suitable for both junior and secondary pupils, adaptable for use both in the classroom and outside.

Kutnick, P. J. (1988) *Relationships in the Primary Classroom*. London: Paul Chapman Publishing.
  A chapter devoted to disruptive behaviour proposes an 'alternative' approach involving the 'enhanced use' of pupils in the classroom, i.e., instead of the teacher taking all responsibility for classroom control, pupils are encouraged to take responsibility for their own and others' behaviour. Makes suggestions for ways to structure classroom activities to promote the social responsibilities of caring, sharing and sensitivity.

Schmuck, R. A. and Schmuck, P. A. (1979) *Group Processes in the Classroom*. Dubuque, Iowa: Wm. C. Brown.
  Provides a framework for analysing and understanding group processes, and offers a series of 'action-ideas for change', with descriptions of activities teachers can use to help pupils develop trust and a sense of belonging and co-operate more effectively with one another.

Watkins, C. and Wagner, P. (1987) *School Discipline: a whole-school approach*. Oxford: Basil Blackwell.
  A practical easy-to-read book providing detailed help in tackling behavioural difficulties constructively. Recommended here for

help with analysing peer group relationships and the roles different individuals are playing in a group as a first step to developing effective intervention strategies to prevent or reduce problems.

Pupils' perceptions/expectations of school and of teacher

Holt, J. (1964) *Why Children Fail*. Harmondsworth, Middx: Penguin Books Ltd.

This classic account of pupils' feelings about and strategies for dealing with school (and how these may be completely at odds with teachers' intentions) is still entirely relevant today.

Nash, R. (1976) 'Pupils' expectations of their teachers'. In Stubbs, M. and Delamont, S. *Explorations in Classroom Observation*. Chichester: John Wiley & Sons.

Trouble may arise if teachers behave in ways which do not conform to pupils' expectations. A teacher who does not like the rules of behaviour imposed by pupil expectations may have difficulty in trying to renegotiate them alone in an otherwise traditional school setting.

Pollard, A. (1985) *The Social World of the Primary School*. London: Holt Rinehart & Winston.

Explores pupils' strategies for coping with demands of school, their expectations of teachers, and identifies principles teachers may choose to adopt in their own practice to promote positive rather than negative responses from pupils.

Salmon, P. and Claire, H. (1984) *Classroom Collaboration*. London: Routledge & Kegan Paul.

Discusses problems of mis-match between teachers' views of learning/intentions and pupils' expectations in relation to collaborative learning. Pupils' perceptions of teachers as 'repositories of knowledge and disciplinarians in learning' will inevitably present an obstacle to the effective implementation of such learning styles. Similarly, pupils' prior negative experiences of schooling and resultant image of themselves as learners are likely to affect their perceptions of themselves and each other as a resource for learning.

Woods, P. (ed.) (1980) *Pupil Strategies. Explorations in the Sociology of the School*. London: Croom Helm.

Looks at schooling through pupils' eyes. Helpful in gaining insight into the reasons why pupils choose to behave differently with different teachers and the rules which they operate in making these choices.

Pupils' perceptions/expectations of lesson content

Development Education Centre (1986) *Hidden Messages*. Bristol Road, Birmingham B29 6LE.
  The first section is designed to help teachers to work together to identify bias in curricular materials which may lead to pupils' sense of exclusion or marginality from the central concerns of the curriculum. The second presents ideas for classroom activities to introduce pupils to the concept of bias: awareness of stereotypes of all kinds. Provides a useful list of resources/checklists to help teachers detect race/sex/class bias in learning materials.

Hargreaves, D. H. (1982) *The Challenge For the Comprehensive School* London: Routledge & Kegan Paul.
  Argues that for most pupils the traditional grammar-school-style curriculum is mostly irrelevant (equates a day's lessons to 'seven very dull television programmes which could not be switched off') and makes the case for a 'community-centred curriculum', with a change of emphasis 'from academic to social subjects and from the learning of information to the acquisition of skills'.

Kohl, H. (1972) *36 Children*. Harmondsworth, Middx: Penguin Books.
  Explores the relationships between pupil alienation, problem behaviour and curricular relevance. Describes an attempt to evolve a negotiated curriculum, building upon the pupils' interests and experiences, and records the children's unwillingness, at first, to relinquish their comfortably familiar, routine curricular tasks.

Pupils' understanding of task

Bennett, N., Desforges, C., Cockburn, A. and Wilkinson, B. (1984) *The Quality of Pupil Learning Experiences*. London: Lawrence Erlbaum Associates Ltd.
  An investigation of the 'match' between pupils' capabilities and the tasks set found that for a considerable proportion of the time the least successful learners were set tasks which were too difficult for them. Though at this age (top infants), this apparently had no significant effect on children's attitudes to work and time spent working on tasks set, the question is raised as to what long-term messages about the meaning, purpose and relevance of school learning may be being subtly conveyed.

Donaldson, M. (1978) *Children's Minds*. London: Fontana.
  Argues that children's failure to accomplish a task may be due to our failure to set that task in a context which makes 'real-life' sense to the child, rather than to a basic failure of understanding on the

part of the child. Problem behaviour might be interpreted, by implication, as a rejection of tasks which, from the child's point of view, appear to be devoid of meaning and purpose.

Mercer, N. and Edwards, D. (1987) *Common Knowledge.* London: Methuen.

A similar implication might be drawn from the arguments in this book. Within the ethos of pupil-centred inductive learning, it is not acceptable to tell pupils what they are supposed to learn for themselves. This can mean that the part of the learning process which involves gradually handing over control to the learner is not realised, with the result that for many pupils education may remain a 'mystery beyond their control'.

Teaching methods and materials

Barnes, D. (1976) *From Communication to Curriculum.* London: Penguin.

Argues that traditional methods of teaching, in which pupils receives knowledge imparted by the teacher, deny learners the opportunity to go to work on new ideas using previous knowledge and experience and make sense of them on their own terms. For pupils who are unable or unwilling to take on the teacher's definitions and meanings, school knowledge remains alien and irrelevant, with the result that they may increasingly opt out and perhaps give vent to their dissatisfaction by disrupting lessons. The book suggests ways of creating 'communication contexts' which open up rather than close off learning opportunities for pupils.

Development Education Centre (1986) *Theme Work.* Bristol Road, Birmingham.

Emphasises active participation of learners and the value of discussion in small groups. Presents ideas for classroom activities based around a number of themes: images/change/transport/Tanzania.

Fisher, S. and Hicks, D. (1984) *World Studies 8–13, A Teacher's Handbook.* Edinburgh: Schools Council/Rowntree Trust.

A valuable source of ideas and activities for co-operative/collaborative learning applied within a non-racist, non-sexist curricular framework.

Graves, D. (1983) *Writing: Teachers and Children at Work.* USA, Portsmouth, New Hampshire: Heinemann.

Suggested here as an alternative model of teacher–pupil relationships in the learning process, with the teacher's skill directed towards tuning in to the meanings and strategies with which the child is operating, and supporting the child's efforts to make

sense of experience, rather than standing in a superior relationship to the child as the keeper/arbiter of knowledge to which the
child must gain access.

Hopson, B. and Scally, M. (1980) *Lifeskills Teaching Programmes*.
Maidenhead, Berks: Lifeskills Associates.
Practical and photocopyable material, with advice for teachers on
how to organise learning activities: e.g., the equipment
needed/when to break into groups/how to evaluate, etc.
Topics include study skills, time management, relationships,
emotions, learning from experience, unemployment, assertive-
ness, finding a job, managing stress, evaluating teaching.

McCall, C. (1983) *Classroom Grouping for Special Need*. Developing
Horizons in Special Education, Series 4. Stratford upon Avon:
National Council for Special Education.
Argues the need for flexibility in pupil groupings, types of activities
and teaching approaches to accommodate pupils' individual
needs and learning styles, and provides practical curriculum-
focused examples of how such flexibility might be achieved.

Montgomery, D. (1983) *Teaching and Learning Strategies, Study Skills*.
Kingston, Surrey: Kingston Polytechnic.
A practical/theory-based handbook for use both in the classroom and for in-service training. Contains lots of useful activities
for developing good study skills.

Willes, M. (1979) 'Early lessons learned too well'. In PE232
Language Development, Supplementary Readings to Block 5. Milton
Keynes: The Open University.
Describes how, within weeks of starting school, children have
already been socialised into the role of pupil, accepting that their
primary function is to please the teacher and provide the answer
that is in the teacher's head rather than to think for themselves.
The passivity and loss of control characteristic of this type of
learner role may be laying the basis for confusion, alienation and,
ultimately, rejection of the aims and purposes of schooling.

Classroom language

Houlton, D. (1985) *All Our Languages – A Handbook for the Multilingual
Classroom*. London: Edward Arnold.
Ideas from Schools Council Mother Tongue Project for theme-
based work in the primary school, designed to support the
learning of bilingual pupils and celebrate linguistic diversity.

Hull, R. (1985) *The Language Gap – How Classroom Dialogue Fails*.
London: Methuen.
Provides a critique of classroom language as used in secondary
subject areas, showing how it may hinder rather than facilitate

learning. Includes teacher talk as a potential barrier to communication, as well as the language of printed materials. Explores what teachers can do to overcome these difficulties, which may create or exacerbate classroom behavioural problems.

Perera, K. (1979) *The Language Demands of School Learning*, in Supplementary Readings to Block 6, PE232 *Language Development*. Milton Keynes: The Open University.

Analyses ways in which the technical language of school subjects, the structure of sentences and discourse of textbooks and worksheets can themselves create obstacles to learning and exclude from participation in the curriculum learners for whom the ideas might be accessible if presented in other ways.

Stubbs, M. (1976) *Language, Schools and Classrooms*. London: Methuen.

Analyses how a gap between the language of school and the language of home may create barriers to learning for pupils for whom such a difference exists, and provides insights into strategies which teachers, aware of these problems, might adopt to overcome them.

Sutton, C. (ed.) (1981) *Communicating in the Classroom*. London: Hodder & Stoughton.

Sub-titled 'A guide for subject teachers on the more effective use of reading, writing and talk', this is a practical activity-based book originally designed for initial training students, but full of useful ideas, applicable to any subject area, for teachers seeking to create better opportunities for pupils to use language for learning.

Tizard, B. and Hughes, M. (1984) *Young Children Learning*. London: Fontana.

Provides evidence to counter 'verbal deprivation' theories to explain relative underachievement of working class children. Documents the differences between children's verbal behaviour at home and at school, arguing that it is not pupils who lack the verbal abilities necessary for school communication, but the conditions under which communication takes place at school which discourage children from expressing curiosity, sustaining conversations or expressing their ideas freely to teachers.

Wells, G. (1987) *The Meaning Makers: Children Learning Language and Using Language to Learn*. London: Hodder & Stoughton.

Reports on a longitudinal study of the development of children's language at home and at school, from the age of fifteen months to the end of primary schooling. Identifies features of schooling and classroom practice which limit opportunities for language development at school, and proposes a collaborative style of teaching and learning as a means of opening up increased opportunities for purposeful interaction in the classroom.

The physical conditions

Rutter, M. (1979) *Fifteen Thousand Hours*. Shepton Mallet: Open Books.
Identifies features of classrooms, such as heating, ventilation, space, seating and general appearance (including messages conveyed by display of pupils' work) as significant in pupils' achievements, attitudes towards learning and behaviour.

(The effect of physical conditions upon pupils' learning and behaviour is usually dealt with as part of a general consideration of classroom organisation and management. See also Hopson and Scally (op. cit.).)

Classroom organisation and management

Montgomery, D. and Rawlings, A. (1987) *Classroom Management*. Leamington Spa: Scholastic Publications.
Practical ideas for improving all aspects of classroom management. Contains a useful chapter on resources and strategies for looking at the behaviour of both teacher and pupil, as well as a checklist for critically examining learning materials and activities as potential sources of difficulty.

(Good and Brophy [op. cit. above] identify good classroom organisation and management as the basis for the prevention of behavioural problems. While agreeing that effective classroom management cannot be reduced to 'cook book recipes', they maintain that there are *general principles* which apply to most situations. 'If practised systematically, they will prevent or resolve most problems and at the same time leave the teacher well-positioned to handle the problems which do require special treatment' [p. 226].)

Appendix 2 Questioning schools

These are some resources which may be of help to schools in carrying out the process of *critical self-questioning* at whole-school policy level:

Curriculum content/organisation/structure/pedagogy

Barnes, D. (1982) *Practical Curriculum Study*. London: Routledge & Kegan Paul.
    Provides a framework and detailed set of activities for review, planning and evaluation of the curriculum (both formal and hidden) at both primary and secondary level.

Booth, T. and Coulby, D. (eds) (1987) *Producing and Reducing Disaffection*. Milton Keynes: The Open University Press.
    Argues that the origins of disaffection and disruption lie, at least in part, in the value placed on pupils in school. Contains an eight-chapter section on ways in which pupils may be devalued through their experiences of schooling, plus suggestions for countering these processes.

Brandt, G. L. (1986) *The Realization of Anti-Racist Teaching*. London: Falmer Press.
    Looks at the theory and practice of anti-racist teaching. Offers questions for teachers to ask themselves in reviewing the content of the curriculum, and provides case study descriptions of actual lessons and lesson planning in primary and secondary schools.

Sarup, M. (1986) *The Politics of Multiracial Education*. London: Routledge & Kegan Paul.
    Presents a critique of current approaches to the education of black pupils and the deficit assumptions upon which many of them are based. Raises the question of why pupils regarded as 'boisterous', 'hyperactive' and with 'discipline problems' in school should present no such problems in their supplementary schools, and argues the need for teachers to challenge the assumptions and content of traditional curricula.

Talk Workshop Group (1982) *Becoming Our Own Experts*. London.
    Describes the work of a group of teachers exploring the relationship between language and learning across the curriculum by focusing upon what was going on in their own classrooms and

considering collaboratively the issues raised. Valuable as a resource both for questions of language policy and as an illustration of the advantages of collaborative, self-sustaining professional development.

Torbe, M. (1980) *Language Policies in Action*. London: Ward Lock.

Looks at the issues involved and the process of developing a school language policy, with practical examples. Includes a detailed description of the development of a marking policy, including involvement of parents to explain to them the principles upon which policy was based.

Trudgill, P. (1975) *Accent, Dialect and the School*. London: Edward Arnold.

Discusses issues of linguistic prejudice and intolerance, and provides a framework which teachers may find helpful in thinking through their responsibilities and deciding policy for developing pupils' linguistic competence.

Verma, G. K. and Bagley, C. (1979) *Race, Education and Identity*. Basingstoke: Macmillan.

Contains a series of papers describing the experience of Afro-Caribbean pupils in British schools and some of the consequences.

Weiner, G. (ed.) (1985) *Just a Bunch of Girls*. Milton Keynes: Open University Press.

Discusses concepts of equality and equal opportunity in relation to feminism and girls' schooling, presents the experience of education as seen through girls' eyes, and describes initiatives in anti-sexist education at both primary and secondary level.

Whyte, J., Deem, R., Kant, L. and Cruickshank, M. (eds) (1985) *Girl Friendly Schooling*. London: Methuen.

Contains an analysis of features of schooling which may make it 'unfriendly' to girls, and presents a section of 'interventions to make schooling more girl friendly'.

School organisation and ethos

Coulby, D. and Harper, T. (1985) *Preventing Classroom Disruption*. London: Croom Helm.

Presents an alternative model of an external support service working with teachers in the classroom to tackle problem behaviour constructively, rather than receiving pupils whom schools can no longer contain themselves. Provides analysis of features of classroom practice and overall school organisation which may contribute to difficulties.

Frude, N. and Gault, H. (1984) *Disruptive Behaviour in Schools*. Chichester: Wiley.

Although relationships between teachers and pupils are a recurring theme of this book, there are short reviews, in chapters 2 and 7, of the main research into pupil–teacher effects.

Reynolds, D. (1985) *Studying School Effectiveness*. Falmer Press. (Also Rutter et al. [op. cit.].)

Reports on research which indicates that where trust in pupils' abilities and maturity leads to the creation of a 'co-operative' rather than a 'coercive' atmosphere, there are beneficial outcomes.

Tattum, D. (1982) *Disruptive Pupils in Schools and Units*. Chichester: Wiley.

Tattum writes, ' ... the official establishment of units facilitates the public labelling process of disrupters. Physical segregation and isolation from "normal" people is an extreme confirmatory act in the minds of both definers and defined.' Chapters 6 and 7 of this book provide useful material for consideration of this interactive analysis of problems in schools.

Watkins, C. and Wagner, P. (1987) *School Discipline: A whole-school approach*. London: Basil Blackwell.

Although already mentioned on page 203, it is worth repeating here, in particular for positive long-term approach to pastoral care, not focused on discipline problems or individual casework. A very helpful book generally for considering the issues of dealing with problem behaviour constructively on a school-wide basis.

Woods, P. (1979) *The Divided School*. London: Routledge & Kegan Paul.

Analyses life in a secondary school, illustrating how the organisation and management of pupils and teachers creates division and conflict.

Ethos and support among staff

Chisholm, B., Kearney, D., Knight, G., Little, H., Morris, S. and Tweddle, D. (1986) *Preventive Approaches to Disruption: Developing Teaching Skills*. London: Macmillan.

Originally designed for use in secondary-school staff-development programmes, but very useful for staff discussions at any level. Provides a series of activities relating to three broad areas – non-verbal communication, lesson organisation and management of pupils – focusing on positive strategies which teachers can use to prevent and respond effectively to 'problem behaviour'.

Hanko, G. (1985) *Special Educational Needs in Ordinary Classrooms*. London: Basil Blackwell.

Describes a consultative approach to work with classroom teachers at both primary and secondary level, which supports teachers working together to find their own solutions to the problems of dealing with children's emotional and behavioural difficulties. Provides many case studies of individual children and the curriculum strategies adopted to help them.

Parental support

Tomlinson, S. (1984) *Home and School in Multicultural Britain.* London: Batsford Academic and Educational Ltd.
Considers the question of how to promote better understanding and co-operation between schools and ethnic minority communities.

Widlake, P. (1986) *Reducing Educational Disadvantage.* Milton Keynes: Open University Press.
Presents a critique of models of parental involvement based upon deficit or paternalistic assumptions, offering an alternative 'participatory' model. Contains a number of case studies describing the process of enlisting active participation of parents/community in the work of the school.

Appendix 3

Galloway (1985): features of one school with 'exceptionally low incidence of disruptive behaviour'

- pupils not labelled as 'remedial' or 'disruptive' and no separate provision made for them;
- disruptive behaviour treated as product of lack of success in curriculum and tackled accordingly;
- resources to support this approach located in subject areas, not separate areas;
- teachers expected to take full responsibility for all pupils in classes;
- support for teachers in meeting special needs offered in classroom;
- teachers work in teams, no criticism attached to lack of success, only to failure to ask for help;
- pastoral systems promote all pupils' adjustment and progress, not just deal with 'problems';
- close co-operation with parents as 'partners'.

Bibliography

Ainscow, M. and Tweddle, D. (1979) *Preventing Classroom Failure*. Chichester: John Wiley and Sons.

Ashton, P. (1981) 'Primary teachers' approaches to personal and social behaviour'. In Simon, B. and Willcocks, J., *Research and Practice in the Primary Classroom*. London: Routledge and Kegan Paul.

Aspy, D., and Roebuck, F. (1977) *Kids Don't Learn From People They Don't Like*. Amherst, Mass.: Human Resource Development Press.

Ball. S. J. (1981) *Beachside Comprehensive*. Cambridge: Cambridge University Press.

Barnes, D. (1977) *From Communication to Curriculum*. London: Penguin.

Barnes, D. and Todd, F. (1976) *Communication and Learning in Small Groups*. London: Routledge & Kegan Paul.

Barons, P. A. (1938) *Backwardness in School*. London: Blackie.

Bennett, N. and Desforges, C. (1985) *Recent Advances in Classroom Research*. Edinburgh: Scottish Academic Press.

Bennett, N., Desforges, C., Cockburn, A. and Williamson, B. (1984) *Quality of Pupil Learning Experiences*. London: Laurence Erlbaum Associates.

Bines, H. (1986) *Redefining Remedial Education*. London: Croom Helm.

Board of Education (1910a) *Annual Report for 1908 of the Chief Medical Officer*. London: HMSO.

Board of Education (1910b) *Annual Report for 1909 of the Chief Medical Officer*. London: HMSO.

Board of Education (1921) *Annual Report for 1920 of the Chief Medical Officer*. London: HMSO.

Board of Education (1928) *Annual Report for 1927 of the Chief Medical Officer*. London: HMSO.

Booth, T. and Coulby, D. (eds) (1987) *Producing and Reducing Disaffection*. Milton Keynes: The Open University Press.

Bowman, I. (1986) 'Maladjustment: a history of the category'. In Swann, W. (ed.) *The Practice of Special Education*. Oxford: Basil Blackwell.

Bridgeland, M. (1971) *Pioneer Work with Maladjusted Children*. London: Staples Press.

Brittan, E. (1976) Multi-racial education. II. Teacher opinion on aspects of school life. *Education Research* 21 (1).

Brown, B. J. (1979) A theoretical and practical account of behaviour modification. *Journal of the Association of Workers for Maladjusted Children* 7 (2), 49–50.

Bruner, J. S. (1968) *Towards a Theory of Instruction*. New York: Norton.

Bruner, J. S. and Haste, H. (1987) *Making Sense*. London: Methuen.

Bullock Report (1975) *A Language for Life*. London: Department of Education and Science.

Burt, C. (1964) 'The school psychological service: its history and development'. Address to the First Annual Conference of the Association of Educational Psychologists.

Burt, C. and Howard, M. (1952) The nature and causes of maladjustment. *British Journal of Psychology* Vol **V** (1) (stat).

Button, L. (1981) *Group Tutoring for the Form Tutor*. London: Hodder & Stoughton.

Cameron, A. C. (1931) 'Reorganisation and the retarded child'. Paper to the meeting of members and officials of LEAs held in Great Yarmouth, April 1931.

Clarricoates, K. (1980) 'All in a day's work'. In Spender, D. and Sarah, E. *'Learning to Lose ... '* London: The Women's Press.

Clemett, T. J. and Pearce, J. S. (1986) *The Evaluation of Pastoral Care and Social Education*. Oxford: Blackwell.

Clift, P. and Sexton, B. (1979) All things nice. *Education Research* **21** (3).

Clunies-Ross, L. and Wimhurst, S. (1983) *The Right Balance: Provision for Slow Learners in Secondary Schools*. Windsor: NFER-Nelson.

Coard, B. (1971) *How the West Indian Child is made ESN in the British Schools System*. London: New Beacon.

Coulby, D. and Harper, T. (1985) *Preventing Classroom Disruption*. London: Croom Helm.

Croll, P. and Moses, D. (1985) *One in Five: The Assessment and Incidence of Special Educational Needs*. London: Routledge & Kegan Paul.

Covill, N., Martin, F., Taylor, J. and Tyson, M. (1984) 'Implications from extreme histories'. In Frude and Gault, op. cit.

Daunt, P. E. (1975) *Comprehensive Values*. London: Heinemann.

Dawson, R. (1981) The place of four pioneer tenets in modern practice and opinion. *New Growth* **1** (2).

Deem, R. (1978) *Women and Schooling*. London: Routledge & Kegan Paul.

Department of Education and Science (1968) *Psychologists in Education Services*. London: HMSO.

Department of Education and Science (1971) *Education Survey no 15: Slow Learners in Secondary Schools*. London: HMSO.

Department of Education and Science (1974) Circular B374: *Child Guidance*. London: HMSO.

Department of Education and Science (1977) *Statistics of Education 1976* Vol. 1. London: HMSO.

Department of Education and Science (1978a) *Report of the Committee of Enquiry into the Education of Handicapped Young People*. (Warnock Report) Cmnd 7212. London: HMSO.

Department of Education and Science (1978b) *'Behavioural Units'*. London: HMSO.

Department of Education and Science (1978c) *Primary Education in England*. London: HMSO.

Department of Education and Science (1978d) *Mixed Ability Work In Comprehensive Schools*. London: HMSO.

Department of Education and Science (1979) *Aspects of Secondary Education in England*. London: HMSO.

Department of Education and Science (1980) *Statistics of Schools*. London: HMSO.

Department of Education and Science (1984) *Slow Learning and Less Successful Pupils in Secondary Schools*. London: HMSO.

Department of Education and Science (1984) *Statistics of Schools*. London: HMSO.

Department of Education and Science (1985a) *Statistics of Schools*. London: HMSO.

Department of Education and Science (1985b) *Education For All*, The Swann Report. London: HMSO.

Department of Education and Science (1988) *National Curriculum: Task Group on Assessment and Testing*. London: HMSO.

Department of Health and Social Security (1985) *Drug Misuse and the Young*. London: HMSO.

Dessent, T. (1978) 'Historical development of the schools psychological service'. In Gillham (1978) op. cit.

Dowling, E. and Osborne, E. (1985) *The Family and the School*. London: Routledge & Kegan Paul.

Driver, G. (1977) Cultural competence, social power and school achievement. West Indian pupils in the West Midlands. *New Community* **V** (4).

Easen, P. (1985) *Making School-Centred INSET Work*. London: Open University in Association with Croom Helm.

Finlayson, D. S. and Loughran, J. L. (1976) Pupils' perceptions in high and low delinquency schools. *Education Research* **18**, 138–145.

Ford, J., Mongon, D. and Whelan, M. (1982) *Special Education and Social Control*. London: Routledge & Kegan Paul.

Foucault, M. (1967) *Madness and Civilisation*. London: Tavistock.

Frazier, N. and Sadker, M. (1978) *Sexism in School and Society*. London. Harper.

Frude, N. and Gault, H. (1984) *Disruptive Behaviour in Schools*. Chichester. John Wiley.

Fullan, M. (1982) *The Meaning of Educational Change*. New York: Columbia University.

Galloway, D. (1985) Meeting special needs in the ordinary school? Or creating them? *Maladjustment and Therapeutic Education* **3** (iii), 3–10.

Galloway, D. and Goodwin, C. (1987) *The Education of Disturbing Children*. London: Longmans.

Galloway, D., Ball, T., Blomfield, D. and Seyd, R. (1982) *Schools and Disruptive Behaviour*. London: Longman.

Galton, M., Simon, B. and Croll, P. (1980) *Inside the Primary Classroom (Oracle).* London: Routledge & Kegan Paul.

Gillham, B. (1978) *Reconstructing Educational Psychology.* London: Croom Helm.

Gillham, B. (1984) 'School organisation and the control of disruptive incidents'. In Frude and Gault (1984) op. cit.

Glavin, J. P. (1972) Persistence of behaviour disorders in children. *Exceptional Children* **38**.

Goodson, I. (1972) 'Towards an alternative pedagogy'. In Whitty et al., op. cit.

Gross, H. and Gipps, C. (1987) *Supporting Warnock's 18%.* London: Falmer Press.

Grunsell, R. (1985) *Finding Answers to Disruption: Discussion Exercises for Secondary Teachers.* York: Schools Curriculum Development Committee/Longman.

Hanko, G. (1985) *Special Educational Needs in Ordinary Classrooms.* London: Basil Blackwell.

Hargreaves, D. H. (1978) 'Deviance, an interactionist approach'. In Gillham, op. cit.

Hargreaves, D. H. (1982) *The Challenge for the Comprehensive School.* London: Routledge & Kegan Paul.

Hargreaves, D. H., Hestor, S. K. and Mellor, F. J. (1975) *Deviance in Classrooms.* London: Routledge & Kegan Paul.

Harris, T. (1973) *I'm OK, You're OK.* London: Pan Books.

Health Education Council (1985) *Drug Abuse.* London: DES.

Hinson, P. (1985) 'Teachers' involvement in curriculum change'. In Smith, C. J. (ed.) *New Directions in Remedial Education.* London: Falmer Press.

Hodgson, A., Clunies-Ross, L. and Hegarty, S. (1982) *Learning Together: Teaching Pupils with Special Educational Needs in the Ordinary School.* Windsor: NFER/Nelson.

Holditch, L. (1985) 'Bridge building between teachers and social workers'. In Dowling and Osborne, op. cit.

Holt, J. (1965) *Why Children Fail.* Harmondsworth, Middx: Penguin Books.

Hopkins, (1985) *The Teacher's Guide to Classroom Research.* Milton Keynes: Open University Press.

Hopkins, D. and Wideen, M. (eds) (1984) *Alternative Perspectives on School Improvement.* London: Falmer Press.

Hopson, B. and Scally, M. (1981) *Lifeskills Teaching.* Maidenhead: McGraw-Hill.

Inner London Education Authority (1984) *Improving Secondary Schools.* The Hargreaves Report. London: ILEA.

Inner London Education Authority (1985) *Educational Opportunities for All?,* The Fish Report. London: ILEA.

Inner London Education Authority (1986) *Educational Opportunities for All? Research Studies.* London: ILEA.

Jay, E. and Kysel, F. (1986) 'Characteristics of pupils in tutorial, opportunity, remedial classes and educational guidance centres'. In ILEA, *Educational Opportunities for All? Research Studies*. London: ILEA.

Johnson, D., Ransom, E., Packwood, T., Bowden, K. and Kogan, M. (1980) *Secondary Schools and the Welfare Network*. London: Allen & Unwin.

Johnson, D. W., Johnson, R. T., Holubec, E. and Roy, P. (1984) *Circles of Learning*. Virginia, USA: Association for Supervision and Curriculum Development.

Jones, C. (1980) The new treatment of the insane in Paris. *History Today* **30** (October).

Jordan, J. (1974) 'The organisation of perspectives in teacher–pupil relations: an interactionist approach'. Unpublished M.Ed. thesis, University of Manchester.

Kaleidoscope (1986) *No Quick Fix*. Basingstoke: Marshall, Morgan & Scott.

Kingston Friends Workshop Group (1988) *Ways and Means*. Kingston: Kingston Polytechnic Learning Difficulties Project.

Kolvin, I., Garside, R. F., Nicol, A. R., Macmillan, A., Wolstenhome, F. and Leitch, I. M. (1986) *Help Starts Here: The Maladjusted Child in the Ordinary School*. London: Tavistock.

Kounin, J. S., Friesen, W. V. and Norton, E. (1966) Managing emotionally disturbed children in regular clas.rooms. *Journal Of Educational Psychology* **57**, 1–13.

Kutnick, P. J. (1988) *Relationships in the Primary Classroom*. London: Paul Chapman Publishing.

Lacey, C. (1970) *Hightown Grammar*. Manchester: Manchester University Press.

Laslett, R. (1977) Disruptive and violent pupils. *Educational Review* **29** (3).

Laslett, R. (1982) *Maladjusted Children in the Ordinary School*. Stratford upon Avon: National Council for Special Education.

Lawrence, J., Steed, D. and Young, P. (1984) *Disruptive Children, Disruptive Schools?* London: Croom Helm.

Leach, D. (1977) Teachers' perceptions and 'problem' pupils. *Educational Review* **29** (3).

Ling, R. and Davies, G. (1984) *A Survey of Off-Site Units in England and Wales*. Birmingham: Birmingham Polytechnic.

Lloyd-Smith, M. (1984) *Disrupted Schooling*. London: John Murray.

Macmillan, K. (1977) *Education Welfare*. New York: Longman.

Marland, M. (1974) *Pastoral Care: organising the care and guidance of the individual child in the comprehensive school*. London: Heinemann.

Maudsley, H. (1879) *Mental Pathology*. London.

Milner, D. (1975) *Children and Race*. Harmondsworth, Middx: Penguin.

Ministry of Education (1955) *Report of the Committee on Maladjusted Children* (Underwood Report). London: HMSO.

Mongon, D. (1987) 'Going against the grain: alternatives to exclusion'. In Booth and Coulby, op. cit.

Montgomery, D. (1981) Teaching thinking skills in the school curriculum. *School Psychology International* **3**, 105–12.

Moody, R. L. (1952) A conflict of discipline and personalities. *British Journal of Educational Psychology* **22**, 308.

Mortimore, P. and Mortimore, J. (1985) 'Education and social class'. In Rogers, R., *Education and Social Class*. London: Falmer Press.

Nash, R. (1973) *Classrooms Observed*. London: Routledge & Kegan Paul.

Norwood (1943) Committee of the Secondary Schools Examinations Council on Curriculum and Examinations in Secondary Schools. London: HMSO.

Oldroyd, D., Smith, K. and Lee, J. (1984) *School-based Staff Development Activities*. York: Schools Council Programme/Longman.

Open University (1980) *P533 Curriculum in Action: Practical classroom evaluation*. Milton Keynes: Open University.

Reeves, C. (1983) Maladjustment: psychodynamic theory and the role of therapeutic education in a residential setting. *Maladjustment and Therapeutic Education* **1** (2).

Rehin, G. (1972) Child guidance at the end of the road. *Social Work Today* **2** (4).

Reid, J. (1987) 'A problem in the family: explanations under strain'. In Booth and Coulby, op. cit.

Reid, K. (1986) *Disaffection from School*. London: Methuen.

Reinert, H. R. (1976) *Children in Conflict*. New York: C. V. Mosby.

Reynolds, D. (1976) Schools do make a difference. *New Society* 37.

Rogers, R. (1986) *Education and Social Class*. London: Falmer Press.

Royal Commission (1889) *Report of The Royal Commission on the Blind and Deaf and Dumb of the United Kingdom*. C.5781. London: HMSO.

Rutter, M. (1967) A child's behaviour questionnaire for completion by teachers. *Journal of Child Psychology and Psychiatry* **8**.

Rutter, M., Maughan, B., Mortimore, P. and Ouston, J. (1979) *Fifteen Thousand Hours*. London: Open Books.

Rutter, M., Tizard, J. and Whitmore, K. (1970) *Education, Health and Behaviour*. London: Longman.

Sammons, P., Kysel, F. and Mortimore, P. (1982) *Educational Priority Indices, a New Perspective* (RS/858/82). London: Inner London Education Authority, Research and Statistics Branch.

Sampson, O. (1980) Child guidance, its history, provenance and future. *British Psychological Society* (3).

Schrag, P. and Divoky, D. (1975) *The Myth of the Hyperactive Child*. London: Pelican.

Sharp, R. and Green, A. (1975) *Education And Social Control*. London: Routledge & Kegan Paul.

Shepherd, M., Oppenheim, B. and Mitchell, S. (1971) *Childhood Behaviour and Mental Health*. London: University of London Press.

Shostak, J. F. (1982) Black side of school. *Times Educational Supplement* (25 June).

Shostak, J. F. (1983) *Maladjusted Schooling: Deviance, Social Control and Individuality in Secondary Schooling*. London: Falmer Press.

Simon, B. and Willcocks, J. (eds) (1981) *Research and Practice in the Primary Classroom*. London: Routledge & Kegan Paul.

Slavin, R. (1983) *Cooperative Learning*. New York: Longman.

Shuttleworth, G. E. and Potts, W. A. (1916) *Mentally Deficient Children*. London: H. K. Lewis.

Smith, C. (1985) *New Directions in Remedial Education*. London: The Falmer Press.

Spender, D. (1982) *Invisible Women – The Schooling Scandal*. London: Writers and Readers Publishing Cooperative.

Spens Report (1938) *Secondary Education*. London: HMSO.

Spradbery, J. (1976) 'Conservative pupils? Pupil resistance to curriculum innovation in mathematics'. In Whitty and Young, op. cit.

Steed, D. (1985) Disruptive pupils, disruptive schools: Which is the chicken? Which is the egg? *Education Research* **27** (1).

Stenhouse, L. (1983) *Authority, Education and Emancipation*. London: Heinemann.

Stenhouse, M. (1975) *An Introduction to Curriculum Research and Development*. London: Heinemann.

Stonier, T. (1979) *Knowledge and Technology: The Impact on Society, Technology, Employment and Education.* Conference Papers, Southampton University.

Stott, D. H. (1974) *Manual to the Bristol Social Adjustment Guide* (5th edition). London: University of London.

Sully, J. (1896) *Studies of Childhood*. London: Longman.

Sully, J. (1913) *The Teacher's Handbook of Psychology*. London: Longman.

Tattum, D. (1982) *Disruptive Pupils in Schools and Units*. Chichester: Wiley.

Tizard, J. (1973) Maladjusted children and the Child Guidance Service. *London Education Review* **2** (2).

Tizard, B., Mortimore, J. and Burchell, B. (1981) *Involving Parents in Nursery and Infant Schools*. London: Grant McIntyre.

Tomlinson, S. (1978) West Indian children and ESN schooling. *New Community* **6** (3).

Tomlinson, S. (1982) *A Sociology of Special Education*. London: Routledge & Kegan Paul.

Topping, K. (1983) *Education Systems for Disruptive Adolescents*. London: Croom Helm.

Warner, F. (1896) Mental and physical conditions amongst fifty thousand children. *Journal of the Royal Statistical Society*.

Watkins, C. and Wagner, P. (1987) *School Discipline: a Whole School Approach*. Oxford: Basil Blackwell.

Wedge, P. and Essen, J. (1982) *Children In Adversity*. London: Pan Books.

Wedge, P. and Prosser, H. (1973) *Born to Fail*. London: Arrow Books.

Wells, G. (1987) *The Meaning Makers*. London: Hodder & Stoughton.

Werthman, C. (1965) 'Delinquents in schools'. In Cosin, B. *School and Society*. London: Open Books.

West, G. (1979) 'Adolescent autonomy, education and pupil deviance'. In Barton, L. et al. *Schools, Pupils and Deviance*. London: Nafferton.

Westmacott, E. V. and Cameron, R. J. (1981) *Behaviour Can Change*. London: Macmillan Education.

Where? (1980) Disruptive units – labelling a new generation. *Where?* (158). Sin bins – the integration argument. *Where?* (160).

Whitty, G. (1974) 'Sociology and the Problem of Radical Educational Change'. In Flude, M. and Ahier, J. *Educability, Schools and Ideology*. London: Croom Helm.

Whitty, G. and Young, M. (1976) *Explorations in the Politics of School Knowledge*. London: Nafferton Books.

Widlake, P. (1986) *Reducing Educational Disadvantage*. Milton Keynes: Open University Press.

Willis, P. E. (1977) *Learning to Labour*. London: Saxon House.

Wilson, M. and Evans, M. (1980) *Education of Disturbed Pupils*. London: Methuen.

Winter, R. (1986) Fictional critical writing: an approach to case study research'. *Cambridge Journal of Education* **10** (3).

Winter, R. (1987) 'Collaboration? The dialectics of practice and reflection in action research'. In Somekh, B. et al. (eds) *Action Research in Development, CARN Bulletin* 8. Cambridge: Cambridge Institute of Education.

Woolfe, R. (1981) 'Maladjustment in the context of local authority decision making'. In Barton, L. and Tomlinson, S. (eds) *Special Education Policies, Practices and Social Issues*. London: Harper & Row.

Wright-Mills, C. (1971) 'Situated actions and vocabulary of motive'. In Cosin, B. *School and Society*. London: Routledge & Kegan Paul.

Young, P., Steed, D. and Lawrence, J. (1980) Local Education Authorities and autonomous off-site units. *Cambridge Journal of Education* **10** (2).

Name Index

Advisory Centre for Education 56, 68
Ainscow, M. 66
Ashton, P. 135
Aspy, D. 78

Bagley, C. 212
Ball, S. 101
Barnes, D. 82, 85, 104, 207, 211
Barons, P. A. 51
Barton, L. 97
Bennett, N. 130, 149, 206
Bines, H. 152
Binet, A. 48
Booth, T. 83, 183, 212
Bowers, T. 154
Bowman, I. 45, 50
Brandt, G. L. 211
Bridgeland, M. 28, 46, 51, 65
Brittan, E. 80
Brophy, J. E. 202, 210
Brown, B. 66
Bruner, J. 130, 175
Burt, C. 51
Button, L. 124, 129

Cameron, A. 48
Caspari, I. 203
Chazan, M. 141
Chisholm, B. 192, 213
Claire, H. 205
Clarricoates, K. 80
Clemett, T. S. 54
Clift, P. 80
Clunies-Ross, L. 52, 53
Cockburn, A. 206
Coulby, D. 183, 190, 211, 212
Covill, N. 196
Croll, P. 52, 74, 81, 135, 149

Daunt, P. 88
Dawson, R. 65
Deem, R. 80, 212
DES xii, 52, 53, 54, 56, 57, 59
  TGAT 86–7, 101, 156, 197
Desforges, C. 206
Dessent, T. 48

Development Education Centre 206,
  207
Divoky, D. 65
Docker-Drysdale, B. 65
Donaldson, M. 206

Edward, D. 207
Easen, P. 152, 153
Essen, J. 75

Finlayson, D. S. 79
Fisher, S. 207
Ford, J. 58
Frazier, N. 80
Freud, A. 65
Freud, S. 46
Frude, N. 212
Fullan, M. 95, 150, 152, 180

Galloway, D. 52, 72, 77, 78, 91, 116,
  177, 184, 215
Galton, F. 46
Galton, M. 81
Gault, H. 212
Georgiades, N. J. 115, 152
Gillham, B. 193
Gipps, C. 154
Glavin, J.P. 59
Goldstein, H. 154
Good, T. L. 202, 210
Goodson, I. 106
Goodwin, C. 72, 77, 91
Graves, D. 207
Gray, J. 202
Green, A. 80
Grunsell, R. 192, 193

Hanko, G. 38, 153, 174, 175, 183, 192,
  193, 213
Hargreaves, D. 31, 45, 79, 81–2, 123,
  130, 203, 206
Harper, T. 183, 212
Harris, T. 154
Haste, H. 130
HMI 53, 56, 63, 85
Health Education Council 197

Hestor, S. K. 203
Hicks, D. 207
Hinson, P. 52
Holditch, L. 195, 196
Holt, J. 31, 81, 205
Hopkins, D. 36, 155, 202
Hopson, B. 126, 204, 208
Houlton, D. 208
Hoyson, J. 202
Hughes, M. 209
Hull, R. 208

ILEA 58, 59, 80, 84, 85, 89, 130, 196

Johnson, D. 53
Johnson, D. W. 129
Jordan, J. 79

Kant, L. 212
Kearney, D. 213
Kingston Friends Workshop Group 204
Klein, M. 65
Knight, G. 213
Kohl, H. 206
Kolyin, I. 66, 69, 70
Kounin, J. S. 35, 86
Kutnick, P. J. 204

Lacey, C. 40
Laslett, R. 68, 74, 86
Lawrence, J. 31, 52, 141, 183, 191
Leach, D. 79
Lee, J. 154
Ling, R. 56, 57, 68, 196
Little, H. 213
Lloyd-Smith, M. 17, 57, 63, 190
Loughran, J. 79

McCall, C. 208
McDermott, P. 30
Macmillan, K. 55
Marland, M. 53
Maudsley, H. 46
Mellor, F. J. 203
Mercer, N. 207
Milner, D. 80
Mongon, D. 193
Montgomery, D. 202–3, 210
Moody, R. L. 51
Morris, S. 213
Mortimore, P. 75
Moses, D. 52, 74, 149

Nash, R. 79, 203, 205

Oldroyd, D. 154
Open University 203

Pearce, J. S. 54
Perera, K. 209
Phillimore, L. 115, 152
Pollard, A. 53, 203, 205
Prosser, H. 75

Rawlings, A. 210
Reeves, C. 65
Rehin, G. 59
Reid, K. 54
Reinert, H. 63, 71
Reynolds, D. 78, 213
Richer, J. 202
Roebuck, F. 78
Ruddock, J. 155
Rutter, M. 27, 78, 210

Salman, P. 205
Sammons, P. 75
Sarup, M. 211
Scally, M. 126, 208, 209
Schmuck, R. A. and P. A. 126, 204
Schrag, P. 65
Sharp, R. 80
Shepherd, M. 59
Shostak, J. 9, 85, 133
Simon, B. 81, 135
Skinner, B. F. 66
Slavin, R. 129
Smith, C. 154
Smith, K. 154
Spender, D. 80
Spradbery, J. 84
Steed, D. 190, 191
Steiner, R. 65
Stonier, T. 139
Stott, D. 27, 126
Stubbs, M. 209
Sully, J. 46
Sutton, C. 209

Talk Workshop Group 211
Tattum, D. 30, 213
Taylor, D. 59
Thorndike, E. L. 65
Tizard, B. 209
Tizard, J. 59, 77
Tomlinson, S. 214
Topping, K. 67
Torbe, M. 212

Trudgill, P. 212

Verma, G. K. 212

Wagner, P. 170, 213
Warner, F. 46
Watkins, C. 170, 213
Watson, J. B. 65
Wedge, P. 75
Weiner, G. 212
Wells, G. 209
West, G. 93, 97
Westmacott, E. V. 66
Whitty, G. 150

Whyte, J. 212
Widlake, P. 76, 212
Wilkinson, B. 206
Willcocks, J. 135
Willes, M. 208
Willis, P. 31
Wilson, M. 65
Winnicott, D. 65
Winter, R. 25, 176
Woods, P. 205, 213
Woolfe, R. 22
Wright-Mills, C. 63

Young, P. 30, 181

Subject Index

Absenteeism 54, 83
Action research 25, 177
Adjustments to teaching 37, 89, 150, 171–4
Alienation 75, 86, 197
  from schooling 37, 40, 105, 123
Association for Therapeutic Education 196
Association of Workers for Maladjusted Children 196
Attitudes
  of parents 76–7
  of pupils 39, 170
  of teachers 78–81
Authority 34, 116, 163, 165, 170
Autonomy
  of pupils 169
  of teachers 40, 90, 111, 177

Background factors 71–7
Behaviour contract 142
Behavioural approaches 64, 65–6, 71, 192
Biophysical explanations 64
Bizarre behaviour 105
British Education Index 29
British Social Adjustment Guide 27

Care (residential) 195
'Causes' of problem behaviour 37, 39, 63–6, 73–87
  see also Factors
Change
  processes of 40, 113–5, 150–6
  resistance to 40, 109, 153, 155
Checklists 27, 124
Child abuse 199
Child Guidance Clinics 49, 50, 58–9
Children 'at risk' 87, 195, 198
Children's rights 120, 169
Classroom
  climate 125, 126, 149, 115
  context 89–90, 160, 165–8
  enquiry 89–91, 202–3
  organisation 89–90, 109, 115, 168
  management 126–9, 168, 210

Clubs 88
Collaboration between teachers 112–4, 132, 179–80
Collaborative learning 103–11, 125, 126
Compensatory education 76
Comprehensive schools 40
Confrontation, avoidance of 173
Consultation 154, 178–9
Co-operative skills 125–7, 139, 145–6
Counselling 55
Critical self-questioning 36, 89–92, 114, 159, 179
Curriculum 32, 35, 82–7, 88, 97–8

Defect model 45, 47
Definition, problems of 9, 25–31
Delicate children 58
Delinquency 27, 28, 195
Devaluation of pupils 40, 82–3
Diagnosis 26, 45, 47, 50
Differentiation 81, 84
Dignity
  of pupils 82, 83
  of teachers 34
Dilemmas 33, 164
Disadvantage
  educational 83–4
  social 75–7
Disaffection 37, 40, 83, 85
Disruptive behaviour
  and curriculum 83–6
  and ethos of school/classroom 78–81
  history of terminology 29
  and home background 74–7
  meaning of term 29–30
  as opportunity for teachers 36, 174
  see also Factors and individual entries
Doctors 46
Drug abuse 120, 197–9

Education Act 1944 28, 51
Education Act 1981 132, 186, 190
Education Reform Act 2, 23, 47
Educational psychologists 46, 52, 55–6
Educational Welfare Services 52, 54–5, 187

Emotional and behavioural
    difficulties 29, 39, 51, 57, 74
Emotional 'disturbance' 24, 27, 37, 39,
    48, 57, 86, 193
Environmental influences Ch. 5 *passim*
Equal opportunities 87, 148
Equality of value 80
Ethnic 'minorities' 75, 77, 87
Ethos 78–81
Evaluation of lessons 90, 128, 131, 137,
    144, 149
Examinations 82, 93
Expertise 113, 123, 151, 193
'Explanations' of behaviour
    problems Ch. 4 *passim*

Factors relating to problem behaviour
    family background 71–7
    individual factors 169–71
    school factors 77–87
    socio-economic factors 39, 71
    susceptible to change by
        teachers 87–93, 169–70
Failure 70, 97, 99
Fear 81
Fiction 25
Fish Report 58, 59, 185

Gender 19, 80, 83, 88, 129
GRIST 151
Group processes
    adult groups 136–7, 153
    in classroom 39, 124, 125–30, 145–6,
        148–9

Head measurement 46
Health authorities 194
Hidden curriculum 81–3, 90–2
History of special services 5, Ch. 3
    passim
Home background 39, 74–7, 87
Home tuition 58
Hospitals 194

Improvements in schooling 35–8, 85,
    87–93, 155, 174–7
Individual pathology 45, 47
Individual programmes 60
In-service training 135, 136–7, 142–3,
    153, 180, 187, 188–9, 190–4
Integration 68, 111
Interaction styles 78–9
Intermediate treatment 195

Judgements about behaviour 26, 38,
    80, 163, 176

Kaleidoscope 197–8

Labelling 1, 20–1, 25–7, 80
Language 83, 90, 92, 138, 143, 167
Language support unit 187
Learning difficulties
    and problem behaviour 52, Ch. 6
        passim, 173–4
    as teaching difficulties 168
Learning environment 98, 115, 166
    see also Classroom context
Liaison
    with colleagues 175
    with outside agencies 185
    with parents 53, 78, 88, 146, 170–1
    primary–secondary 20–1

'Maladjusted' pupils
    emotional and behavioural
        problems 29, 39, 51, 57, 74
    history of use of term 49–51
    importance of context 29, 31
    pioneers working with 49, 50–51
    preventive measures 38, 86, 165–75
    problems of definition 25–9
    special schools 57–8, 67–8
    studies of 69–70, 86
    treatment of 32, 51, 59, 64, 69–70
Maladjustment 22, 28
    history of category 49–51
Meaning
    of behaviour 26, 61–2, 83, 162–4
    of innovation 153
Medical model 45
Medical Officer, Chief 48–9
Medical services 194
MENCAP xiv
Mixed-ability teaching 97, 100–5

National Children's Bureau 75, 76
National curriculum 2
    testing 93
National Deaf Children's Society 196
Needs
    of children 37, 39, 114, 127, 142, 155,
        160, 169–75, 192
    of teachers 36, 40, 154, 175–6, 183
Norwood Committee 49

Observation strategies 140–2
Off-site units 39, 56–7

On-site units 39, 56–7, 121
ORACLE project 81, 135
Organisation of schools 5, 32, 35, 82,
    91–3, 176–7
Ownership of change 113, 154, 177–8,
    180–1

PACT (Parents and Children and
    Teachers) 88
Parents
    expectations of school 115, 135,
        146–7
    good relationships with 78
    helping with behaviour
        problems 170–1
    involvement in school work 53,
        76–77, 88, 135, 146
Pastoral
    curriculum 124–5, 126–9, 130–1
    separation from academic 124–5
    systems 14, 33, 52, 53–4, 123, 124
Peer group 72, 82, 125, 126–9, 166–7,
    170, 197, 204
Perceptions
    of pupils by teachers 79–81, 166
    of teachers by pupils 79, 167, 205
Perspectives, differences in 31, 43,
    62–3, 167, 170
Pioneers 49, 50–1
Prejudice 75
Prevention 5, Ch. 2 *passim*, 87–93
    preventive principles 160–2
    preventive responsibilities 37, 90–2,
        162, 165, 176–7
    preventive strategies 171–5
Problem-solving 127, 138, 142, 147
Professional
    association 196
    attitudes 48
    development 25, 91
        see also In-service training
    judgement 38, 163–4
    responsibility 37, 63, 88–93, 156, 162
Professionalism 91
Profiling 93
Psychoanalysis 51
Psychodynamic approaches 64–5, 71,
    192
Psychologists 46
Pupils *see under individual headings*

Qualifications 52
Questioning frameworks 89–93

Race 83, 88, 129
Records 53, 139
Records of achievement 93
Referral system
    to outside agencies 188
    within school 117, 118, 125
Reinforcement 66, 142
Rejection 33–4, 74, 83
Relationships
    between pupils *see* Peer Group *and*
        Group processes
    teacher–pupil 27, 32, 53, 78–81, 110,
        129
    between teachers 177, 180
Remedial 52
Responses
    to behaviour 38, 62–3, 64–6, 80–1,
        89–93, 160–77
    to schooling 81–5, 89–92, 166–8
Responsibility
    of school 37, 92, 176
    of teacher *see* Professional
        responsibility
ROSLA (Raising of School Leaving
    Age) 84
Rules 128, 161, 163

Schooling, processes of 77–93
Schools Psychological Service 122, 139,
    187
Self-esteem 52, 129, 148
Self-evaluation 90–1, 114, 165, 176
Single-parent families 120
Social problems 37, 58
Social services 195
Socio-ecological explanations 62, 74
Socio-economic factors 72–7, 88
Spastics Society 196
Special educational needs 37, 39, 60,
    132, 148, 175, 187
Special schools 22, 52, 57–8, 67–8
Spens Report 49
Standards 86, 129
Stereotyping 88
Summerfield Report 55
Support
    departments 52, 114, 179–80, 185
    in-class 114, 124, 131, 179, 189
    services 139, Ch. 11 *passim*
    skills 154, 179, 189
    for teachers 114, 168, 175–6, 183, 191–2
Suspension 77
Swann Report 75, 86–7

Talk   104, 138, 174
Teacher training   27
Teacher-as-researcher   36
Teachers *see under individual headings*
Teaching
  materials   89–90, 107–8, 167
  methods   37,89–90, 97, 101–8, 129,
    145, 167
Techniques   27, 47, 124, 140–2
Testing   2, 93
Therapy   45, 51, 57, 65
Transfer of specialist methods   69–71
Truancy   83, 119

Underachievement   85, 87

Underwood Report   46
Unified teaching service   188–90
Units   35, 37, 52, 56–7, 68, 93, 120, 133

Voluntary work   196

Warning signs   37
Warnock Report   28–9, 156, 196
Whole-school approach   156, Ch. 10
    passim
Whole-school policy   91, 132, 156, 176,
    178–9
Withdrawal   36, 52–3, 100, 123, 124